Holy in Christ

Thoughts on the Calling of God's Children to be
Holy as He is Holy

Andrew Murray

Holy in Christ: Thoughts on the Calling of God's Children to be Holy as He is Holy

ISBN: 978-1-64799-919-3

PREFACE

There is not in Scripture a word more distinctly Divine in its origin and meaning than the word holy. There is not a word that leads us higher into the mystery of Deity, nor deeper into the privilege and the blessedness of God's children. And yet it is a word that many a Christian has never studied or understood.

There are not a few who can praise God that during the past twenty years the watchword Be Holy has been taken up in many a church and Christian circle with greater earnestness than before. In books and magazines, in conventions and conferences, in the testimonies and the lives of believers, we have abundant tokens that what is called the Holiness-movement is a reality.

And yet how much is still wanting! What multitudes of believing Christians there are who have none but the very vaguest thoughts of what holiness is! And of those who are seeking after it 6how many who have hardly learnt what it is to come to God's Word and to God Himself for the teaching that can alone reveal this part of the mystery of Christ and of God! To many, holiness has simply been a general expression for the Christian life in its more earnest form, without much thought of what the term really means.

In writing this little book, my object has been to discover in what sense God uses the word, that so it may mean to us what it means to Him. I have sought to trace the word through some of the most important passages of Holy Scripture where it occurs, there to learn what God's holiness is, what ours is to be, and what the way by which we attain it. I have been specially anxious to point out how many and various the elements are that go to make up true holiness as the Divine expression of the Christian life in all its fulness and perfection. I have at the same time striven continually to keep in mind the wonderful unity and simplicity there is in it, as centred in the person of Jesus. As I proceeded in my work, I felt ever more deeply how high the task was I had undertaken in offering to guide others even into the outer courts of the Holy Place of the Most High. And yet the very difficulty of the task convinced me of how needful it was.

I fear there are some to whom the book may 7be a disappointment. They have heard that the entrance to the life of holiness is often but a step. They have heard of or seen believers who could tell of the blessed change that has come over their lives since they found the wonderful secret of holiness by faith. And now they are seeking for this secret. They cannot understand that the secret comes to those who seek it not, but only seek Jesus. They might fain have a book in which all they need to know of Holiness and the way to it is gathered into a few simple lessons, easy to learn, to remember, and to practise. This they will not find. There is such a thing as a Pentecost still to the disciples of Jesus; but it comes to him who has forsaken all to follow Jesus only, and in following fully has allowed the Master to reprove and instruct him. There are often very blessed revelations of Christ, as a Saviour from sin, both in the secret chamber and in the meetings of the saints; but these are given to those for whom they have been prepared, and who have been prepared to receive. Let all learn to trust in Jesus, and rejoice in Him, even though their experience be not what they would wish. He will make us holy. But whether we have entered the blessed life of faith in Jesus as our sanctification, or are still longing for it from afar, we all need one thing, the simple, believing, 8and obedient acceptance of each word that our God has spoken. It has been my earnest desire that I might be a helper of the faith of my brethren in seeking to trace with them the wondrous revelation of God's Holiness through the ages as recorded in His blessed Word. It has been my continual prayer that God might use what is written to increase in His children the conviction that we must be holy, the knowledge of how we are to be holy, the joy that we may be holy, the faith that we can be holy. And may He stir us all to cry day and night to Him for a visitation of the Spirit and the Power of Holiness upon all His people, that the name of Christian and of saint may be synonymous, and every believer be a vessel made holy and meet for the Master's use.

A. M.
Wellington, 16th November 1887.

CONTENTS

First Day

HOLY IN CHRIST

God's Call to Holiness

'Like as He which called you is holy, be ye yourselves also holy in all manner of living; because it is written, Ye shall be holy, for I am holy.'—1 Pet. i. 15, 16.

The call of God is the manifestation in time of the purpose of eternity: 'Whom He predestinated, them He also called.' Believers are 'the called according to His purpose.' In His call He reveals to us what His thoughts and His will concerning us are, and what the life to which He invites us. In His call He makes clear to us what the hope of our calling is; as we spiritually apprehend and enter into this, our life on earth will be the reflection of His purpose in eternity.

Holy Scripture uses more than one word to indicate the object or aim of our calling, but none more frequently than what Peter speaks of here—God has called us to be holy as He is holy. Paul addresses believers twice as 'called to be holy' (Rom. i. 7; 1 Cor. i. 2). 'God called us', he says, 'not for uncleanness, but in sanctification' (1 Thess. 12iv. 7). When he writes, 'The God of peace sanctify you wholly,' he adds, 'Faithful is He which calleth you, who also will do it' (1 Thess. v. 24). The calling itself is spoken of as 'a holy calling.' The eternal purpose of which the calling is the outcome, is continually also connected with holiness as its aim. 'He hath chosen us in Him, that we should be holy and without blame' (Eph. i. 4). 'Whom God chose from the beginning unto salvation in sanctification' (2 Thess. ii. 12). 'Elect according to the foreknowledge of the Father, through sanctification of the Spirit' (1 Pet. i. 2). The call is the unveiling of the purpose that the Father from eternity had set His heart upon: that we should be holy.

It needs no proof that it is of infinite importance to know aright what God has called us to. A misunderstanding here may have fatal results. You may have heard that God calls you to salvation or to happiness, to receive pardon or to obtain heaven, and never noticed that all these were subordinate. It was to

1

'salvation in sanctification,' it was to Holiness in the first place, as the element in which salvation and heaven are to be found. The complaints of many Christians as to lack of joy and strength, as to failure and want of growth, are simply owing to this—the place God gave Holiness in His call they have not given it in their response. God and they have never yet come to an agreement on this.

No wonder that Paul, in the chapter in which he had spoken to the Ephesians of their being 'chosen to be holy' prays for the spirit of wisdom and revelation in the knowledge of God to be given to believers, that they might know 'the hope of their calling' (i. 17, 18). Let all of us, who feel that we have too little realized that we are called to Holiness, pray this prayer. It is just what we need. Let us ask God to show us how, as He who hath called us is Himself holy, so we are to be holy too; our calling is a holy calling, a calling before and above everything, to Holiness. Let us ask Him to show us what Holiness is, His Holiness first, and then our Holiness; to show us how He has set His heart upon it as the one thing He wants to see in us, as being His own image and likeness; to show us too the unutterable blessedness and glory of sharing with Christ in His Holiness. Oh! that God by His Spirit would teach us what it means that we are called to be holy as He is holy. We can easily conceive what a mighty influence it would exert.

'Like as He which called you is holy, be ye yourselves also holy'. How this call of God shows us the true motive to Holiness. 'Be ye holy, for I am holy.' It is as if God said, Holiness is my blessedness and my glory: without this you cannot, in the very nature of things, see me or enjoy me. Holiness is my blessedness and my glory: there is nothing higher to be conceived; I invite you to share with me in it, I invite you to likeness to myself: 'Be ye holy, for I am holy.' Is it not enough, has it no attraction, does it not move and draw you mightily, the hope of being with me, partakers of my Holiness? I have nothing better to offer—I offer you myself: 'Be holy, for I am holy.' Shall we not cry earnestly to God to show us the glory of His Holiness, that our souls may be made willing to give everything in response to this wondrous call?

As we listen to the call, it shows also the nature of true Holiness. 'Like as He is holy, so be ye also holy.' To be holy is to be Godlike, to have a disposition, a will, a character like God. The thought almost looks like blasphemy, until we listen again, 'He

2

hath chosen us in Christ to be holy.' In Christ the Holiness of God appeared in a human life: in Christ's example, in His mind and Spirit, we have the Holiness of the Invisible One translated into the forms of human life and conduct. To be Christlike is to be Godlike; to be Christlike is to be holy as God is holy.

The call equally reveals the power of Holiness. 'There is none holy but the Lord;' there is no Holiness but what He has, or rather what He is, and gives. Holiness is not something we do or attain: it is the communication of the Divine life, the inbreathing of the Divine nature, the power of the Divine Presence resting on us. And our power to become holy is to be found in the call of God: the Holy One calls us to Himself, that He may make us holy in possessing Himself. He not only says 'I am holy,' but 'I am the Lord, who make holy.' It is because the call to Holiness comes from the God of infinite Power and Love that we may have the confidence: we can be holy.

The call no less reveals the standard of Holiness. 'Like as He is holy, so ye also yourselves,' or (as in margin, R.V.), 'Like the Holy One, which calleth you, be ye yourselves also holy.' There is not one standard of Holiness for God and another for man. The nature of light is the same, whether we see it in the sun or in a candle: the nature of Holiness remains unchanged, whether it be God or man in whom it dwells. The Lord Jesus could say nothing less than, 'Be perfect, even as your Father in heaven is perfect.' When God calls us to Holiness, He calls us to Himself and His own life: the more carefully we listen to the voice, and let it sink into our hearts, the more will all human standards fall away, and only the words be heard, Holy, as I am holy.

And the call shows us the path to Holiness. The calling of God is one of mighty efficacy, an effectual calling. Oh! let us but listen to it, let us but listen to Him, and the call will with Divine power work what it offers. He calleth the things that are not as though they were: His call gives life to the dead, and holiness to those whom He has made alive. He calls us to listen as He speaks of His Holiness, and of our holiness like His. He calls us to Himself, to study, to fear, to love, to claim His Holiness. He calls us to Christ, in whom Divine Holiness became human Holiness, to see and admire, to desire and accept what is all for us. He calls us to the indwelling and the teaching of the Spirit of Holiness, to yield ourselves that He may bring home to us and breathe within us what is ours in Christ. Christian! listen to God calling thee to

3

Holiness. Come and learn what His Holiness is, and what thine is and must be.

Yes, be very silent and listen. When God called Abraham, he answered, Here am I. When God called Moses from the bush, he answered, Here am I, and he hid his face, for he was afraid to look upon God. God is calling thee to Holiness, to Himself the Holy One, that He may make thee holy. Let thy whole soul answer, Here am I, Lord! Speak, Lord! Show Thyself, Lord! Here am I. As you listen, the voice will sound ever deeper and ever stiller: Be holy, as I am holy. Be holy, for I am holy. You will hear a voice coming out of the great eternity, from the council-chamber of redemption, and as you catch its distant whisper, it will be, Be holy, I am holy. You will hear a voice from Paradise, the Creator making the seventh day holy for man whom He had created, and saying, Be holy. You will hear the voice from Sinai, amid thunderings and lightnings, and still it is, Be holy, as I am holy. You will hear a voice from Calvary, and there above all it is, Be holy, for I am holy.

Child of God, have you ever realized it, our Father is calling us to Himself, to be holy as He is holy? Must we not confess that happiness has been to us more than holiness, salvation than sanctification? Oh! it is not too late to redeem the error. Let us now band ourselves together to listen to the voice that calls, to draw nigh, and find out and know what Holiness is, or rather, find out and know Himself the Holy One. And if the first approach to Him fill us with shame and confusion, make us fear and shrink back, let us still listen to the Voice and the Call, 'Be holy, as I am holy.' 'Faithful is He which calleth, who also will do it.' All our fears and questions will be met by the Holy One who has revealed His Holiness, with this one purpose in view, that we might share it with Him. As we yield ourselves in deep stillness of soul to listen to the Holy Voice that calls us, it will waken within us new desire and strong faith, and the most precious of all promises will be to us this word of Divine command:

Be holy, for I am holy

O Lord! the alone Holy One, Thou hast called us to be holy, even as Thou art holy. Lord! how can we, unless Thou reveal to us Thy Holiness. Show us, we pray Thee, how Thou art holy, how holy Thou art, what Thy holiness is, that we may know how we

4

are to be holy, how holy we are to be. And when the sight of Thy Holiness only shows us the more how unholy we are, teach us that Thou makest partakers of Thy own Holiness those who come to Thee for it.

O God! we come to Thee, the Holy One. It is in knowing and finding and having Thyself, that the soul finds Holiness. We do beseech Thee, as we now come to Thee, establish it in the thoughts of our heart, that the one object of Thy calling us, and of our coming to Thee, is Holiness. Thou wouldst have us like Thyself, partakers of Thy Holiness. If ever our heart becomes afraid, as if it were too high, or rests content with a salvation less than Holiness, Blessed God! let us hear Thy voice calling again, Be holy, I am holy. Let that call be our motive and our strength, because faithful is He that calleth, who also will do it. Let that call mark our standard and our path; oh! let our life be such as Thou art able to make it.

Holy Father! I bow in lowly worship and silence before Thee. Let now Thine own voice sound in the depths of my heart calling me, Be holy, as I am holy. Amen.

1. Let me press it upon every reader of this little book, that if it is to help him in the pursuit of Holiness, he must begin with God Himself. You must go to Him who calls you. It is only in the personal revelation of God to you, as He speaks, I am holy, that the command, Be ye holy, can have life or power.

2. Remember, as a believer, you have already accepted God's call, even though you did not fully understand it. Let it be a settled matter, that whatever you see to be the meaning of the call, you will at once accept and carry out. If God calls me to be holy, holy I will be.

3. Take fast hold of the word: 'The God of peace sanctify you wholly: faithful is He which calleth you, who also will do it.' In that faith listen to God calling you.

4. Do be still now, and listen to your Father calling you. Ask for and count upon the Holy Spirit, the Spirit of Holiness, to open your heart to understand this holy calling. And then speak out the answer you have to give to this call.

Second Day

HOLY IN CHRIST

God's Provision for Holiness

'To those that are made holy in Christ Jesus, called to be holy.'—1 Cor. i. 2.

'To all the holy ones in Christ Jesus which are at Philippi. Salute every holy one in Christ Jesus.' [1] —Phil. i. 1, iv. 21.

Holy! In Christ! In these two expressions we have perhaps the most wonderful words of all the Bible.

Holy! the word of unfathomable meaning, which the Seraphs utter with veiled faces. Holy! the word in which all God's perfections centre, and of which His glory is but the streaming forth. Holy! the word which reveals the purpose with which God from eternity thought of man, and tells what man's highest glory in the coming eternity is to be; to be partaker of His Holiness!

In Christ! the word in which all the wisdom and love of God are unveiled! The Father giving His Son to be one with us! the Son dying on the cross to make us one with Himself! the Holy Spirit of the Father dwelling in us to establish and maintain that union! In Christ! what a summary of what redemption has done, and of the inconceivably blessed life in which the child of God is permitted to dwell. In Christ! the one lesson we have to study on earth. God's one answer to all our needs and prayers. In Christ! the guarantee and the foretaste of eternal glory.

---

[1] There is one disadvantage in English in our having synonyms of which some are derived from Saxon and others from Latin. Ordinary readers are apt to forget that in our translation of the Bible we may use two different words for what in the original is expressed by one term. This is the case with the words holy, holiness, keep holy, hallow, saint, sanctify, and sanctification. When God or Christ is called the Holy One, the word in Hebrew and Greek is exactly the same that is used when the believer is called a saint: he too is a holy one. So the three words hallow, keep holy, sanctify, all represent but one term in the original, of which the real meaning is to make holy, as it is in Dutch, heiliging (holying), and heiligmaking (holy-making).

What wealth of meaning and blessing in the two words combined: Holy in Christ! Here is God's provision for our holiness, God's response to our question, How to be holy? Often and often as we hear the call, Be ye holy, even as I am holy, it is as if there is and ever must be a great gulf between the holiness of God and man. In Christ! is the bridge that crosses the gulf; nay rather, His fulness has filled it up. In Christ! God and man meet; In Christ! the Holiness of God has found us, and made us its own; has become human, and can indeed become our very own. To the anxious cries and the heart-yearnings of thousands of thirsty souls who have believed in Jesus and yet know not how to be holy, here is God's answer: Ye are Holy in Christ Jesus. Would they but hearken, and believe; would they but take these Divine words, and say them over, if need be, a thousand times, how God's light would shine, and fill their hearts with joy and love as they echo them back: Yes, now I see it. Holy in Christ! Made holy in Christ Jesus!

As we set ourselves to study these wondrous words, let us remember that it is only God Himself who can reveal to us what Holiness truly is. Let us fear our own thoughts, and crucify our own wisdom. Let us give up ourselves to receive, in the power of the life of God Himself, working in us by the Holy Spirit, that which is deeper and truer than human thought, Christ Himself as our Holiness. In this dependence upon the teaching of the Spirit of Holiness, let us seek simply to accept what Holy Scripture sets before us; as the revelation of the Holy One of old was a very slow and gradual one, so let us be content patiently to follow step by step the path of the shining light through the Word; it will shine more and more unto the perfect day.

We shall first have to study the word Holy in the Old Testament. In Israel as the holy people, the type of us who now are holy in Christ, we shall see with what fulness of symbol God sought to work into the very constitution of the people some apprehension of what He would have them be. In the law we shall see how Holy is the great keyword of the redemption which it was meant to serve and prepare for. In the prophets we shall hear how the Holiness of God is revealed as the source whence the coming redemption should spring: it is not so much Holiness as the Holy One they speak of, who would, in redeeming love and saving righteousness, make Himself known as the God of His people.

And when the meaning of the word has been somewhat

7

opened up, and the deep need of the blessing made manifest in the Old Testament, we shall come to the New to find how that need was fulfilled. In Christ, the Holy One of God, Divine Holiness will be found in human life and human nature; a truly human will being made perfect and growing up through obedience into complete union with all the Holy Will of God. In the sacrifice of Himself on the cross, that holy nature gave itself up to the death, that, like the seed-corn, it might through death live again and reproduce itself in us. In the gift from the throne of the Spirit of God's Holiness, representing and revealing and communicating the unseen Christ, the holy life of Christ descends and takes possession of His people, and they become one with Him. As the Old Testament had no higher word than that Holy, the New has none deeper than this, in Christ. The being in Him, the abiding in Him, the being rooted in Him, the growing up in Him and into Him in all things, are the Divine expressions in which the wonderful and complete oneness between us and our Saviour are brought as near us as human language can do.

And when Old and New Testament have each given their message, the one in teaching us what Holy, the other what in Christ means, we have in the word of God, that unites the two, the most complete summary of the Great Redemption that God's love has provided. The everlasting certainty, the wonderful sufficiency, the infinite efficacy of the Holiness that God has prepared for us in His Son, are all revealed in this blessed, Holy in Christ.

'The Holy Ones in Christ Jesus!' Such is the name, beloved fellow-believers, which we bear in Holy Scripture, in the language of the Holy Spirit. It is no mere statement of doctrine, that we are holy in Christ: it is no deep theological discussion to which we are invited; but out of the depths of God's loving heart, there comes a voice thus addressing His beloved children. It is the name by which the Father calls His children. That name tells us of God's provision for our being holy. It is the revelation of what God has given us, and what we already are; of what God waits to work in us, and what can be ours in personal practical possession. That name, gratefully accepted, joyfully confessed, trustfully pleaded, will be the pledge and the power of our attainment of the Holiness to which we have been called.

And so we shall find that as we go along, all our study and all God's teaching will be comprised in three great lessons. The first a revelation, 'I am holy;' the second a command, 'Be ye holy;' the third a gift, the link between the two, 'Ye are holy in Christ.'

First comes the revelation, 'I am holy.' Our study must be on bended knee, in the spirit of worship and deep humility. God must reveal Himself to us, if we are to know what Holy is. The deep unholiness of our nature and all that is of nature must be shown us; with Moses and Isaiah, when the Holy One revealed Himself to them, we must fear and tremble, and confess how utterly unfit we are for the revelation or the fellowship, without the cleansing of fire. In the consciousness of the utter impotence of our own wisdom or understanding to know God, our souls must in contrition, brokenness from ourselves and our power or efforts, yield to God's Spirit, the Spirit of Holiness, to reveal God as the Holy One. And as we begin to know Him in His infinite righteousness, in His fiery burning zeal against all that is sin, and His infinite self-sacrificing love to free the sinner from his sin, and to bring him to His own perfection, we shall learn to wonder at and worship this glorious God, to feel and deplore our terrible unlikeness to Him, to long and cry for some share in the Divine beauty and blessedness of this Holiness.

And then will come with new meaning the command, 'Be holy, as I am holy.' Oh, my brethren! ye who profess to obey the commands of your God, do give this all-surpassing and all-including command that first place in your heart and life which it claims. Do be holy with the likeness of God's Holiness. Do be holy as He is holy. And if you find that the more you meditate and study, the less you can grasp this infinite holiness; that the more you at moments grasp of it, the more you despair of a holiness so Divine; remember that such breaking down and such despair is just what the command was meant to work. Learn to cease from your own wisdom as well as your own goodness; draw near in poverty of spirit to let the Holy One show you how utterly above human knowledge or human power is the holiness He demands; to the soul that ceases from self, and has no confidence in the flesh, He will show and give the holiness He calls us to.

It is to such that the great gift of Holiness in Christ becomes intelligible and acceptable. Christ brings the Holiness of God nigh by showing it in human conduct and intercourse. He brings it nigh by removing the barrier between it and us, between God and us. He brings it nigh, because He makes us one with Himself. 'Holy in Christ:' our holiness is a Divine bestowment, held for us, communicated to us, working mightily in us because we are in Him. 'In Christ!' oh, that wonderful in! our very life rooted in the life of Christ. That holy Son and Servant of the Father, beautiful in His life of love and obedience on earth, sanctifying Himself for us—that life of Christ, the ground in which I am planted and rooted, the soil from which I draw as my nourishment its every quality and its very nature. How that word sheds its light both on the revelation, 'I am holy,' and on the command, 'Be ye holy, as I am,' and binds them in one! In Christ I see what God's Holiness is, and what my holiness is. In Him both are one, and both are mine. In Him I am holy; abiding and growing up in Him, I can be holy in all manner of living, as God is holy.

Be ye holy, as I am holy

O Most Holy God! we do beseech Thee, reveal Thou to Thy children what it meaneth that Thou hast not only called them to holiness, but even called them by this name, 'the holy ones in Christ Jesus.' Oh that every child of Thine might know that He bears this name, might know what it means, and what power there is in it to make Him what it calls him. Holy Lord God! oh that the time of Thy visitation might speedily come, and each child of Thine on earth be known as a holy one!

To this end we pray Thee to reveal to Thy saints what Thy Holiness is. Teach us to worship and to wait until Thou hast spoken unto our souls with Divine Power Thy word, 'I am holy.' Oh that it may search out and convict us of our unholiness!

And reveal to us, we pray Thee, that as holy as Thou art, even a consuming fire, so holy is Thy command in its determined and uncompromising purpose to have us holy. O God! let Thy voice sound through the depth of our being, with a power from which there is no escape: Be holy, be holy.

And let us thus, between Thine infinite Holiness on the one hand and our unholiness on the other, be driven and be drawn to accept of Christ as our sanctification, to abide in Him as our life and our power to be what Thou wouldst have us—'Holy in Christ Jesus.'

O Father! let Thy Spirit make this precious word life and truth within us. Amen.

1. You are entering anew on the study of a Divine mystery. 'Trust not to your own understanding;' wait for the teaching of the Spirit of truth.

2. In Christ. A commentator says, 'The phrase denotes two moral facts—first, the act of faith whereby a man lays hold of Christ; second, the community of life with Him contracted by means of this faith.' There is still another fact, the greatest of all: that it is by an act of Divine power that I am in Christ and am kept in Him. It is this I want to realize: the Divineness of my position in Jesus.

3. Grasp the two sides of the truth. You are holy in Christ with a Divine holiness. In the faith of that, you are to be holy, to become holy with a human holiness, the Divine Holiness manifest in all the conduct of a human life.

4. This Christ is a Living Person, a Loving Saviour: how He will delight to get complete possession, and do all the work in you! Keep hold of this all along as we go on: you have a claim on Christ, on His Love and Power, to make you holy. As His redeemed one, you are at this moment, whatever and wherever you be, in Him. His Holy Presence and Love are around you. You are in Him, in the enclosure of that tender love, which ever encircles you with His Holy Presence. In that Presence, accepted and realized, is your holiness.

Third Day

HOLY IN CHRIST

Holiness and Creation

'And God blessed the Sabbath day, and sanctified it, because that in it He had rested from all the work which God created and made.'—Gen. ii. 3.

In Genesis we have the Book of Beginnings. To its first three chapters we are specially indebted for a Divine light shining on the many questions to which human wisdom never could find an answer. In our search after Holiness, we are led thither too. In the whole book of Genesis the word Holy occurs but once. But that once in such a connection as to open to us the secret spring whence flows all that the Bible has to teach or to give us of this heavenly blessing. The full meaning of the precious word we want to master, of the priceless blessing we want to get possession of, 'Sanctified in Christ,' takes its rise in what is here written of that wondrous act of God, by which He closed His creation work, and revealed how wonderfully it would be continued and perfected. When God blessed the seventh day, and sanctified it, He lifted it above the other days, and set it apart to a work and a revelation of Himself, excelling in glory all that had preceded. In this simple expression, Scripture reveals to us the character of God as the Holy One, who makes holy; the way in which He makes holy, by entering in and resting; and the power of blessing with which God's making holy is ever accompanied. These three lessons we shall find it of the deepest importance to study well, as containing the root-principles of all the Scripture will have to teach us in our pursuit of Holiness.

1. God sanctified the Sabbath day. Of the previous six days the keyword was, from the first calling into existence of the heaven and the earth, down to the making of man: God created. All at once a new word and a new work of God, is introduced: God sanctified. Something higher than creation, that for which creation is to exist, is now to be revealed; God Almighty is now to be known as God Most Holy. And just as the work of creation shows His Power, without that Power being mentioned, so His

12

making holy the seventh day reveals His character as the Holy One. As Omnipotence is the chief of His natural, so Holiness is the first of His moral attributes. And just as He alone is Creator, so He alone is Sanctifier; to make holy is His work as truly and exclusively as to create. Blessed is the child of God who truly and fully believes this!

God sanctified the Sabbath day. The word can teach us what the nature is of the work God does when He makes holy. Sanctification in Paradise cannot be essentially different from Sanctification in Redemption. God had pronounced all His works, and man the chief of them, very good. And yet they were not holy. The six days' work had nought of defilement or sin, and yet it was not holy. The seventh day needed to be specially made holy, for the great work of making holy man, who was already very good. In Exodus, God says distinctly that He sanctified the Sabbath day, with a view to man's sanctification. 'That ye may know that I am the Lord that doth sanctify you.' Goodness, innocence, purity, freedom from sin, is not Holiness. Goodness is the work of omnipotence, an attribute of nature, as God creates it: holiness is something infinitely higher. We speak of the holiness of God as His infinite moral perfection; man's moral perfection could only come in the use of his will, consenting freely to and abiding in the will of God. Thus alone could he become holy. The seventh day was made holy by God as a pledge that He would make man holy. In the ages that preceded the seventh day, the Creation period, God's Power, Wisdom, and Goodness had been displayed. The age to come, in the seventh day period, is to be the dispensation of holiness: God made holy the seventh day.

2. God sanctified the Sabbath day, because in it He rested from all His work. This rest was something real. In Creation, God had, as it were, gone out of Himself to bring forth something new: in resting He now returns from His creating work into Himself, to rejoice in His love over the man He has created, and communicate Himself to him. This opens up to us the way in which God makes holy. The connection between the resting and making holy was no arbitrary one; the making holy was no after-thought; in the very nature of things it could not be otherwise: He sanctified because He rested in it; He sanctified by resting. As He regards His finished work, more especially man, rejoices in it, and, as we have it in Exodus, 'is refreshed,' this time of His Divine rest is the time in which He will carry on unto perfection

13

what He has begun, and make man, created in His image, in very deed partaker of His highest glory, His Holiness.

Where God rests in complacency and love, He makes holy. The Presence of God revealing itself, entering in, and taking possession, is what constitutes true Holiness. As we go down the ages, studying the progressive unfolding of what Holiness is, this truth will continually meet us. In God's indwelling in heaven, in His temple on earth, in His beloved Son, in the person of the believer through the Holy Spirit, we shall everywhere find that Holiness is not something that man is or does, but that it always comes where God comes. In the deepest meaning of the words: where God enters to rest, there He sanctifies. And when we come to study the New Testament revelation of the way in which we are to be holy, we shall find in this one of our earliest and deepest lessons. It is as we enter into the rest of God that we become partakers of His Holiness. 'We which have believed do enter into that rest;' 'He that hath entered into his rest hath himself also rested from his works, as God did from His.' It is as the soul ceases from its own efforts, and rests in Him who has finished all for us, and will finish all in us, as the soul yields itself in the quiet confidence of true faith to rest in God, that it will know what true Holiness is. Where the soul enters into the Sabbath stillness of perfect trust, God comes to keep His Sabbath holy; and the soul where He rests He sanctifies. Whether we speak of His own day, 'He sanctified it,' or His own people 'sanctified in Christ,' the secret of Holiness is ever the same: 'He sanctified because he rested.'

3. And then we read, 'He blessed and sanctified it.' As used in the first chapter and throughout the book of Genesis, the word 'God blessed' is one of great significance. 'Be fruitful and multiply' was, as to Adam, so later to Noah and Abraham, the Divine exposition of its meaning. The blessing with which God blessed Adam and Noah and Abraham was that of fruitfulness and increase, the power to reproduce and multiply. When God blessed the seventh day, He filled it so with the living power of His Holiness, that in it that Holiness might increase and reproduce itself in those who, like Him, seek to enter into its rest and sanctify it. The seventh day is that in which we are still living. Of each of the creation days it is written, up to the last, 'There was evening, and there was morning, the sixth day.' Of the seventh the record has not yet been made; we are living in it now, God's own day of rest and holiness and blessing. Entering into it

14

in a very special manner, and taking possession of it, as the time for His rejoicing in His creature, and manifesting the fulness of His love in sanctifying him, He has made the dispensation we now live in one of Divine and mighty blessing. And He has at the same time taught us what the blessing is. Holiness is blessedness. Fellowship with God in His holy rest is blessedness. And as all God's blessings in Christ have but one fountain, God's Holiness, so they all have but one aim, making us partakers of that Holiness. God created, and blessed; with the creation blessing. God sanctified, and blessed; with the Sabbath blessing of His rest. The Creation blessing, of goodness and fruitfulness and dominion, is to be crowned by the Sabbath blessing of rest in God and holiness in fellowship with Him.

God's finished work of Creation was marred by sin, and our fellowship with Him in the blessing of His holy rest cut off. The finished work of redemption opened for us a truer rest and a surer entrance into the Holiness of God. As He rested in His holy day, so He now rests in His Holy Son. In Him we now can enter fully into the rest of God. 'Made holy in Christ,' let us rest in Him. Let us rest, because we see that as wonderfully as God by His mighty power finished His work of Creation, will He complete and perfect His work of sanctification. Let us yield ourselves to God in Christ, to rest where He rested, to be made holy with His own holiness, and to be blessed with God's own blessing. God the Sanctifier is the name now inscribed upon the throne of God the Creator. At the threshold of the history of the human race there shines this word of infinite promise and hope: 'God blessed and sanctified the seventh day because in it He rested.'

Be ye holy, for I am holy

Blessed Lord God! I bow before Thee in lowly worship. I adore Thee as God the Creator, and God the Sanctifier. Thou hast revealed Thyself as God Almighty and God Most Holy. I beseech Thee, teach me to know and to trust Thee as such.

I humbly ask Thee for grace to learn and hold fast the deep spiritual truths Thou hast revealed in making holy the Sabbath day. Thy purpose in man's creation is to show forth Thy Holiness, and make him partaker of it. Oh, teach me to believe in Thee as God my Creator and Sanctifier, to believe with my whole heart that the same Almighty power which gave the sixth-day blessing of creation, secures to us the seventh-day blessing of sanctification. Thy will is our sanctification.

And teach me, Lord, to understand better how this blessing comes. It is where Thou enterest to rest, to refresh and reveal Thyself, that Thou makest holy. O my God! may my heart be Thy resting-place. I would, in the stillness and confidence of a restful faith, rest in Thee, believing that Thou doest all in me. Let such fellowship with Thee, and Thy love, and Thy will be to me the secret of a life of holiness. I ask it in the name of our Lord Jesus, in whom Thou hast sanctified us. Amen.

1. God the Creator is God the Sanctifier. The Omnipotence that did the first work does the second too. I can trust God Almighty to make me holy. God is holy: if God is everything to me, His presence will be my holiness.

2. Rest is ceasing from work, not to work no more, but to begin a new work. God rests and begins at once to make holy that in which He rests. He created by the word of His power; He rests in His love. Creation was the building of the temple; sanctification is the entering in and taking possession. Oh, that wonderful entering into human nature!

3. God rests only in what is restful, wholly at His disposal. It is in the restfulness of faith that we must look to God the Sanctifier; He will come in and keep His holy Sabbath in the restful soul. We rest in God's rest; God rests in our rest.

4. The God that rests in man whom He made, and in resting sanctifies, and in sanctifying blesses: this is our God; praise and worship Him. And trust Him to do His work.

5. Rest! what a simple word. The Rest of God! what an inconceivable fulness of Life and Love in that word. Let us meditate on it and worship before Him, until it overshadow us and we enter into it—the Rest of God. Rest belongeth unto God: He alone can give it, by making us share His own.

Fourth Day

HOLY IN CHRIST

Holiness and Revelation

'And when the Lord saw that Moses turned aside to see, He called unto him out of the midst of the bush, and said, Moses, Moses. And he said, Here am I. And He said, Draw not nigh hither; put off thy shoes from thy feet, for the place where thou standest is holy ground. And Moses hid his face, for He was afraid to look upon God.'—Ex. iii. 4–6.

And why was it holy ground? Because God had come there and occupied it. Where God is, there is holiness; it is the presence of God makes holy. This is the truth we met with in Paradise when man was just created; here, where Scripture uses the word Holy for the second time, it is repeated and enforced. A careful study of the word in the light of the burning bush will further open its deep significance. Let us see what the sacred history, what the revelation of God, and what Moses teaches us of this holy ground.

1. Note the place this first direct revelation of God to man as the Holy One takes in sacred history. In Paradise we found the word Holy used of the seventh day. Since that time twenty-five centuries have elapsed. We found in God's sanctifying the day of rest a promise of a new dispensation—the revelation of the Almighty Creator to be followed by that of the Holy One making holy. And yet throughout the book of Genesis the word never occurs again; it is as if God's Holiness is in abeyance; only in Exodus, with the calling of Moses, does it make its appearance again. This is a fact of deep import. Just as a parent or teacher seeks, in early childhood, to impress one lesson at a time, so God deals in the education of the human race. After having in the flood exhibited His righteous judgment against sin, He calls Abraham to be the father of a chosen people. And as the foundation of all His dealings with that people, He teaches him and his seed first of all the lesson of childlike trust—trust in Him as the Almighty, with whom nothing is too wonderful, and trust in Him as the Faithful One, whose oath could not be broken. With the growth of Israel to a people we see the revelation

17

advancing to a new stage. The simplicity of childhood gives way to the waywardness of youth, and God must now interfere with the discipline and restriction of law. Having gained a right to a place in their confidence as the God of their fathers, He prepares them for a further revelation. Of the God of Abraham the chief attribute was that He was the Almighty One; of the God of Israel, Jehovah, that He is the Holy One.

And what is to be the special mark of the new period that is now about to be inaugurated, and which is introduced by the word holy? God tells Moses that He is now about to reveal Himself in a new character. He had been known to Abraham as God Almighty, the God of Promise (Ex. vi. 3). He would now manifest Himself as Jehovah, the God of Fulfilment, especially in the redemption and deliverance of His people from the oppression He had foretold to Abraham. God Almighty is the God of Creation: Abraham believed in God, 'who quickeneth the dead, and calleth the things that are not as though they were.' Jehovah is the God of Redemption and of Holiness. With Abraham there was not a word of sin or guilt, and therefore not of redemption or holiness. To Israel the law is to be given, to convince of sin and prepare the way for holiness; it is Jehovah, the Holy One of Israel, the Redeemer, who now appears. And it is the presence of this Holy One that makes the holy ground.

2. And how does this Presence reveal itself? In the burning bush God makes Himself known as dwelling in the midst of the fire. Elsewhere in Holy Scripture the connection between fire and the Holiness of God is clearly expressed: 'The light of Israel shall be for a fire, and the Holy One for a flame.' The nature of fire may be either beneficent or destructive. The sun, the great central fire, may give life and fruitfulness, or may scorch to death. All depends upon occupying the right position, upon the relation in which we stand to it. And so wherever God the Holy One reveals Himself, we shall find the two sides together: God's Holiness as judgment against sin, destroying the sinner who remains in it, and as Mercy freeing His people from it. Judgment and Mercy ever go together. Of the elements of nature there is none of such spiritual and mighty energy as Fire: what it consumes it takes and changes into its own spiritual nature, rejecting as smoke and ashes what cannot be assimilated. And so the Holiness of God is that infinite Perfection by which He keeps Himself free from all that is not Divine, and yet has fellowship

with the creature, and takes it up into union with Himself, destroying and casting out all that will not yield itself to Him.

It is thus as One who dwells in the fire, who is a fire, that God reveals Himself at the opening of this new redemption period. With Abraham and the patriarchs, as we have said, there had been little teaching about sin or redemption; the nearness and friendship of God had been revealed. Now the law will be given, sin will be made manifest, the distance from God will be felt, that man, in learning to know himself and his sinfulness, may learn to know and long for God to make him holy. In all God's revelation of Himself we shall find the combination of the two elements, the one repelling, the other attracting. In His house He will dwell in the midst of Israel, and yet it will be in the awful unapproachable solitude and darkness of the holiest of all within the veil. He will come near to them, and yet keep them at a distance. As we study the Holiness of God, we shall see in increasing clearness how, like fire, it repels and attracts, how it combines into one His infinite distance and His infinite nearness.

3. But the distance will be that which comes out first and most strongly. This we see in Moses: he hid his face, for He feared to look upon God. The first impression which God's Holiness produces is that of fear and awe. Until man, both as a creature and a sinner, learns how high God is above him, how different and distant he is from God, the Holiness of God will have little real value or attraction. Moses hiding his face shows us the effect of the drawing nigh of the Holy One, and the path to His further revelation.

How distinctly this comes out in God's own words: 'Draw not nigh hither; put off thy shoes from off thy feet.' Yes, God had drawn nigh, but Moses may not. God comes near: man must stand back. In the same breath God says, Draw nigh, and, Draw not nigh. There can be no knowledge of God or nearness to Him, where we have not first heard His, Draw not nigh. The sense of sin, of unfitness for God's presence, is the groundwork of true knowledge or worship of Him as the Holy One. 'Put off thy shoes from off thy feet.' The shoes are the means of intercourse with the world, the aids through which the flesh or nature does its will, moves about and does its work. In standing upon holy ground, all this must be put away. It is with naked feet, naked and stript of every covering, that man must bow before a holy God. Our utter unfitness to draw nigh or have any dealings with the Holy One, is the very first lesson we have to learn, if ever we are to participate in His Holiness. That Put off! must exercise its condemning power through our whole being, until we come to realize the full extent of its meaning in the great, 'Put off the old man; put on the Lord Jesus,' and what 'the putting off of the body of the flesh, in the circumcision of Christ,' is. Yes, all that is of nature and the flesh, all that is of our own doing or willing or working—our very life, must be put off and given unto the death, if God, as the Holy One, is to make Himself known to us.

We have seen before that Holiness is more than goodness or freedom from sin: even unfallen nature is not holy. Holiness is that awful glory by which Divinity is separated from all that is created. Therefore even the seraphs veil their faces with their wings when they sing the Thrice Holy. But oh! when the distance and the difference is not that of the creature only, but of the sinner, who can express, who can realize, the humiliation, the fear, the shame with which we ought to bow before the voice of the Holy One? Alas! this is one of the most terrible effects of sin, that it blinds us. We know not how unholy, how abominable, sin and the sinful nature are in God's sight. We have lost the power of recognising the Holiness of God: heathen philosophy had not even the idea of using the word as expressive of the moral character of its gods. In losing the light of the glory of God, we have lost the power of knowing what sin is. And now God's first work in drawing nigh to us is to make us feel that we may not draw nigh as we are; that there will have to be a very real and a very solemn putting off, and even giving up to the death, of all that appears most lawful and most needful. Not only our shoes are soiled with contact with this unholy earth; even our face must be covered and our eyes closed, in token that the eyes of our heart, all our human wisdom and understanding, are incapable of beholding the Holy One. The first lesson in the school of personal holiness is, to fear and hide our face before the Holiness of God. 'Thus saith the High and Lofty One, whose name is holy, I dwell in the High and Holy Place, and with him that is of a contrite and humble spirit.' Contrition, brokenness of spirit, fear and trembling are God's first demand of those who would see His Holiness.

Moses was to be the first preacher of the Holiness of God. Of the full communication of God's Holiness to us in Christ, His first revelation to Moses was the type and the pledge. From Moses' lips the people of Israel, from his pen the Church of

Christ, was to receive the message, 'Be holy: I am holy: I make holy.' His preparation for being the messenger of the Holy One was here, where he hid his face, because he was afraid to look upon God. It is with the face in the dust, it is in the putting off not only of the shoes, but of all that has been in contact with the world and self and sin, that the soul draws nigh to the fire, in which God dwells, and which burns, but does not consume. Oh that every believer, who seeks to witness for God as the Holy One, might thus learn how the fulfilment of the type of the Burning Bush is the Crucified Christ, and how, as we die with Him, we receive that Baptism of Fire, which reveals in each of us what it means: the Holy One dwelling in a Burning Bush. Only so can we learn what it is to be holy, as He is holy.

Be ye holy, for I am holy

Most Holy God! I have seen Thee, who dwellest in the fire. I have heard Thy voice, Draw not nigh hither; put thy shoes off from thy feet. And my soul has feared to look upon God, the Holy One.

And yet, O my God! I must see Thee. Thou didst create me for Thy likeness. Thou hast taught that this likeness is Thy Holiness: 'Be holy, as I am holy.' O my God! how shall I know to be holy, unless I may see Thee, the Holy One? To be holy, I must look upon God.

I bless Thee for the revelation of Thyself in the flames of the thorn-bush, in the fire of the accursed tree. I bow in amazement and deep abasement at the great sight: Thy Son in the weakness of His human nature, in the fire, burning but not consumed. O my God! in fear and trembling I have yielded myself as a sinner to die like Him. Oh, let the fire consume all that is unholy in me! Let me too know Thee as the God that dwelleth in the fire, to melt down and purge out and destroy what is not of Thee, to save and take up into Thine own Holiness what is Thine own.

O Holy Lord God! I bow in the dust before this great mystery. Reveal to me Thy Holiness, that I too may be its witness and its messenger on earth. Amen.

1. Holiness as the fire of God. Praise God that there is a Power that can consume the vile and the dross, a Power that will

21

not leave it undisturbed. 'The bush burning but not consumed' is not only the motto of the Church in time of persecution; it is the watchword of every soul in God's sanctifying work.

2. There is a new Theology, which only speaks of the love of God as seen in the cross. It sees not the glory of His Righteousness, and His righteous judgment. This is not the God of Scripture. 'Our God is a consuming fire,' is New Testament Theology. To 'offer service with reverence and awe,' is New Testament religion. In Holiness, Judgment and Mercy meet.

3. Holiness as the fear of God. Hiding the face before God for fear, not daring to look or speak,—this is the beginning of rest in God. It is not yet the true rest, but on the way to it. May God give us a deep fear of whatever could grieve or anger Him. May we have a deep fear of ourselves, and all that is of the old, the condemned nature, lest it rise again. 'The spirit of the fear of the Lord' is the first manifestation of the spirit of holiness, and prepares the way for the joy of holiness. 'Walking in the fear of the Lord, and in the comfort of the Holy Ghost;' these are the two sides of the Christian life.

4. The Holiness of God was revealed to Moses that he might be its messenger. The Church needs nothing so much to-day as men and women who can testify for the Holiness of God. Will you be one?

NOTE

The connection between the fear of God and holiness is most intimate. There are some who seek most earnestly for holiness, and yet never exhibit it in a light that will attract the world or even believers, because this element is wanting. It is the fear of the Lord that works that meekness and gentleness, that deliverance from self-confidence and self-consciousness, which form the true groundwork of a saintly character. The passages of God's Word in which the two words are linked together are well worthy of a careful study. 'Who is like unto Thee, glorious in holiness, fearful in praises?' 'In Thy fear will I worship towards Thy holy temple.' 'O fear the Lord, ye His holy ones.' 'O worship the Lord, in the beauty of holiness; fear before Him, all the earth.' 'Let them praise Thy great and terrible name; holy is He.' 'The fear of the Lord is the beginning of wisdom; and the knowledge of the Holy One is understanding.' 'The Lord of hosts,

Him shall ye sanctify; let Him be your fear, and let Him be your dread.' 'Perfecting holiness in the fear of the Lord.' 'Like as He which called you is holy, be ye yourselves also holy; and if ye call on Him as father, pass the time of your sojourning in fear.' And so on through the whole of Scripture, from the Song of Moses on to the Song of the Lamb: 'Who shall not fear Thee, O Lord! and glorify Thy name, for Thou only art holy.' If we yield ourselves to the impression of such passages, we shall feel more deeply that the fear of God, the tender fear of in any way offending Him, the fear especially of entering into His holy presence with what is human and carnal, with aught of our own wisdom and effort, is of the very essence of the holiness we are to follow after. It is this fear of God will make us, like Moses, fall down and hide our face in God's presence, and wait for His own Holy Spirit to open in us the eyes, and breathe in us the thoughts and the worship, with which we draw nigh to Him, the Holy One. It is in this holy fear that that stillness of soul is wrought which leads it to rest in God, and opens the way for what we saw in Paradise to be the secret of holiness: God keeping His Sabbath, and sanctifying the soul in which He rests.

Fifth Day

HOLY IN CHRIST

Holiness and Redemption

'Sanctify unto me all the first-born.'—Ex. xiii. 2.

'All the first-born are mine; for on the day I smote all the first-born in the land of Egypt I sanctified unto me all the first-born in Israel: mine they shall be: I am the Lord.'—Num. iii. 13, viii. 17.

'For I am the Lord your God that bringeth you up out of the land of Egypt to be your God: ye shall therefore be holy, for I am holy.'—Lev. xi. 45.

'I have redeemed thee; thou art mine.'—Isa. xliii. 1.

At Horeb we saw how the first mention of the word holy in the history of fallen man was connected with the inauguration of a new period in the revelation of God, that of Redemption. In the passover we have the first manifestation of what Redemption is; and here the more frequent use of the word holy begins. In the feast of unleavened bread we have the symbol of the putting off of the old and the putting on of the new, to which redemption through blood is to lead. Of the seven days we read: 'In the first day there shall be an holy convocation, and in the seventh day there shall be an holy convocation;' the meeting of the redeemed people to commemorate its deliverance is a holy gathering; they meet under the covering of their Redeemer, the Holy One. As soon as the people had been redeemed from Egypt, God's very first word to them was, 'Sanctify—make holy unto me all the first-born: it is mine.' (See Ex. xiii. 2.) The word reveals how proprietorship is one of the central thoughts both in redemption and in sanctification, the link that binds them together. And though the word is here only used of the first-born, they are regarded as the type of the whole people. We know how all growth and organization commence from a centre, around which in ever-widening circles the life of the organism spreads.

24

If holiness in the human race is to be true and real, free as that of God, it must be the result of a self-appropriating development. And so the first-born are sanctified, and afterwards the priests in their place, as the type of what the whole people is to be as God's first-born among the nations, His peculiar treasure, 'an holy nation.' This idea of proprietorship as related to redemption and sanctification comes out with especial clearness when God speaks of the exchange of the priests for the first-born (Num. iii. 12, 13, viii. 16, 17): 'The Levites are wholly given unto me; instead of the first-born have I taken them unto me; for all the first-born are mine; in the day that I smote every first-born in the land of Egypt I sanctified them for myself.'

Let us try and realize the relation existing between redemption and holiness. In Paradise we saw what God's sanctifying the seventh day was: He took possession of it, He blessed it, He rested in it and refreshed Himself. Where God enters and rests, there is holiness: the more perfectly the object is fitted for Him to enter and dwell, the more perfect the holiness. The seventh day was sanctified as the period for man's sanctification. At the very first step God took to lead him to His Holiness—the command not to eat of the tree—man fell. God did not give up His plan, but had now to pursue a different and slower path. After twenty-five centuries' slow but needful preparation, He now reveals Himself as the Redeemer. A people whom He had chosen and formed for Himself He gives up to oppression and slavery, that their hearts may be prepared to long for and welcome a Deliverer. In a series of mighty wonders He proves Himself the Conqueror of their enemies, and then, in the blood of the Paschal Lamb on their doors, teaches them what redemption is, not only from an unjust oppressor here on earth, but from the righteous judgment their sins had deserved. The Passover is to be to them the transition from the seen and temporal to the unseen and spiritual, revealing God not only as the Mighty but as the Holy One, freeing them not only from the house of bondage but the Destroying Angel.

And having thus redeemed them, He tells them that they are now His own. During their stay at Sinai and in the wilderness, the thought is continually pressed upon them that they are now the Lord's people, whom He has made His own by the strength of His arm, that He may make them holy for Himself, even as He is holy. The purpose of redemption is

25

Possession, and the purpose of Possession is likeness to Him who is Redeemer and Owner, is Holiness.

In regard to this Holiness, and the way it is to be attained as the result of redemption, there is more than one lesson the sanctifying of the first-born will teach us.

First of all, we want to realize how inseparable redemption and holiness are. Neither can exist without the other. Only redemption leads to holiness. If I am seeking holiness, I must abide in the clear and full experience of being a redeemed one, and as such of being owned and possessed by God. Redemption is too often looked at from its negative side as deliverance from: its real glory is the positive element of being redeemed unto Himself. Full possession of a house means occupation: if I own a house without occupying it, it may be the home of all that is foul and evil. God has redeemed me and made me His own with the view of getting complete possession of me. He says of my soul, 'It is mine,' and seeks to have His right of ownership acknowledged and made fully manifest. That will be perfect holiness, where God has entered in and taken complete and entire possession. [2] It is redemption gives God His right and power over me; it is redemption sets me free for God now to possess and bless: it is redemption realized and filling my soul, that will bring me the assurance and experience of all His power will work in me. In God, redemption and sanctification are one: the more redemption as a Divine reality possesses me, the closer am I linked to the Redeemer-God, the Holy One.

And just so, only holiness brings the assurance and enjoyment of redemption. If I am seeking to hold fast redemption on lower ground, I may be deceived. If I have become unwatchful or careless, I should tremble at the very idea of trusting in redemption apart from holiness as its object. To Israel God spake, 'I brought you up out of the land of Egypt: therefore ye shall be holy, for I am holy.' It is God the Redeemer who made us His own, who calls us too to be holy: let Holiness be to us the most essential, the most precious part of redemption: the yielding of ourselves to Him who has taken us as His own, and has undertaken to make us His own entirely.

A second lesson suggested is the connection between God's and man's working in sanctification. To Moses the Lord speaks, 'Sanctify unto me all the first-born.' He afterwards says, 'I

---

[2] See Note A on Holiness as Proprietorship.

sanctified all the first-born for myself.' What God does He does to be carried out and appropriated through us. When He tells us that we are made holy in Christ Jesus, that we are His holy ones, He speaks not only of His purpose, but of what He has really done; we have been sanctified in the one offering of Christ, and in our being created anew in Him. But this work has a human side. To us comes the call to be holy, to follow after holiness, to perfect holiness. God has made us His own, and allows us to say that we are His: but He waits for us now to yield Him an enlarged entrance into the secret places of our inner being, for Him to fill it all with His fulness. Holiness is not something we bring to God or do for Him. Holiness is what there is of God in us. God has made us His own in redemption, that He might make Himself our own in sanctification. And our work in becoming holy is the bringing our whole life, and every part of it, into subjection to the rule of this holy God, putting every member and every power upon His altar.

And this teaches us the answer to the question as to the connection between the sudden and the gradual in sanctification: between its being a thing once for all complete, and yet imperfect and needing to be perfected. What God sanctifies is holy with a Divine and perfect holiness as His gift: man has to sanctify by acknowledging and maintaining and carrying out that holiness in relation to what God has made holy. God sanctified the Sabbath day: man has to sanctify it, that is, to keep it holy. God sanctified the first-born as His own: Israel had to sanctify them, to treat them and give them up to God as holy. God is holy: we are to sanctify Him in acknowledging and adoring and honouring that holiness. God has sanctified His great name, His name is Holy: we sanctify or hallow that name as we fear and trust and use it as the revelation of His Holiness. God sanctified Christ: Christ sanctified Himself, manifesting in His personal will and action perfect conformity to the Holiness with which God had made Him holy. God has sanctified us in Christ Jesus: we are to be holy by yielding ourselves to the power of that holiness, by acting it out, and manifesting it in all our life and walk. The objective Divine gift, bestowed once for all and completely, must be appropriated as a subjective personal possession; we must cleanse ourselves, perfecting holiness. Redeemed unto holiness: as the two thoughts are linked in the mind and work of God, they must be linked in our heart and life.

When Isaiah announced the second, the true redemption,

it was given to him, even more clearly and fully than to Moses, to reveal the name of God as 'The Redeemer, the Holy One of Israel.' The more we study this name, and hallow it, and worship God by it, the more inseparably will the words become connected, and we shall see how, as the Redeemer is the Holy One, the redeemed are holy ones too. Isaiah says of 'the way of holiness,' the 'redeemed shall walk therein.' The redemption that comes out from the Holiness of God must lead up into it too. We shall understand that to be redeemed in Christ is to be holy in Christ, and the call of our redeeming God will acquire new meaning: 'I am holy: be ye holy.'

Be ye holy, for I am holy

O Lord God! the Holy One of Israel and his Redeemer! I worship before Thee in deep humility. I confess with shame that I so long sought Thee more as the Redeemer than as the Holy One. I knew not that it was as the Holy One Thou hadst redeemed, that redemption was the outcome and the fruit of Thy Holiness; that a participation in Thy Holiness was its one purpose and its highest beauty. I only thought of being redeemed from bondage and death: like Israel, I understood not that without fellowship and conformity to Thyself redemption would lose its value.

Most holy God! I praise Thee for the patience with which Thou bearest with the selfishness and the slowness of Thy redeemed ones. I praise Thee for the teaching of the Spirit of Thy Holiness, leading Thy saints, and me too, to see how it is Thy Holiness, and the call to become partaker of it, that gives redemption its value; how it is for Thyself as the Holy One, to be Thine own, possessed and sanctified of Thee, that we are redeemed.

O my God! with a love and a joy and a thanksgiving that cannot be uttered, I praise Thee for Christ, who has been made unto us of Thee sanctification and redemption. In Him Thou art my Redeemer, my Holy One. In Him I am Thy redeemed, Thy holy one. O God! in speechless adoration I fall down to worship the love that passeth knowledge, that hath done this for us, and to believe that in one who is now before Thee, holy in Christ, Thou wilt fulfil all Thy glorious purposes according to the greatness of Thy power. Amen.

1. 'Redemption through His blood.' The blood we meet at the threshold of the pathway of Holiness. For it is the blood of the sacrifice which the fire of God consumed, and yet could not consume. That blood has such power of holiness in it, that we read, 'Sanctified by His own blood.' Always think of holiness, or pray for it, as one redeemed by blood. Live under the covering of the blood in its daily cleansing power.

2. It is only as we know the Holiness of God as Fire, and bow before His righteous judgment, that we can appreciate the preciousness of the blood or the reality of the redemption. As long as we only think of the love of God as goodness, we may aim at being good; faith in God who redeems will waken in us the need and the joy of being holy in Christ.

3. Have you understood the right of property God has in what He has redeemed? Have you heard a voice say, Mine. Thou art Mine. Ask God very humbly to speak it to you. Listen very gently for it.

4. The holiness of the creature has its origin in the Divine will, in the Divine election, redemption, and possession. Give yourself up to this will of God and rejoice in it.

5. As God created, so He redeemed, to sanctify. Have great faith in Him for this.

6. Let God have the entire possession and disposal of you. Holiness is His; our holiness is to let Him, the Holy One, be all.

Sixth Day

HOLY IN CHRIST

Holiness and Glory

'Who is like unto Thee, O Lord! among the gods?
Who is like unto Thee, glorious in holiness,
Fearful in praises, doing wonders?
Thou in Thy mercy hast led Thy people which Thou hast
redeemed:
Thou hast guided them in Thy strength to the habitation of
Thy holiness ...
The holy place, O Lord, which Thy hands have
established.'
—Ex. xv. 11–17.

In these words we have another step in advance in the revelation of Holiness. We have here for the first time Holiness predicated of God Himself. He is glorious in holiness: and it is to the dwelling-place of His Holiness that He is guiding His people.

Let us first note the expression used here: glorious in holiness. Throughout Scripture we find the glory and the holiness of God mentioned together. In Ex. xxix. 43 we read, 'And the tent shall be made holy by my glory,' that glory of the Lord of which we afterwards read that it filled the house. The glory of an object, of a thing or person, is its intrinsic worth or excellence: to glorify is to remove everything that could hinder the full revelation of that excellence. In the Holiness of God His glory is hidden; in the glory of God His Holiness is manifested: His glory, the revelation of Himself as the Holy One, would make the house holy. In the same way the two are connected in Lev. x. 3, 'I will be sanctified in them that come nigh unto me, and before all the people I will be glorified.' The acknowledgment of His Holiness in the priests would be the manifestation of His glory to the people. So, too, in the song of the Seraphim (Isa. vi. 3), 'Holy, holy, holy, Lord God of Hosts: the whole earth is full of His glory.' God is He who dwelleth in a light that is unapproachable, whom no man hath seen or can see: it is the light of the knowledge of the glory of God that He gives into our hearts. The glory is that which can be seen and known of the

30

invisible and unapproachable light: that light itself, and the glorious fire of which that light is the shining out, that light is the Holiness of God. Holiness is not so much an attribute of God, as the comprehensive summary of all His perfections.

It is on the shore of the Red Sea that Israel thus praises God: 'Who is like unto Thee, O Lord! Who is like unto Thee, glorious in holiness?' He is the Incomparable One, there is none like Him. And wherein has He proved this, and revealed the glory of His Holiness? With Moses in Horeb we saw God's glory in the fire, in its double aspect of salvation and destruction: consuming what could not be purified, purifying what was not consumed. We see it here too in the song of Moses: Israel sings of judgment and of mercy. The pillar of fire and of the cloud came between the camp of the Egyptians and the camp of Israel: it was a cloud and darkness to those, but it gave light by night to these. The two thoughts run through the whole song. But in the two verses that follow the ascription of holiness, we find the sum of the whole. 'Thou stretchedst out Thy right hand: the earth swallowed them.' 'The Lord looked forth upon the host of the Egyptians from the pillar of fire and discomfited them.' This is the glory of Holiness as judgment and destruction of the enemy. 'Thou in Thy mercy hast led Thy people which thou hast redeemed. Thou hast guided them in Thy strength to the habitation of Thy Holiness.' This is the glory of Holiness in mercy and redemption—a Holiness that not only delivers but guides to the habitation of holiness, where the Holy One is to dwell with and in His people. In the inspiration of the hour of triumph it is thus early revealed that the great object and fruit of redemption, as wrought out by the Holy One, is to be His indwelling: with nothing short of this can the Holy One rest content, or the full glory of His Holiness be made manifest.

And now, observe further, how, as it is in the redemption of His people that God's Holiness is revealed, so it is in the song of redemption that the personal ascription of Holiness to God is found. We know how in Scripture, after some striking special interposition of God as Redeemer, the special influence of the Spirit is manifested in some song of praise. It is remarkable how it is in these outbursts of holy enthusiasm, God is praised as the Holy One. See it in the song of Hannah (1 Sam. ii. 2), 'There is none holy as the Lord.' The language of the Seraphim (Isa. vi.) is that of a song of adoration. In the great day of Israel's deliverance the song will be, 'The Lord Jehovah is become my strength and song. Sing unto the Lord, for He hath done excellent things. Cry aloud and shout, thou inhabitant of Zion, for great is the Holy One of Israel in the midst of thee.' Mary sings, 'For He that is mighty hath done great things to me: and holy is His name.' The book of Revelation reveals the living creatures giving glory and honour and thanks to Him that sitteth on the throne; 'and they have no rest day and night, saying, Holy, holy, holy is the Lord God, the Almighty, which was, and which is, and which is to come.' And when the song of Moses and of the Lamb is sung by the sea of glass, it will still be, 'Who shall not fear, O Lord, and glorify Thy name? for Thou only art holy.' It is in the moments of highest inspiration, under the fullest manifestation of God's redeeming power, that His servants speak of His Holiness. In Ps. xcvii. we read, 'Rejoice in the Lord, ye righteous, and give thanks at the remembrance of His Holiness.' And in Ps. xcix., which has, with its thrice repeated holy, been called the echo on earth of the Thrice Holy of heaven, we sing—

> Let them praise Thy great and terrible name.
> Holy is He.
>
> Exalt ye the Lord our God,
> and worship at His footstool:
> Holy is He.
>
> Exalt ye the Lord our God,
> and worship at His holy hill:
> For the Lord our God is HOLY.

It is only under the influence of high spiritual elevation and joy that God's holiness can be fully apprehended or rightly worshipped. The sentiment that becomes us as we worship the Holy One, that fits us for knowing and worshipping Him aright, is the spirit of praise that sings and shouts for joy in the experience of His full salvation.

But is not this at variance with the lesson we learnt at Horeb, when God spake, 'Draw not nigh hither: put off thy shoes,' and where Moses feared and hid his face? And is not this in very deed the posture that becomes us as creatures and sinners? It is indeed: and yet the two sentiments are not at variance: rather they are indispensable to each other; the fear is the preparation for the praise and the glory. Or is it not that same

Moses who hid his face and feared to look upon God, who afterwards beheld His glory until his own face shone with a brightness that men could not bear to look upon? And is not the song that sings here of God as glorious in holiness, also the song of Moses who feared and hid his face? Have we not seen in the fire, and in God, and specially in His Holiness, the twofold aspect; consuming and purifying, repelling and attracting, judging and saving, with the latter in each case not only the accompaniment but the result of the former? And so we shall find that the deeper the humbling and the fear in God's Holy Presence, and the more real and complete the putting off of all that is of self and of nature, even to the putting off, the complete death of the old man and his will, the more hearty the giving up to be consumed of what is sinful, the deeper and fuller will be the praise and joy with which we daily sing our song of redemption: 'Who is like unto Thee, O Lord, glorious in holiness, fearful in praises, doing wonders?'

'Glorious in holiness; fearful in praises:' the song itself harmonizes the apparently conflicting elements. Yes, I will sing of judgment and of mercy. I will rejoice with trembling as I praise the Holy One. As I look upon the two sides of His Holiness, as revealed to the Egyptians and the Israelites, I remember that what was there separated is in me united. By nature I am the Egyptian, an enemy doomed to destruction; by grace, an Israelite chosen for redemption. In me the fire must consume and destroy; only as judgment does its work, can mercy fully save. It is only as I tremble before the Searching Light and the Burning Fire and the Consuming Heat of the Holy One, as I yield the Egyptian nature to be judged and condemned and slain, that the Israelite will be redeemed to know aright his God as the God of salvation, and to rejoice in Him.

Blessed be God! the judgment is past. In Christ, the burning bush, the fire of the Divine Holiness did its double work: in Him sin was condemned in the flesh; in Him we are free. In giving up His will to the death, and doing God's will, Christ sanctified Himself; and in that will we are sanctified too. His crucifixion, with its judgment of the flesh, His death, with its entire putting off of what is of nature, is not only for us, but is really ours; a life and a power working within us by His Spirit. Day by day we abide in Him. Tremblingly but rejoicingly we take our stand in Him, for the Power of Holiness as Judgment to vindicate within us its fierce vengeance against what is sin and flesh, and so to let the Power of Holiness as Redemption accomplish that glorious work that makes us give thanks at the remembrance of His Holiness. And so the shout of Salvation rings ever deeper and truer and louder through our life, 'Who is like unto Thee, O Lord, among the gods? Who is like unto Thee, glorious in holiness, fearful in praises, doing wonders?'

Be ye holy, as I am holy

'Who is like unto Thee, O Lord! glorious in holiness, fearful in praises, doing wonders?' With my whole heart would I join in this song of redemption, and rejoice in Thee as the God of my salvation.

O my God! let Thy Spirit, from whom these words of holy joy and triumph came, so reveal within me the great redemption as a personal experience, that my whole life may be one song of trembling and adoring wonder.

I beseech Thee especially, let my whole heart be filled with Thyself, glorious in holiness, fearful in praises, who alone doest wonders. Let the fear of Thy Holiness make me tremble at all there is in me of self and flesh, and lead me in my worship to deny and crucify my own wisdom, that the Spirit of Thy Holiness may breathe in me. Let the fear of the Lord give its deep undertone to all my coming in and going out in Thy Holy Presence. Prepare me thus for giving praise without ceasing at the remembrance of Thy holiness. O my God! I would rejoice in Thee as my Redeemer, my Holy One, with a joy unspeakable and full of glory. As my Redeemer, Thou makest me holy. With my whole heart do I trust Thee to do it, to sanctify me wholly. I do believe in Thy promise. I do believe in Thyself, and believing I receive Thee, the Holy One, my Redeemer.

Who is like unto Thee, O Lord! glorious in holiness, fearful in praises, doing wonders?

1. God's Holiness as Glory. God is glorified in the holiness of His people. True holiness always gives glory to God alone. Live to the glory of God: that is holiness. Live holily: that will glorify God. To lose sight of self, and seek only God's glory, is holiness.

2. Our Holiness as Praise. Praise gives glory to God, and is thus an element of holiness. 'Thou art holy, Thou that inhabitest the praises of Israel.'

3. God's Holiness, His holy redeeming love, is cause of unceasing joy and praise. Praise God every day for it. But you cannot do this unless you live in it. May God's holiness become so glorious to us, as we understand that whatever we see of His glory is just the outshining of His holiness, that we cannot help rejoicing in it, and in Him the Holy One.

4. The spirit of the fear of the Lord and the spirit of praise may, at first sight, appear to be at variance. But it is not so. The humility that fears the Holy One will also praise Him: 'Ye that fear the Lord: praise the Lord.' The lower we lie in the fear of God, and the fear of self, the more surely will He lift us up in due time to praise Him.

Seventh Day

HOLY IN CHRIST

Holiness and Obedience

'Ye have seen what I did to the Egyptians, and how I bare you on eagles' wings, and brought you unto myself. Now therefore, if ye will obey my voice indeed, and keep my covenant, ye shall be a peculiar treasure unto me above all people: ye shall be unto me an holy nation.'—Ex. xix. 4–6.

Israel has reached Horeb. The law is to be given and the covenant made. Here are God's first words to the people; He speaks of redemption and its blessing, fellowship with Himself: 'Ye have seen how I brought you unto myself.' He speaks of holiness as His purpose in redemption: 'Ye shall be unto me an holy nation.' And as the link between the two He places obedience: 'If ye will indeed obey my voice, ye shall be unto me an holy nation.' God's will is the expression of His holiness; as we do His will, we come into contact with His holiness. The link between Redemption and Holiness is Obedience.

This takes us back to what we saw in Paradise. God sanctified the seventh day as the time for sanctifying man. And what was the first thing He did with this purpose? He gave him a commandment. Obedience to that commandment would have opened the door, would have been the entrance, into the Holiness of God. Holiness is a moral attribute; and moral is that which a free will chooses and determines for itself. What God creates and gives is only naturally good; what man wills to have of God and His will, and really appropriates, has moral worth, and leads to holiness. In creation God manifested His wise and good will. His holy will He speaks in His commands. As that holy will enters man's will, as man's will accepts and unites itself with God's will, he becomes holy. After creation, in the seventh day, God took man up into His work of sanctification to make him holy. Obedience is the path to holiness, because it is the path to union with God's holy will; with man unfallen, as with fallen man, in redemption here and in glory above, in all the holy angels, in Christ the Holy One of God Himself, obedience is the

36

path of holiness. It is not itself holiness: but as the will opens itself to accept and to do the will of God, God communicates Himself and His Holiness. To obey His voice is to follow Him as He leads in the way to the full revelation and communication of Himself and His blessed nature as the Holy One.

Obedience. Not knowledge of the will of God, not even approval, not even the will to do it, but the doing of it. Knowledge, and approval, and will must lead to action; the will of God must be done. 'If ye indeed obey my voice, ye shall be unto me an holy nation.' It is not faith, and not worship, and not profession, that God here asks in the first place from His people when He speaks of holiness; it is obedience. God's will must be done on earth, as in heaven. 'Remember and do all my commandments, that ye may be holy to your God' (Num. xv. 40). 'Sanctify yourselves therefore, and be ye holy; and ye shall keep my statutes and do them. I am the Lord which sanctify you' (Lev. xx. 7, 8). 'Therefore shall ye keep my commandments and do them: I am the Lord: I will be hallowed among the children of Israel: I am the Lord which hallow you, that brought you up out of the land of Egypt' (xxii 21, 33).

A moment's reflection will make the reason of this clear to us. It is in a man's work that he manifests what he is. I may know what is good, and yet not approve it. I may approve, and yet not will it. I may in a certain sense will it, and yet be wanting in the energy, or the self-sacrifice, or the power that will rouse and do the thing. Thinking is easier than willing, and willing is easier than doing. Action alone proves whether the object of my interest has complete mastery over me. God wants His will done. This alone is obedience. In this alone it is seen whether the whole heart, with all its strength and will, has given itself over to the will of God; whether we live it, and are ready at any sacrifice to make it our own by doing it. God has no other way for making us holy. 'Ye shall keep my statutes and do them: I am the Lord which make you holy.'

To all seekers after holiness this is a lesson of deep importance. Obedience is not holiness; holiness is something far higher, something that comes from God to us, or rather, something of God coming into us. But obedience is indispensable to holiness: it cannot exist without it. While, therefore, your heart seeks to follow the teaching of God's word, and looks in faith to what God has done, as He has made you holy in Christ, and to what God is still to do through the Spirit of Holiness as He

37

fulfils the promise, 'The very God of peace sanctify you wholly,' never for one moment forget to be obedient. 'If ye shall indeed obey my voice, ye shall be an holy nation to me.' Begin by doing at once whatever appears right to do. Give up at once whatever conscience tells that you dare not say is according to the will of God. Not only pray for light and strength, but act; do what God says. 'He that doeth the will of God is my brother,' Jesus says. Every son of God has been begotten of the will of God: in it he has his life. To do the Father's will is the meat, the strength, the mark, of every son of God.

It is nothing less than the surrender to such a life of simple and entire obedience that is implied in becoming a Christian. There are, alas! too many Christians who, from the want either of proper instruction, or of proper attention to the teaching of God's word, have never realized the place of supreme importance that obedience takes in the Christian life. They know not that Christ, and redemption, and faith all lead to it, because through it alone is the way to the fellowship of the Love, and the Likeness, and the Glory of God. We have all, possibly, suffered from it ourselves: in our prayers and efforts after the perfect peace and the rest of faith, after the abiding joy and the increasing power of the Christian life, there has been a secret something hindering the blessing, or causing the speedy loss of what had been apprehended. A wrong impression as to the absolute necessity of obedience was probably the cause. It cannot too earnestly be insisted on that the freeness and mighty power of grace has this for its object from our conversion onwards, the restoring us to the active obedience and harmony with God's will from which we had fallen through the first sin in Paradise. Obedience leads to God and His Holiness. It is in obedience that the will is moulded, and the character fashioned, and an inner man built up which God can clothe and adorn with the beauty of holiness.

When a Christian discovers that this has been the missing link, the cause of failure and darkness, there is nothing for it but, in a grand act of surrender, deliberately to choose obedience, universal, whole-hearted obedience, as the law of his life in the power of the Holy Spirit. Let him not fear to make his own the words of Israel at Sinai, in answer to the message of God we are considering: 'All that the Lord hath spoken, we will do;' 'All that the Lord hath said will we do, and be obedient.' What the law could not do, in that it was weak through the flesh, God hath done by the gift of His Son and Spirit. The law-giving of Sinai on tables of stone has been succeeded by the law-giving of the Spirit on the table of the heart: the Holy Spirit is the power of obedience, and is so the Spirit of Holiness, who, in obedience, prepares our hearts for being the dwelling of the Holy One. Let us in this faith yield ourselves to a life of obedience: it is the New Testament path to the realization of the promise: 'If ye will obey my voice indeed, ye shall be unto me an holy nation.'

We have already seen how holiness in its very nature supposes the personal relation to God, His personal presence. 'I have brought you unto myself; if ye obey, ye shall be unto me an holy nation.' It is as we understand and hold fast this personal element that obedience will become possible, and will lead to holiness. Mark well God's words: 'If ye will obey my voice, and keep my covenant.' The voice is more than a law or a book; it always implies a living person and intercourse with him. It is this that is the secret of gospel obedience: hearing the voice and following the lead of Jesus as a personal friend, a living Saviour. It is being led by the Spirit of God, having Him to reveal the Presence, and the Will, and the Love of the Father, that will work in us that personal relation which the New Testament means when it speaks of doing everything unto the Lord, as pleasing God.

Such obedience is the pathway of holiness. Its every act is a link to the living God, a surrender of the being for God's will, for God Himself to take possession. In the process of assimilation, slow but sure, by which the will of God, as the meat of our souls, is taken up into our inmost being, our spiritual nature is strengthened, is spiritualized, growing up into an holy temple in which God can reveal Himself and take up His abode.

Let every believer study to realize this. When God sanctified the seventh day as His period of making holy, He taught us that He could not do it at once. The revelation and communication of holiness must be gradual, as man is prepared to receive it. God's sanctifying work with each of us, as with the race, needs time. The time it needs and seeks is the life of daily, hourly obedience. All that is spent in self-will, and not in the living relation to the Lord, is lost. But when the heart seeks day by day to hearken to the voice and to obey it, the Holy One Himself watches over His words to fulfil them: 'Ye shall be unto me an holy nation.' In a way of which the soul beforehand can have but little conception, God will overshadow and make His abode in the obedient heart. The habit of always listening for the voice and obeying it will only be the building of the temple: the Living God Himself, the Holy One, will come to take up His abode. The glory of the Lord will fill the house, and the promise be made true, 'I will sanctify it by my glory.'

'I brought you unto myself; if ye will obey my voice in deed, ye shall be unto me an holy nation.' Seekers after holiness! God has brought you to Himself. And now His voice speaks to you all the thoughts of His heart, that as you take them in, and make them your own, and make His will your own by living and doing it, you may enter into the most complete union with Himself, the union of will as well as of life, and so become a holy people unto Him. Let obedience, the listening to and the doing the will of God, be the joy and the glory of your life; it will give you access unto the Holiness of God.

Be holy, as I am holy

O my God! Thou hast redeemed me for Thyself, that Thou mightest have me wholly as Thine own, possessing, filling my inmost being with Thy own likeness, Thy perfect will, and the glory of Thy Holiness. And Thou seekest to train me, in the power of a free and loving will, to take Thy will and make it my own, that in the very centre of my being I may have Thine own perfection dwelling in me. And in Thy words Thou revealest Thy will, that as I accept and keep them I may master their Divine contents, and will all that Thou willest.

O my God! let me live day by day in such fellowship with Thee, that I may indeed in everything hear Thy voice, the living voice of the living God speaking to me. Let the Holy Spirit, the Spirit of Thy Holiness, be to me Thy voice guiding me in the path of simple, childlike obedience. I do bless Thee that I have seen that Christ, in whom I am holy, was the obedient one, that in obedience He sanctified Himself to become my sanctification, and that abiding in Him, Thy obedient, holy Child, is abiding in Thy will as once done by Him, and now to be done by me. O my God! I will indeed obey Thy will: make Thou me one of Thy holy nation, a peculiar treasure above all people. Amen.

1. 'He became obedient unto death.' 'Though He was a Son, yet He learned obedience by the things which He suffered.' 'I come to do Thy will.' 'In which will we are sanctified.' Christ's

40

example teaches us that obedience is the only path to the Holiness or the glory of God. Be this your consecration: a surrender in everything to seek and do the will of God.

2. We are 'holy in Christ'—in this Christ who did the will of God and was obedient to the death. In Him it is we are; in Him we are holy. His obedience is the soil in which we are planted, and must be rooted. 'It is my meat to do His will;' obedience was the sustenance of His life; in doing God's will He drew down Divine nourishment; it must be so with us too.

3. As you study what it is to be and abide in Christ, as you rejoice you are in Him, always remember it is Christ who obeyed in whom God has planted you.

4. If ever you feel perplexed about holiness, just yield yourself again to do God's will, and go and do it. It is ours to obey, it is God's to sanctify.

5. Holy in Christ. Christ sanctified Himself by obedience, by doing the will of God, and in that will, as done by Him, we have been sanctified. In accepting that will as done by Him, in accepting Him, I am holy. In accepting that will of God, as to be done by me, I become holy. I am in Him; in every act of living obedience, I enter into living fellowship with Him, and draw the power of His life into mine.

6. Obedience depends upon hearing the voice. Do not imagine you know the will of God. Pray and wait for the inward teaching of the Spirit.

Eighth Day

HOLY IN CHRIST

Holiness and Indwelling

'And let them make me a holy place, that I may dwell among them.'—Ex. xxv. 8.

'And the tent shall be sanctified by my glory, and I will dwell among the children of Israel, and will be their God.'—Ex. xxix. 43, 45.

The Presence of God makes holy, even when it descends but for a little while, as at Horeb, in the burning bush. How much more must that Presence make holy the place where it dwells, where it fixes its permanent abode! So much is this the case, that the place where God dwells came to be called the holy place, 'the holy place of the habitation of the Most High.' All around where God dwelt was holy: the holy city, the mountain of God's Holiness, His holy house, till we come within the veil, to the most holy place, the holy of holies. It is as the indwelling God that He sanctifies His house, that He reveals Himself as the Holy One in Israel, that He makes us holy too.

Because God is holy, the house in which He dwells is holy too. This is the only attribute of God which He can communicate to His house; but this one He can and does communicate. Among men there is a very close link between the character of a house and its occupants. When there is no obstacle to prevent it, the house unintentionally reflects the master's likeness. Holiness expresses not so much an attribute as the very being of God in His infinite perfection, and His house testifies to this one truth, that He is holy, that where He dwells He must have holiness, that His indwelling makes holy. In His first command to His people to build Him a holy place, God distinctly said that it was that He might dwell among them: the dwelling in the house was to be the shadowing forth of His dwelling in the midst of His people. The house with its holiness thus leads us on to the holiness of His dwelling among His redeemed ones.

The holy place, the habitation of God's Holiness, was the

centre of all God's work in making Israel holy. Everything connected with it was holy. The altar, the priests, the sacrifices, the oil, the bread, the vessels, all were holy, because they belonged to God. From the house there issued the twofold voice—God's call to be holy, God's promise to make holy. God's claim was manifested in the demand for cleansing, for atonement, for holiness, in all who were to draw near, whether as priests or worshippers. And God's promise shone forth from His house in the provision for making holy, in the sanctifying power of the altar, of the blood and the oil. The house embodied the two sides that are united in holiness, the repelling and the attracting, the condemning and the saving. Now by keeping the people at a distance, then by inviting and bringing them nigh, God's house was the great symbol of His own Holiness. He had come nigh even to dwell among them; and yet they might not come nigh, they might never enter the secret place of His presence.

All these things are written on our behalf. It is as the Indwelling One that God is the sanctifier of His people still: the Indwelling Presence alone makes us holy. This comes out with special clearness if we note how, the nearer the Presence was, the greater the degree of holiness. Because God dwelt among them, the camp was holy: all uncleanness was to be removed from it. But the holiness of the court of the tabernacle was greater: uncleanness which did not exclude from the camp would not be tolerated there. Then the holy place was still holier, because still nearer God. And the inner sanctuary, where the Presence dwelt on the mercy-seat, was the Holiest of All, was most holy. The principle still holds good: holiness is measured by nearness to God; the more of His Presence, the more of true holiness; perfect indwelling will be perfect holiness. There is none holy but the Lord; there is no holiness but in Him. He cannot part with somewhat of His holiness, and give it to us apart from Himself; we have only so much of holiness as we have of God Himself. And to have Himself truly and fully, we must have Him as the Indwelling One. And His indwelling in a house or locality, without life or spirit, is only a faint shadow of the true indwelling as the Living One, when He enters into and penetrates our very being, and fills us, our very selves, with His own life.

There is no union so intimate, so real, so perfect, as that of an indwelling life. Think of the life that circulates through a large and fruitful tree. How it penetrates and fills every portion; how inseparably it unites the whole as long as it really is to exist!—in wood and leaf, in flower and fruit, everywhere the indwelling life flows and fills. This life is the life of nature, the life of the Spirit of God which dwells in nature. It is the same life that animates our bodies, the spirit of nature pervading every portion of them with the power of sensibility and action.

Not less intimate, yea rather, far more wonderful and real, is the indwelling of the Spirit of the New Life, through whom God dwells in the heart of the believer. And it is as this indwelling becomes a matter of conscious longing and faith, that the soul obeys the command, 'Let them make me a holy place, that I may dwell among them,' and experiences the truth of the promise, 'The tent shall be sanctified by my glory, and I will dwell among the children of Israel.'

It was as the Indwelling One that God revealed Himself in the Son, whom He sanctified and sent into the world. More than once our Lord insisted upon it, 'Believe me, that I am in the Father and the Father in me; the Father abiding in me doeth the works.' It is specially as the temple of God that believers are more than once called holy in the New Testament: 'The temple of God is holy, which temple ye are.' 'Your body is a temple of the Holy Spirit.' 'All the building groweth unto an holy temple in the Lord.' It is—we shall later on learn to understand this better— just because it is through the Spirit that the heart is prepared for the indwelling, and the indwelling effected and maintained, that the Spirit so peculiarly takes the attribute of Holy. The Indwelling Spirit is the Holy Spirit. The measure of His indwelling, or rather of His revealing the Indwelling Christ, is the measure of holiness.

We have seen what the various degrees of nearness to God's Presence in Israel were. They are still to be found. You have Christians who dwell in the camp, but know little of drawing nigh to the Holy One. Then you have outer court Christians: they long for pardon and peace, they come ever again to the altar of atonement; but they know little of true nearness or holiness; of their privilege as priests to enter the holy place. Others there are who have learnt that this is their calling, and long to draw near, and yet hardly understand the boldness they have to enter into the Holiest of all, and to dwell there. Blessed they to whom this, the secret of the Lord, has been revealed. They know what the rent veil means, and the access into the immediate Presence. The veil hath been taken away from their hearts: they have found the secret of true holiness in

44

the Indwelling of the Holy One, the God who is holy and makes holy.

Believer! the God who calls you to holiness is the God of the Indwelling Life. The tabernacle typifies it, the Son reveals it, the Spirit communicates it, the eternal glory will fully manifest it. And you may experience it. It is your calling as a believer to be God's Holy Temple. Oh, do but yield yourself to His full indwelling! seek not holiness in the first place in what you are or do; seek it in God. Seek it not even as a gift from God, seek it in God Himself, in His indwelling Presence. Worship Him in the beauty of holiness, as He dwells in the high and holy place. And as you worship, listen to His voice: 'Thus saith the high and lofty One, that inhabiteth eternity, whose name is Holy: I dwell in the high and holy place, with him also that is of a contrite and humble spirit.' It is as the Spirit strengthens us mightily in the inward man, so that Christ dwells in our heart by faith, and the Father comes and makes with Him His abode in us, that we are truly holy. Oh, let us but, in true, true-hearted consecration, yield ourselves to be, as distinctly as was the tabernacle or the temple, given up entirely to be the dwelling of the Most High, the habitation of His Holiness. A house filled with the glory of God, a heart filled with all the fulness of God, is God's promise, is our portion. Let us in faith claim and accept and hold fast the blessing: Christ, the Holy One of God, will in His Father's Name, enter and take possession. Then faith will bring the solution of all our difficulties, the victory over all our failures, the fulfilment of all our desires: 'The tent, the heart, shall be sanctified by my glory; and I will dwell among them.' The open secret of true holiness, the secret of the joy unspeakable, is Christ dwelling in the heart by faith.

Be holy, as I am holy

We bow our knees to the Father of our Lord Jesus, that He would grant unto us, according to the riches of His glory, what He Himself has taught us to ask for. We ask nothing less than this, that Christ may dwell in our hearts by faith. We long for that most blessed, permanent, conscious indwelling of the Lord Jesus in the heart, which He so distinctly promised as the fruit of the Holy Spirit's coming. Father! we ask for what He meant when He spake of the loving, obedient disciple: 'I will come and manifest

myself to him. We will come and take up our abode with him.'
Oh, grant unto us this indwelling of Christ in the heart by faith!

And for this, we beseech Thee, grant us to be strengthened
with might by Thy Spirit in the inner man. O Most Mighty God!
let the spirit of Thy Divine Power work mightily within us,
renewing our mind, and will, and affections, so that the heart be
all prepared and furnished as a temple, as a home, for Jesus. Let
that Blessed Spirit strengthen us to the faith that receives the
Blessed Saviour and His indwelling Presence.

O Most Gracious Father! hear our cry. We do bow our knee
to Thee. We plead the riches of Thy glory. We praise Thee who
art mighty to do above what we can ask or think. We wait on
Thee, O our Father: oh, grant us a mighty strengthening by the
Spirit in the inner man, that this bliss may be ours in its full
blessedness, our Lord Jesus dwelling in the heart.

We ask it in His Name. Amen.

1. God's dwelling in the midst of Israel was the great
central fact to which all the commands concerning holiness were
but preparatory and subordinate. So the work of the Holy Spirit
also culminates in the personal indwelling of Christ. (John xiv.
21, 23. Eph. iii. 16, 17.) Aim at this and expect it.

2. The tabernacle with its three divisions was, as of other
spiritual truths, so the image of man's threefold nature. Our
spirit is the Holiest of all, where God is meant to dwell, where the
Holy Spirit is given. The life of the soul, with its powers of
feeling, knowing, and willing, is the holy place. And the outer life
of the body, of conduct and action, is the outer court. Begin by
believing that the Spirit dwells in the inmost sanctuary, where
His workings are secret and hidden. Honour Him by trusting
Him to work, by yielding to Him in silent worship before God.
From within He will take possession of thought and will; He will
even fill the outer court, the body, with the Holiness of God. 'The
God of peace Himself sanctify you wholly; and may your spirit,
and soul, and body, be preserved entire, without blame. Faithful
is He which calleth you, who will also do it.'

3. God's indwelling was within the veil, in the unseen, the
secret place. Faith knew it, and served Him with holy fear. Our
faith knows that God the Holy Spirit has His abode in the hidden
place of our inner life. Set open your inmost being to Him; bow
in lowly reverence before the Holy One as you yield yourself to
His working. Holiness is the presence of the Indwelling One.

Ninth Day

HOLY IN CHRIST

Holiness and Mediation

'And thou shalt make a plate of pure gold, and grave upon it, Holiness to the Lord. And it shall be upon Aaron's forehead, that Aaron may bear the iniquity of the holy things, which the children of Israel shall hallow in all their holy gifts; and it shall always be upon his forehead, that they may be accepted before the Lord.'—Ex. xxviii. 36, 38.

God's house was to be the dwelling-place of His Holiness, the place where He was to reveal Himself; as the Holy One, not to be approached but with fear and trembling; as the Holy-making One, drawing to Himself all who would be made partakers of His Holiness. Of the revelation of His Holy and His Holy-making Presence, the centre is found in the person of the high priest, in his double capacity of representing God with man, and man with God. He is the embodiment of the Divine Holiness in human form, and of human holiness as a Divine gift, as far as the dispensation of symbol and shadow could offer and express it. In him God came near to sanctify and bless the people. In him the people came their very nearest to God. And yet the very Day of Atonement, in which he might enter into the Most Holy, was but the proof of how unholy man was, and how unfit to abide in God's Presence. In himself a proof of Israel's unholiness, he yet was a type and picture of the coming Saviour, our blessed Lord Jesus, a wondrous exhibition of the way in which hereafter the holiness of God should become the portion of His people.

Among the many points in which the high priest typified Christ as our sanctification, there is, perhaps, none more suggestive or beautiful than the holy crown he wore on his forehead. Everything about him was to be holy. His garments were holy garments. But there was to be one thing in which this holiness reached its fullest manifestation. On his forehead he was always to wear a plate of gold, with the words engraved on it, Holiness to the Lord. Every one was to read there that the whole object of his existence, the one thing he lived for, was, to be the embodiment and the bearer of the Divine holiness, the chosen one through whom God's holiness might flow out in blessing upon the people.

The way in which the blessing of the holy crown was to act was a most remarkable one. In bearing Holiness to the Lord on his forehead, he is, we read, 'to bear the iniquity of the holy things which the children of Israel hallow; that they may be accepted before the Lord.' For every sin some sacrifice or way of atonement had been devised. But how about the sin that cleaves to the very sacrifice and religious service itself? 'Thou desirest truth in the inward parts.' How painfully the worshipper might be oppressed by the consciousness that his penitence, his faith, his love, his obedience, his consecration, were all imperfect and defiled! For this need, too, of the worshipper, God had provided. The holiness of the high priest covered the sin and the unholiness of his holy things. The holy crown was God's pledge that the holiness of the high priest rendered the worshipper acceptable. If he was unholy, there was one among his brethren who was holy, who had a holiness that could avail for him too, a holiness he could trust in. He could look to the high priest not only to effect atonement by his blood-sprinkling, but in his person to secure a holiness too that made him and his gifts most acceptable. In the consciousness of personal unholiness he might rejoice in a mediator, in the holiness of Another than himself, the priest whom God had provided.

Have we not here a most precious lesson, leading us a step farther on in the way of holiness? To our question, How God makes holy, we have the Divine answer: Through a man whom the Divine Holiness has chosen to rest upon, and whose holiness belongs to us, as His brethren, the very members of His own body. Through a holiness which is of such efficacy, that the very sins of our holy things disappear, and we can enter the Holy Presence with the assurance of being altogether well-pleasing.

And is not just this the lesson that many earnest seekers after holiness need? They know all that the Word teaches of the blessed Atonement, and the full pardon it has brought. They believe in the Father's wonderful love, and what He is ready to do for them. And yet, when they hear of the childlike simplicity, the assurance of faith, the loving obedience, and the blessed surrender with which the Father expects them to come and receive the blessing, their heart fails for fear. It is as if the blessing were all beyond their reach. What avails that the Holy One is said to come so nigh? their unholiness renders them incapable of claiming or grasping the Presence that offers itself to them. Just see how the Holy One here reveals His way of making holy, and preparing for the fellowship of His Holiness. In His Elect One as Mediator, holiness is prepared and treasured up enough for all who come through Him. As I bow to pray or worship, and feel how much there is still wanting of that humility, and fervency, and faith, that God has a right to demand, I may look up to the High Priest in His Holiness, to the holy crown upon His forehead, and believe that the iniquity of my holy things is borne and taken away. I may, with all my deficiency and unworthiness, know most assuredly that my prayer is acceptable, a sweet-smelling savour. I may look up to the Holy One to see Him smiling on me, for the sake of His Anointed One. 'The holy crown shall always be on His forehead, that they may be accepted before the Lord.' It is the blessed truth of Substitution—One for all—of Mediatorship; God's way of making us holy. The sacrifice of the worshipping Israelite is holy and acceptable in virtue of the holiness of Another.

The Old Testament shadow can never adequately set forth the New Testament reality with its fulness of grace and truth. As we proceed in our study, we shall find that the holiness of Jesus our sanctification is not only imputed but imparted, because we are in Him; the new man we have put on is created in true holiness. We are not only counted holy; we are holy, we have received a new holy nature in Christ Jesus. 'He that sanctifieth and they who are sanctified are all of One; therefore He is not ashamed to call them brethren.' It is our living union with Jesus, God's Holy One, that has given us the new and holy nature, and with that a claim and a share in all the holiness there is in Jesus. And so, as often as we are conscious of how unholy we are, we have only to come under the covering of the Holiness of Jesus, to enjoy the full assurance that we and our gifts are most acceptable. However great be the weakness of our faith, the shortcoming in our desire for God's glory, the lack in our love or zeal, as we see Jesus, with Holiness to the Lord on His forehead, we lift up our faces to receive the Divine smile of full approval and perfect acceptance.

This is God's way of making holy. Not only with the holy place, as we have seen, but with the holy persons too, He begins with a centre, and from that in ever-widening circle makes holy. And that this Divine method will be crowned with success we may be sure. In the Word we find a most remarkable illustration of the extent to which it will be realized. We find the words on the holy crown once again in the Old Testament at its close. In the day of the Lord, 'there shall be upon the bells of the horses, Holiness to the Lord.' The high priest's motto shall then have become the watchword of daily life; every article of beauty or of service shall be holy too; from the head it shall have extended to the skirts of the garments. Let us begin with realizing the Holiness of Jesus in its power to cover the iniquity of our holy things; let us make proof of it, and no longer suffer our unworthiness to keep us back or make us doubt; let us believe that we and our holy things are acceptable, because in Christ holy to the Lord; let us live in this consciousness of acceptance, and enter into fellowship with the Holy One. As we enter in and abide in the holiness of Jesus, it will enter in and abide in us. It will take possession and spread its conquering power through our whole life, until with us too upon everything that belongs to us the word shall shine, Holiness to the Lord. And we shall again find how God's way of holiness is ever from a centre, here the centre of our renewed nature, throughout the whole circumference of our being, to make His Holiness prove its power. Let us but dwell under the covering of the Holiness of Jesus, as He takes away the iniquity of our holy things, He will make us and our life holy to the Lord.

Be ye holy, for I am holy

O my God and Father! my soul doth bless Thee for this wondrous revelation of what Thy way and Thy grace is with those whom Thou hast called 'Holy in Christ.' Thou knowest, O Lord, how continually our hearts have limited our acceptance with Thee by our attainments, and conscious shortcoming has wrought condemnation. We knew too little how, in the Holiness of Him who makes us holy, there is a Divinely infinite efficacy to cover our iniquities, and give us the assurance of perfect acceptance. Blessed Father! open our eyes to see, and our hearts to understand this holy crown of our blessed Jesus, with its wondrous and most blessed, Holiness to the Lord.

And when our hearts condemn us, because our prayers are so little consciously according to the will or to the glory of God, or truly in the name of Jesus, O most Holy Father, be pleased by Thy Spirit to show us how bright the smile and how hearty the welcome is we still have with Thee. Teach us to come in the Holiness of our High Priest, and enter into Thine, until it take possession of us, and permeate our whole being, and all that is in us be holy to the Lord. Amen.

1. Holiness is not something I can see or admire in myself: it is covering myself, losing myself, in the Holiness of Jesus. How wonderfully this is typified in Aaron and the holy crown. And the more I see and have apprehended of the Holiness of Jesus, the less shall I see or seek of holiness in myself.

2. He will make me holy: my tempers and dispositions will be renewed; my heart and mind cleansed and sanctified; holiness will be a new nature; and yet there will be all along the consciousness, humbling and yet full of joy: it is not I; Christ liveth in me.

3. Let us lie very low and tender before God, that the Holy Spirit may reveal to us what it is to be holy in the Holiness of Another, in the Holiness of Jesus, that is, in the Holiness of God.

4. Do not trouble or weary too much to grasp this with the intellect. Just believe it, and look in simplicity and trust to Jesus to make it all right for you.

5. Holy in Christ. In childlike faith I take Christ's holiness afresh as my covering before God. In loving obedience I take it into my will and life. I trust and I follow Jesus: this is the path of holiness.

6. If we gather up the lessons we have found in the Word from Paradise downward, we see that the elements of holiness in us are these, each corresponding to some special aspect of God's holiness: deep Restfulness (ch. 3), humble Reverence (ch. 4), entire Surrender (ch. 5), joyful Adoration (ch. 6), simple Obedience (ch. 7). These all prepare for the Divine Indwelling (ch. 8), and this again we have through the Abiding in Jesus with the Crown of Holiness on His head.

Tenth Day

HOLY IN CHRIST

Holiness and Separation

'I am the Lord your God, which have separated you from other people. And ye shall be holy unto me, for I the Lord am holy, and have separated you from other people that ye should be Mine.'—Lev. xx. 24, 26.

'Until the days be fulfilled, in the which he separateth himself unto the Lord, he shall be holy.... All the days of his separation he is holy unto the Lord.'—Num. vi. 5, 8.

'Wherefore Jesus also, that He might sanctify the people through His own blood, suffered without the gate. Let us therefore go forth unto Him without the camp, bearing His reproach.'—Heb. xiii. 12, 13.

Separation is not holiness, but is the way to it. Though there can be no holiness without separation, there can be separation that does not lead to holiness. It is of deep importance to understand both the difference and the connection, that we may be kept from the right-hand error of counting separation alone as holiness, as well as the left-hand error of seeking holiness without separation.

The Hebrew word for holiness possibly comes from a root that means to separate. But where we have in our translation 'separate' or 'sever' or 'set apart,' we have quite different words. [3] The word for holy is used exclusively to express that special idea. And though the idea of holy always includes that of separation, it is itself something infinitely higher. It is of great importance to understand this well, because the being set apart to God, the surrender to His claim, the devotion or consecration to His service, is often spoken of as if this constituted holiness. We cannot too earnestly press the thought that this is only the beginning, the presupposition: holiness itself is infinitely more;

---

[3] See Note B.

not what I am, or do, or give, is holiness, but what God is, and gives, and does to me. It is God's taking possession of me that makes me holy; it is the Presence and the glory of God that really makes holy. A careful study of God's words to Israel will make this clear to us. Eight times we find the expression in Leviticus, 'Ye shall be holy, for I am holy.' Holiness is the highest attribute of God, expressive not only of His relation to Israel, but of His very being and nature, His infinite moral perfection. And though it is by very slow and gradual steps that He can teach the carnal darkened mind of man what this means, yet from the very commencement He tells His people that His purpose is that they should be like Himself—holy because and as He is holy. To tell me that God separates men for Himself to be His, even as He gives Himself to be theirs, tells me of a relation that exists, but tells me nothing of the real nature of this Holy Being, or of the essential worth of the holiness He will communicate to me. Separation is only the setting apart and taking possession of the vessel to be cleansed and used; it is the filling of it with the precious contents we entrust to it that gives it its real value. Holiness is the Divine filling without which the separation leaves us empty. Separation is not holiness.

But separation is essential to holiness. 'I have separated you from other people, and ye shall be holy.' Until I have chosen out and separated a vessel from those around it, and, if need be, cleansed it, I cannot fill or use it. I must have it in my hand, full and exclusive command of it for the time being, or I will not pour into it the precious milk or wine. And just so God separated His people when He brought them up out of Egypt, separated them unto Himself when He gave them His covenant and His law, that He might have them under His control and power, to work out His purpose of making them holy. This He could not do until He had them apart, and had wakened in them the consciousness that they were His peculiar people, wholly and only His, until He had so taught them also to separate themselves to Him. Separation is essential to holiness.

The institution of the Nazarite will confirm this, and will also bring out very clearly what separation means. Israel was meant to be a holy nation. Its holiness was specially typified in its priests. With regard to the individual Israelite, we nowhere read in the books of Moses of his being holy. But there were ordinances through which the Israelite, who would fain prove his desire to be entirely holy, could do so. He might separate himself

53

from the ordinary life of the nation around him, and live the life of a Nazarite, a separated one. This separation was accepted, in those days of shadow and type, as holiness. 'All the days of his separation he is holy unto the Lord.'

The separation consisted specially in three things—temperance, in abstinence from the fruit of the vine; humiliation, in not cutting or shaving his hair ('it is a shame for a man if he have long hair'); self-sacrifice, in not defiling himself for even father or mother, on their death. What we must specially note is that the separation was not from things unlawful, but things lawful. There was nothing sinful in itself in Abraham living in his father's house, or in Israel dwelling in Egypt. It is in giving up, not only what can be proved to be sin, but all that may hinder the full intensity of our surrender into God's hands to make us holy, that the spirit of separation is manifested.

Let us learn the lessons this truth suggests. We must know the need for separation. It is no arbitrary demand of God, but has its ground in the very nature of things. To separate a thing is to set it free for one special use or purpose, that it may with undivided power fulfil the will of him who chose it, and so realize its destiny. It is the principle that lies at the root of all division of labour; complete separation to one branch of study or labour is the way to success and perfection. I have before me an oak forest with the trees all shooting up straight and close to each other. On the outskirts there is one tree separated from his fellows; its heavy trunk and wide-spreading branches prove how its being separated, and having a large piece of ground separated to its own use, over which roots and branches can spread, is the secret of growth and greatness. Our human powers are limited; if God is to take full possession, if we are fully to enjoy Him, separation to Him is nothing but the simple, natural, indispensable requisite. God wants us all to Himself, that He may give Himself all to us.

We must know the purpose of separation. It is to be found in what God has said, 'Ye shall be holy unto me, for I the Lord am holy, and have separated you from the people, that ye should be Mine.' God has separated us for Himself in the deepest sense of the word; that He might enter into us, and show forth Himself in us. His holiness is the sum and the centre of all His perfections; it is that He may make us holy like Himself that He has separated us. Separation never has any value in itself; it may become most wrong or hurtful; everything depends upon the object proposed.

It is as God gets and takes full possession of us, as the eternal life in Christ has the mastery of our whole being, as the Holy Spirit flows fully and freely through us, so that we dwell in God, and God in us, that separation will be, not a thing of ordinances and observances, but a spiritual reality. And it is as this purpose of God is seen and accepted and followed after, that difficult questions as to what we must be separated from, and how much sacrifice separation demands, will find an easy answer. God separates from all that does not lead us into His holiness and fellowship.

We need, above all, to know the power of separation, the power that leads us into it in the spirit of desire and of joy, of liberty and of love. The great separating word in human language is the word Mine. In this we have the great spring of effort and of happiness: in the child with its toys, in labour with its gains and rewards, in the patriot who dies for his country, it is this Mine that lays its hand on what it sets apart from all else. It is the great word that love uses. Be it the child that says to its mother, My own mamma, and calls forth the response, My own child; the bridegroom who draws the daughter from her beloved home and parents to become his; or the Holy God who speaks: 'I have separated you from the people, that ye should be Mine;' it is always with that Mine that love exerts its mighty power, and draws from all else to itself. God Himself knows no mightier argument, can put forth no more powerful attraction than this, 'that ye should be Mine.' And the power of separation will come to us, and work in us, just as we yield ourselves to study and realize that holy purpose, to listen to and appropriate that wondrous Mine, to be apprehended and possessed of that Almighty Love.

Let us study step by step the wondrous path in which Divine Love does it separating work. In redemption it prepares the way. Israel is separated from Egypt by the blood of the Lamb and the guiding pillar of fire. In its command, 'Come out and be separate,' it wakens man to action; in its promises, 'I will be your God,' it stirs desire and strengthens faith. In all the holy saints and servants of God, and at last in Him who was holy, harmless, undefiled, separate from sinners, it points the way. In the power of the Holy Spirit, the Spirit of Holiness, it seals the separation by the Presence of the Indwelling God. This is indeed the power of separation. The separating power of the Presence of God; this it is we need to know. 'Wherein now shall it be known that I have found grace in Thy sight, I and Thy people?' said Moses: 'is it not in that Thou goest with us? so shall we be separated, I and Thy people, from all the people that are upon the face of the earth.' It is the consciousness of God's Indwelling Presence, making and keeping us His very own, that works the true separateness from the world and its spirit, from ourselves and our own will. And it is as this separation is accepted and prized and persevered in by us, that the holiness of God will enter in and take possession. And we shall realize that to be the Lord's property, a people of His own, is infinitely more than merely to be accounted or acknowledged as His, that it means nothing less than that God, in the power and indwelling of the Holy Ghost, fills our being, our affections, and our will with His own life and holiness. He separates us for Himself, and sanctifies us to be His dwelling. He comes Himself to take personal possession by the indwelling of Christ in the heart. And we are then truly separate, and kept separate, by the presence of God within us.

Be ye Holy, for I am holy

O my God! who hast separated me for Thyself, I beseech Thee, by Thy mighty power, to make this Divine separation deed and truth to me. May within, in the depths of my own spirit, and without, in all my intercourse, the crown of separation of my God be upon me.

I pray Thee especially, O my God, to perfect in power the separation from self! Let Thy Presence in the indwelling of my Lord Jesus be the power that banishes self from the throne. I have turned from it with abhorrence; oh, my Father, reveal Thy Son fully in me! it is His enthronement in my heart can keep me as Thy own, as Himself takes the place of myself.

And give me grace, Lord, in my outward life to wait for a Divine wisdom, that I may know to witness, for Thy glory and for what Thy people need, to the blessedness of an entire giving up of everything for God, a separation that holds back nothing, to be His and His alone.

Holy Lord God! visit Thy people. Oh, withdraw Thou them from the world and conformity to it. Separate, Lord, separate Thine own for Thyself. Separate, Lord, the wheat from the chaff; separate, as by fire, the gold from the dross; that it may be seen who are the Lord's, even His holy ones. Amen.

1. Love separates effectually. With what jealousy a husband claims his wife, a mother her children, a miser his possessions! Pray that the Holy Spirit may show how God brought you to Himself, that you should be His. 'He is a holy God; He is a Jealous God.' God's love shed abroad in the heart makes separation easy.

2. Death separates effectually. If I reckon myself to be indeed dead in Christ, I am separated from self by the power of Christ's death. Life separates still more mightily. As I say, 'Not I, but Christ liveth in me,' I am lifted up out of the life of self.

3. Separation must be manifest; it is meant as a witness to others and ourselves; it must find expression in the external, if internally it is to be real and strong. It is the characteristic of a symbolic action that it not merely expresses a feeling, but nourishes and strengthens the feeling to which it corresponds. When the soul enters the fellowship of God, it feels the need of external separation, sometimes even from what appears to others harmless. If animated by the spirit of lowly consecration to God, the external may be a great strengthening of the true separateness.

4. Separation to God and appropriation by Him go together. This has been the blessing that has come to martyrs, confessors, missionaries,—all who have given distinct expression to the forsaking all.

5. Separation begins in love, and ends in love. The spirit of separation is the spirit of self-sacrifice, of surrender to the love of God; the truly separate one will be the most loving and love-winning, given up to serve God and man. Is not what separates, what distinguishes Jesus from all others, His self-sacrificing love? This is His separateness, in which we are to be made like Him.

6. God's holiness is His separateness; let us enter into His separateness from the world; that will be our holiness. Unite thyself to God. Then art thou separate and holy. God separates for Himself, not by an act from without, but as His Will and Presence take possession of us.

Eleventh Day

HOLY IN CHRIST

The Holy One of Israel

'I am the Lord that brought you up out of the land of Egypt, to be your God; ye shall therefore be holy, for I am holy. I the Lord which make you holy, am holy.'—Lev. xi. 45, xxi. 8.

'I am the Lord Thy God, the Holy One of Israel, Thy Saviour. Thus saith the Lord, your Redeemer, the Holy One of Israel: I am the Lord, your Holy One, the Creator of Israel, your King.'—Isa. xliii. 3, 14, 15.

In the book of Exodus we found God making provision for the Holiness of His people. In the holy times and holy places, holy persons, holy things, and holy services, He had taught His people that everything around Him, that all that would come near Him, must be holy. He would only dwell in the midst of holiness; His people must be a holy people. But there is no direct mention of God Himself as holy. In the book of Leviticus we are led on a step further. Here first we have God speaking of His own holiness, and making it the plea for the holiness of His people, as well as its pledge and power. Without this the revelation of holiness were incomplete, and the call to holiness powerless. True holiness will come to us as we learn that God Himself alone is holy. It is He alone makes holy; it is as we come to Himself, and in obedience and love are linked to Himself, that His Holiness can rest on us. 4

---

4 'I am the Lord your God; ye shall therefore make holy yourselves, and be holy, for I am holy' (Lev. xi. 44).

'I am the Lord that bringeth you out of the land of Egypt to be your God: ye shall therefore be holy, for I am holy' (Lev. xi. 45).

'Ye shall be holy, for I the Lord your God am holy' (Lev. xix. 2).

'Make holy yourselves therefore, and be ye holy, for I am the Lord your God; ye shall keep my statutes and do them: I am the Lord which make you holy' (Lev. xx. 7, 8).

From the books of Moses onwards we shall find that the name of God as holy is found but seldom in the inspired writings, until we come to Isaiah, the evangelist prophet. There it occurs twenty-six times, and has its true meaning opened up in the way in which it is linked with the name of Saviour and Redeemer. The sentiments of joy and trust and praise, with which a redeemed people would look upon their Deliverer, are all mentioned in connection with the name of the Holy One. 'Cry aloud and shout, thou inhabitant of Zion, for great is the Holy One of Israel in the midst of thee.' 'The poor among men shall rejoice in the Holy One of Israel.' 'Thou shalt rejoice in the Lord, and shalt glory in the Holy One of Israel.' In Paradise we saw that God the Creator was God the Sanctifier, perfecting the work of His hands. In Israel we saw that God the Redeemer was ever God the Sanctifier, making holy the people He had chosen for Himself. Here in Isaiah we see how it is God the Sanctifier, the Holy One, who is to bring about the great redemption of the New Testament: as the Holy One, He is the Redeemer. God redeems because He is holy, and loves to make holy: Holiness will be Redemption perfected. Redemption and Holiness together are to be found in the personal relation to God. The key to the secret of holiness is offered to each believer in that word: 'Thus saith the Lord, your Redeemer, the Holy One of Israel: I am the Lord, your Holy One.' To come near, to know, to possess the Holy One, and be possessed of Him, is Holiness.

If God's Holiness is thus the only hope for ours, it is right that we seek to know what that Holiness is. And though we may find it indeed to be something that passeth knowledge, it will not be in vain to gather up what has been revealed in the Word concerning it. Let us do so in the spirit of holy fear and worship, trusting to the Holy Spirit to be our teacher.

And let us first notice how this Holiness of God, though it is often mentioned as one of the Divine attributes, can hardly be counted such, on a level with the others. The other attributes all

---

'Ye shall be holy unto me, for I the Lord am holy, and have separated you from other people, that ye should be mine' (Lev. xx. 26).

'The priest shall be holy unto thee, for I the Lord which make you holy, am holy' (Lev. xxi. 8).

'I will be hallowed among the children of Israel; I am the Lord which make you holy' (Lev. xxii. 32).

'I am the Lord which make them holy' (Lev. xxi. 15, 23; xxii. 9, 16).

refer to some special aspect or characteristic of the Divine Nature; Holiness appears to express what is the very essence or perfection of the Divine Being Himself. None of the attributes can be predicated of all that belongs to God; but Scripture speaks of His Holy Name, His Holy Day, His Holy Habitation, His Holy Word. In the word Holy we have the nearest possible approach to a summary of all the Divine perfections, the description of what Divinity is. We speak of the other attributes as Divine perfections, but in this we have the only human expression for the Divine Perfection itself. It is for this reason that theologians have found such difficulty in framing a definition that can express all the word means. 5

The original Hebrew word, whether derived from a root signifying to separate, or another with the idea of shining, expressed the idea of something distinguished from others, separate from them by superior excellence. God is Separate and different from all that is created, keeps Himself separate from all that is not God; as the Holy One He maintains His Divine glory and perfection against whatever might interfere with it: 'There is none holy, but the Lord;' 'To whom will you liken me? or shall I be equal? saith the Holy One.' As Holy, God is indeed the Incomparable One; Holiness is His alone; there is nothing like it in heaven or earth, except when He gives it. And so our holiness will consist, not in a human separation in which we attempt to imitate God's,—no, but in entering into His separateness; belonging entirely to Him; set apart by Him and for Himself.

Closely connected with this is the idea of Exaltation: 'Thus saith the High and Holy One, whose name is Holy.' It was the Holy One who was seen sitting upon a throne high and lifted up, the object of the worship of the seraphim. In Psalm xcix. God's Holiness is specially spoken of in connection with His exaltation. For this reason, too, His Holiness is so often connected with His Glory and Majesty (see 'Sixth Day'). And here our holiness will be seen to be nothing but the poverty and humility which comes when 'the loftiness of man is brought low, and the Lord alone is exalted.'

If we inquire more closely wherein the infinite excellence of this Separateness and Exaltation consists, we are led to think of the Divine Purity, and that not only in its negative aspect—as

---

5 See Note C for some account of the different definitions that have been given.

hatred of sin—but with the more positive element of perfect beauty. Because we are sinners, and the revelation of God's Holiness is in a world of sin, it is natural, it is right and meet, that the first, that the abiding impression of God's Holiness should be that of an Infinite Purity that cannot look upon sin, in whose Presence it becomes the sinner to hide his face and tremble. The Righteousness of God, forbidding and condemning and punishing sin, has its root in His Holiness, is one of its two elements—the devouring and destroying power of the consuming fire. 'God the Holy One is sanctified in righteousness' (Isa. v. 16); in righteousness the Holiness of the Holy One is maintained and revealed. But Light not only discovers what is impure, that it may be purified, but is in itself a thing of infinite beauty. And so some of our holiest men have not hesitated to speak of God's Holiness as the infinite Pulchritude or Beauty of the Divine Being, the Perfect Purity and Beauty of that Light in which God dwelleth. And if the Holiness of God is to become ours, to rest upon us, and enter into us, there must be, without ceasing, the holy fear that trembles at the thought of grieving the infinite sensitiveness of this Holy One by our sins, and yet side by side, and in perfect harmony with it, the deep longing to behold the Beauty of the Lord, an admiration of its Divine glory, and a joyful surrender to be His alone.

We must go one step further. When God says, 'I am holy: I make holy,' we see that one of the chief elements of His Holiness is this, that it seeks to communicate itself, to make partaker of its own perfection and blessedness. This is nought but Love. In the wonderful revelation in Isaiah of what the Holy One is to His people, we must beware of misreading God's precious Word. It is not said, that though God is the Holy One, and hates sin, and ought to punish and destroy, that notwithstanding this He will save. By no means. But we are taught that as the Holy One, just because He is the Holy One, who delights to make holy, He will be the Deliverer of His people. (See Hos. xi. 9.) It is Holiness above everything else that we are invited to look to, to trust in, to rejoice in. The Holy One is the Holy-making One: He redeems and saves that He may win our confidence for Himself, that He may draw us to Himself as the Holy One, that in the personal attachment to Himself we may learn to obey, to become of one mind with Him, to be holy as He is holy.

The Divine Holiness is thus that infinite Perfection of Divinity in which Righteousness and Love are in perfect harmony, out of which they proceed, and which together they reveal. It is that Energy of the Divine life in the power of which God not only keeps Himself free from all creature weakness or sin, but unceasingly seeks to lift the creature into union with Himself and the full participation of His own purity and perfection. The glory of God as God, as the God of Creation and Redemption, is His Holiness. It is in this that the Separateness and Exaltation of God, even above all thought of man, really consists. 'God is Light;' in His infinite Purity He reveals all darkness, and yet has no fellowship with it. He judges and condemns it; He saves out of it, and lifts up into the fellowship of His own purity and blessedness. This is the Holy One of Israel.

It is this God who speaks to us, 'I am the Lord your God: I am holy: I make holy.' It is in the adoring contemplation of His Holiness, in the trustful surrender to it, in the loving fellowship with Himself, the Holy One, that we can be made holy. My brother! would you be holy? listen again, and let, in the deep silence of trust, God's words sink into your heart—'Your Holy One.' Come to Himself and claim Him as your God, and claim all that He, as the Holy One who makes holy, can do for you. Just remember that Holiness is Himself. Come to Him; worship Him; give Him the glory. Seek not, even from Him, holiness in yourself; let self be abased, and be content that the Holiness is His. As His presence fills your heart, as His Holiness and Glory are your one desire, as His holy Will and Love are your delight,— as the Holy One becomes all in all to you,—you will be holy with the holiness He loves to see. And as, to the end, you see nothing to admire in self, and only Beauty in Him, you will know that He has laid of His glory on you; and your holiness will be found in the song, There is none holy, but the Lord.

Be ye holy, as I am holy

O God! we have again heard the wonderful revelation of Thyself, 'I am holy.' And as we felt how infinitely exalted above all our conceptions Thy Holiness is, we heard Thy call, almost still more wonderful, 'Be ye holy, as I am holy.' And as every thought of how we were to be holy, as Thou art holy, failed us, we heard Thy voice once again, in this most wonderful word of all, 'I make you holy.' I am 'your Holy One.'

Most Holy God! we do beseech Thee, give us in some due

measure to realize how unholy we are, and so to take the place that becomes us in Thy presence. Oh that the sinfulness of our nature, and all that is of self, may be so discovered to us, that it may be no longer possible to live in it! May the Light that reveals this, reveal too, how Thy Holiness is our only hope, our sure refuge, our complete deliverance. O Lord! speak into our souls the word, 'The Holy One, your Redeemer,' 'Your Holy One,' with such power by Thy Spirit, that our faith may grow into the assured confidence that we can be holy as Thou art holy.

Holy Lord God! we wait for Thee. Reveal Thyself in power within us, and fit us to be the messengers of Thy Holiness, to tell Thy people how holy Thou art, and how holy we must be, and how holy Thou dost make us. Amen.

1. This Holy One is God Almighty. Before He revealed Himself to Israel as the Holy One, He made Himself known to Abraham as the Almighty, 'who quickeneth the dead.' In all your dealings with God for holiness, remember He is the Almighty One, who can do wonders in you. Say often, 'Glory to Him who is mighty to do exceeding abundantly above all we ask or think.'

2. This Holy One is the Righteous God, a consuming fire. Cast yourself into it, that all that is sinful may be destroyed. As you lay yourself upon the altar, expect the fire. 'And yield your members unto God as instruments of Righteousness.'

3. This Holy One is the God of Love. He is your Father; yield yourself to let the Holy Spirit cry in you, Abba Father! that is, to let Him shed abroad and fill your heart with God's father-love. God's Holiness is His fatherliness; our holiness is childlikeness. Be simple, loving, trustful.

4. This Holy One is God. Let Him be God to you; ruling all, filling all, working all. Worship Him, come near to Him, live with and in and for Him: He will be your holiness.

Twelfth Day

HOLY IN CHRIST

The Thrice Holy One

'I saw the Lord sitting on a throne, high and lifted up. Above Him stood the seraphim. And one cried to another, and said, Holy, holy, holy is the Lord of hosts: the whole earth is full of His glory.'—Isa. vi. 1–3.

'And the four living creatures, they have no rest day and night, saying, Holy, holy, holy is the Lord God, the Almighty, which was, and which is, and which is to come.'—Rev. iv. 8.

It is not only on earth, but in heaven too, that the Holiness of God is His chief and most glorious attribute. It is not only on earth, but in heaven too, that the highest inspiration of adoration and praise makes mention of His Holiness. The brightest of living beings, they who are ever before and around and above the throne, find their glory in adoring and proclaiming the Holiness of God: surely there can be for us no higher honour than to study and to know, to worship and adore, to proclaim and show forth the glory of the Thrice Holy One.

After Moses, as we know, Isaiah was the chief messenger of the Holiness of God. Each had a special preparation for his commission to make known the Holy One. Moses saw the Holy One in the fire, and hid his face and feared to look upon God, and so was prepared for being His messenger, and for praising Him as 'glorious in holiness.' Isaiah, as he heard the song of the seraphim, and saw the fire on the altar, and the house filled with the smoke, cried out, 'Woe is me.' It was not till, in the deep sense of the need of cleansing, he had received the touch of the fire and the purging of his sin, that he might bear to Israel the Gospel of the Holy One as its Redeemer. May it be in the spirit of fear and lowly worship that we listen to the song of the seraphim, and seek to know and worship the Thrice Holy One. And may ours too be the cleansing with the fire, that we may be found fit to tell God's people that He is the Holy One of Israel, their Redeemer.

The threefold repetition of the Holy has at all times by the

Church of Christ been connected with the Holy Trinity. The song of the living creatures around the throne (Rev. iv.) is evidence of the truth of this thought. We there find it followed by the adoration of Him who was, and is, and is to come, the Almighty: the Eternal Source, the present manifestation in the Son, the future perfecting of the revelation of God in the Spirit's work in His Church. The truth of the Holy Trinity is often regarded as an abstract doctrine, with little direct bearing on practical life. So far is this from being the case, that a living faith must root in it: some spiritual insight into the relation and the operation of each of the Three, and the reality of their living Oneness, is an essential element of true growth in knowledge and spiritual understanding. [6] Let us here regard the Trinity specially in its relation to God's Holiness and as the source of ours. What does it mean that we adore the Thrice Holy One? God is not only holy, but makes holy: in the revelation of the Three Persons we have the revelation of the way in which God makes holy.

The Trinity teaches us that God has revealed Himself in two ways. The Son is the Form of God, His manifestation as He shows Himself to man, the Image in which His unseen glory is embodied, and to which man is to be conformed. The Spirit is the Power of God, working in man, and leading him up to that Image. In Jesus, He who had been in the form of God took the form of man; and the Divine Holiness was literally manifested in the form of a human life and the members of a human body. A new holy human nature was formed in Christ, to be communicated to us. In His death His own personal holiness was perfected as human obedience, and so the power of sin conquered and broken. Therefore in the resurrection, through the Spirit of Holiness, He was declared to be the Son of God with

---

[6] The Divine necessity and meaning of the doctrine of the Trinity is seen from the counterpart we have of it in nature. In every living object that exists we distinguish first the life, then the form or shape in which that life manifests itself, then the power or effect as seen in the result which the life acting in its form or manifestation produces. And so we have God as the Unseen One, the Fountain of life; the Son as the Form or Image of God, the manifestation of the Unseen Life; and the Holy Spirit as the Power of that life proceeding from the Father and the Son, and working out the purpose of God's will in the Church. Applying this thought to God as the Holy One, we shall understand better the place of the Son and the Spirit as they bring to us the Holiness of God.

power to impart His life to us. There the Spirit of Holiness was set free from the veil of the flesh, the trammels that hindered it, and obtained power to enter and dwell in man. The Holy Spirit was poured out as the fruit of Resurrection and Ascension. And the Spirit is now the Power of God in us, working upwards towards Christ, to reproduce His life and Holiness in us, to fit us for fully receiving and showing forth Him in our lives. Christ from above comes to us as the embodiment of the Unseen Holiness of God: the Spirit from within lifts us up to meet Him, and fits us to receive and make our own all that is in Him.

The Triune God whom we adore is the Thrice Holy One: the mystery of the Trinity is the mystery of Holiness: the Glory and the Power of the Trinity is the Glory and Power of God who makes us holy. There is God dwelling in light inaccessible, a consuming fire of Holy Love, destroying all that resists, glorifying into its own purity all that yields. There is the Son, casting Himself into that consuming fire, whether in its eternal blessedness in heaven, or its angry wrath on earth, a willing sacrifice, to be its food and its satisfaction, as well as the revelation of its power to destroy and to save. And there is the Spirit of Holiness, the flames of that mighty fire spreading on every side, convicting and judging as the Spirit of Burning, and then transforming into its own brightness and holiness all that it can reach. All the relations of the Three Persons to each other and to us have their root and their meaning in the revelation of God as the Holy One. As we know and partake of Him, we shall know and partake of Holiness.

And how shall we know Him? Let us learn to know the Holiness of God as the seraphs do: in the worship of the Thrice Holy One. Let us with veiled faces join in the ceaseless song of adoration: 'Holy, holy, holy is the Lord of hosts.' Each time we meditate on the Word, each prayer to the Holy God, each act of faith in Christ the Holy One, each exercise of waiting dependence on the Holy Spirit, let it be in the spirit of worship: Holy, holy, holy. Let us learn to know the Holiness of God as Isaiah did. He was to be the chosen messenger to reveal and interpret to the people the name, the Holy One of Israel. His preparation was the vision that made him cry out, 'Woe is me! for mine eyes have seen the King, the Lord of hosts.' Let us bow in silence before the Holy One, until our comeliness too be turned into corruption. And then let us believe in the cleansing fire from the altar, the touch of the live coals of the burning holiness, which not only consumes, but purges lips and heart to say, 'Here am I, send me.' Yes, let us worship, whether like the adoring seraphim, or like the trembling prophet, until we know that our service too is accepted, to tell forth the praise of the Thrice Holy One.

Holy, holy, holy: if we are indeed to be the messengers of the Holy One, let us seek to enter fully into what this Thrice Holy means. Holy, the Father, God above us, High and Lifted up, whom no man hath seen or can see, whose Holiness none dare approach, but who doth Himself in His Holiness draw nigh to make holy. Holy, the Son, God with us, revealing Divine Holiness in human life, maintaining it amid the suffering of death for us, and preparing a holy life and nature for His people. Holy, the Spirit, God in us, the Power of Holiness within us, reaching out to and embracing Christ, and transforming our inner life into the union and communion of Him in whom we are holy. Holy, holy, holy! it is all holiness. It is only holiness—perfect holiness. This is Divine holiness: holiness hidden and unapproachable; holiness manifested and maintained in human nature; holiness communicated and made our very own.

The mystery of the Holy Trinity is the mystery of the Christian life, the mystery of Holiness. The Three are One, and we need to enter ever more deeply into the truth that neither of the Three ever works separate or independent of the other. The Son reveals the Father, and the Father reveals the Son. The Father gives not Himself, but the Spirit: the Spirit speaks not of Himself, but cries Abba Father! The Son is our Sanctification, our Life, our All: the fulness is in Him. And yet we have ever to bow our knees to the Father for Him to reveal Christ in us, for Him to establish us in Christ. And the Father does not this without the Spirit: so that we have to ask to be strengthened mightily by the Spirit, that Christ may dwell in us. Christ gives the Spirit to them that believe and love and obey; the Spirit again gives Christ, formed within and dwelling in the heart. And so in each act of worship, and each step of growth, and each blessed experience of grace, all the Three Persons are actively engaged: the One is ever Three, the Three are ever One.

Would you apply this in the life of holiness, let faith in the Holy Trinity be a living practical reality. In every prayer to the Father to sanctify you, take up your position in Christ, and do it in the power of the Spirit within you. In every exercise of faith in Christ as your Sanctification, let your posture be that of prayer to the Father and trust in Him as He delights to honour the Son, and of quiet expectancy of the Spirit's working, through whom the Father glorifies the Son. In every surrender of the soul to the sanctification of the Spirit, to His leading as the Spirit of Holiness, look to the Father who grants His mighty working, and who sanctifies through faith in the Son, and expect the Spirit's power to manifest itself in showing the will of God, and Jesus as your Sanctification. If for a time this appears at variance with the simplicity of childlike faith and prayer, be assured that as God has thus revealed Himself, He will teach you so to worship and believe. And so the Holy, holy, holy will become the deep undertone of all our worship and all our life.

Children of God! called to be holy as He is holy, oh, come let us bow down and worship in His holy presence! Come and veil the face: withdraw eye and mind from gazing on what passes knowledge, and let the soul be gathered into that inner stillness, in which the worship of the heavenly Sanctuary alone can be heard. Come and cover the feet: withdraw from the rush of work and haste, be it worldly or religious, and learn to worship. Come, and as you fall down in self-abasement, the glory of the Holy One will shine upon you. And as you hear and take up and sing the song, Holy, Holy, Holy, you will find how in such knowledge and worship of the Thrice Holy One is the power that makes you holy.

Be holy, for I am holy

Holy, holy, holy, the Lord God Almighty! which wast, and art, and art to come! I worship Thee as the Triune God. With face veiled and feet covered, I would bow in deep humility and silence, till Thy mercy lift me as on eagles' wings to behold Thy glory.

Most merciful God! who hast called me to be holy as Thou art holy, oh, reveal to me somewhat of Thy Holiness! As it shines upon me and strikes death into the creature and the flesh, may even the most involuntary taint of sin, and its slightest movement, become unbearable. As it shines and revives the hope of being partaker of Thy Holiness, may the confidence grow strong that Thou Thyself art making me holy, wilt even make me a messenger of Thy Holiness.

Thrice Holy God! I worship Thee as my God. Holy! the Father; holy and making holy; making holy His own Son and sending Him into the world, that we might behold the very glory of God in a human face, the face of Jesus Christ. Holy! the Son; the Holy One of God, fulfilling the will of the Father, and so making holy Himself that He might be our holiness. Holy! the Spirit; the Spirit of Holiness, dwelling within us, making the Son and His Holiness our own, and so making us partakers of the Holiness of God. O my God! I bow down, and worship, and adore.

May even now the worship of heaven that rests not day or night be the worship my soul renders Thee without ceasing. May its song be, down in the depths of the heart, the keynote of my life: Holy, Holy, Holy, Lord God Almighty! which wast, and art, and art to come. Amen.

1. Thought always needs to distinguish and separate: in life alone there is perfect unity. The more we know the living God, the more we shall realize how truly the Three are One. In each act of One Person the other Two are present. There is not a prayer rises but the Presence of the Holy Three is needed through Christ, in the Spirit, we speak to the Father.

2. In faith to apprehend this is to have the secret of holiness. The Holy God above us, ever giving and working; the Holy One of God, the living gift, who has possession of us, in whom we are; the Holy Spirit, God within us, through whom the Father works, and the Son is revealed: this is the God who says, I am holy, I make holy. In the perfect unity of the work of the Three, holiness is found.

3. No wonder that the love of the Father and the grace of the Son do not accomplish more, when the fellowship of the Holy Spirit is little understood or sought or accepted. The Holy Spirit is the fruit and crown of the Divine Revelation, through whom the Son and the Father come to us. If you would know God, if you would be holy, you must be taught and led of the Spirit.

4. As often as you worship the Thrice Holy One, hearken if no voice be heard: Whom shall I send, and who will go for us? Let the answer rise, Here am I, send me, and offer yourself to be a messenger of the holiness of God to those around you.

5. When in meditation and worship you have sought to take in and express what God's word has taught, then comes the time for confessing how you know nothing, and for waiting on God to reveal Himself.

Thirteenth Day

HOLY IN CHRIST

Holiness and Humility

'Thus saith the High and Lofty One that inhabiteth eternity, whose name is Holy: I dwell in the High and Holy place, with him that is of a contrite and humble spirit, to revive the spirit of the humble, and to revive the heart of the contrite ones.'—Isa. lvii. 15.

Very wonderful is the revelation we have in Isaiah of God, the Holy One, as the Redeemer and the Saviour of His people. In the midst of the people whom He created and formed for Himself, He will as the Holy One dwell, showing forth His power and His glory, filling them with joy and gladness. All these promises have, however, reference to the people as a whole. Our text to-day reveals a new and specially beautiful feature of the Divine Holiness in its relation to the individual. The High and Lofty One, whose name is Holy, and whose only fit dwelling-place is eternity, He looks to the man who is of a humble and contrite heart; with him will He dwell. God's Holiness is His condescending Love. As it is a consuming fire against all who exalt themselves before Him, it is to the spirit of the humble like the shining of the sun, heart-reviving and life-giving.

The deep significance of this promise comes out clearly when we connect it with the other promises of New Testament times. The great feature of the New Covenant, in its superiority to the old, is this, that whereas in the law and its institution all was external, in the New the kingdom of God would be within. God's laws given and written into the heart, a new spirit put within us, God's own Spirit given to dwell within our spirit, and so the heart and the inner life fitted to be the temple and home of God; it is this constitutes the peculiar privilege of the ministration of the Spirit. Our text is perhaps the only one in the Old Testament in which this indwelling of the Holy One, not among the people only, but in the heart of the individual believer, is clearly brought out. In this the two aspects of the Divine Holiness would reach their full manifestation: I dwell in the High and Holy place, and with him also that is of a contrite

70

and humble spirit. In His heaven above, the high and lofty place, and in our heart, contrite and humble, God has His home. God's Holiness is His glory that separates Him by an infinite distance, not only from sin, but even from the creature, lifting Him high above it. God's Holiness is His Love, drawing Him down to the sinner, that He may lift him into His fellowship and likeness, and make him holy as He is holy. The Holy One seeks the humble; the humble find the Holy One: such are the two lessons we have to learn to-day.

The Holy One seeks the humble. There is nothing that has such an attraction for God, that has such affinity with holiness, as a contrite and humble spirit. The reason is evident. There is no law in the natural and the spiritual world more simple, than that two bodies cannot at the same moment occupy the same space. Only so much as the new occupant can expel of what the space was filled with can it really possess. In man, self has possession, and self-will the mastery, and there is no room for God. It is simply impossible for God to dwell or rule when self is on the throne. As long as, through the blinding influence of sin and self-love, even the believer is not truly conscious of the extent to which this self-will reigns, there can be no true contrition or humility. But as it is discovered by God's Spirit, and the soul sees how it has just been self that has been secretly keeping out God, with what shame it is broken down, and how it longs to break utterly away from self, that God may have His place! It is this brokenness, and continued breaking down, that is expressed by the word contrition. And as the soul sees what folly and guilt it has been, by its secret honouring of self, to keep the Holy One from the place which He alone has a right to, and which He would so blessedly have filled, it casts itself down in utter self-abasement, with the one desire to be nothing, and to give God the place and the praise that is His due.

Such breaking down and humiliation is painful. Its intense reality consists in this, that the soul can see nothing in itself to trust or hope in. And least of all can it imagine that it should be an object of Divine complacency, or a fit vessel for the Divine blessing. And yet just this is the message which the Word of the Lord brings to our faith. It tells us that the Holy One, who dwells in the High and Lofty place, is seeking and preparing for Himself a dwelling here on this earth. It tells us, just what the truly contrite and humble never could imagine, and even now can

71

hardly believe, that it is even, that it is only, with such that He will dwell. These are they in whom God can be glorified, in whom there is room for Him to take the place of self and to fill the emptied place with Himself. The Holy One seeks the humble. Just when we see that there is nothing in us to admire or rest in, God sees in us everything to admire and to rest in, because there is room for Himself. The lowly one is the home of the Holy One.

The humble find the Holy One. Just when the consciousness of sin and weakness, and the discovery of how much of self there is, makes you fear that you can never be holy, the Holy One gives Himself. Not as you look at self, and seek to know whether now you are contrite and humble enough—no, but when no longer looking at self, because you have given up all hope of seeing anything in it but sin, you look up to the Holy One, you will see how His promise is your only hope. It is in faith that the Holy One is revealed to the contrite soul. Faith is ever the opposite of what we see and feel; it looks to God alone. And it believes that in its deepest consciousness of unholiness, and its fear that it never can be holy, God, the Holy One, who makes holy, is near as Redeemer and Saviour. And it is content to be low, in the consciousness of unworthiness and emptiness, and yet to rejoice in the assurance that God Himself does take possession and revive the heart of the contrite one. Happy the soul who is willing at once to learn the lesson that, all along, it is going to be the simultaneous experience of weakness and power, of emptiness and filling, of deep, real humiliation, and the as real and most wonderful indwelling of the Holy One.

This is indeed the deep mystery of the Divine life. To human reason it is a paradox. When Paul says of himself, 'as dying, and behold we live; as sorrowful, yet always rejoicing; as having nothing, yet possessing all things,' he only gives expression to the law of the kingdom, that as self is displaced and man becomes nothing, God will become all. Side by side with deepest sense of nothingness and weakness, the sense of infinite riches and the joy unspeakable can fill the heart. However deep and blessed the experience becomes of the nearness, the blessing, the love, the actual indwelling of the Holy One, it is never an indwelling in the old self; it is ever a Divine Presence humbling self to make place for God alone to be exalted. The power of Christ's death, the fellowship of His cross, works each moment side by side with the power and the joy of His resurrection. 'He that humbleth himself shall be exalted;' in the blessed life of faith the humiliation and the exaltation are simultaneous, each dependent on the other.

The humble find the Holy One; and when they have found, the possession only humbles all the more. Not that there is no danger or temptation of the flesh exalting itself in the possession, but, once knowing the danger, the humble soul seeks for grace to fear continually, with a fear that only clings more firmly to God alone. Never for a moment imagine that you attain a state in which self or the flesh are absolutely dead. No; by faith you enter into and abide in a fellowship with Jesus, in whom they are crucified; abiding in Him, you are free from their power, but only as you believe, and, in believing, have gone out of self and dwell in Jesus. Therefore, the more abundant God's grace becomes, and the more blessed the indwelling of the Holy One, keep so much the lower. Your danger is greater, but your Help is now nearer: be content in trembling to confess the danger, it will make you bold in faith to claim the victory.

Believers, who profess to be nothing, and to trust in grace alone, I pray you, do listen to the wondrous message. The High and Lofty One, whose name is Holy, and who dwells in the Holy Place, and who can dwell nowhere but in a Holy Place, seeks a dwelling here on earth. Will you give it Him? Will you not fall down in the dust, that He may find in you the humble heart He loves to dwell in? Will you not now believe that even in you, however low and broken you feel, He doth delight to make His dwelling? 'Blessed are the poor in spirit: for theirs is the Kingdom;' with them the King dwells. Oh, this is the path to holiness! be humble, and the holy nearness and presence of God in you will be your holiness. As you hear the command, Be holy, as I am holy, let faith claim the promise, and answer, I will be holy, O Most Holy God! if Thou, the Holy One, wilt dwell with me.

Be holy, as I am holy

O Lord! Thou art the High and Lofty One, whose Name is Holy. And yet Thou speakest, 'I dwell in the high and holy place, and with him that is of a contrite and humble spirit.' Yes, Lord! when the soul takes the low place, and has low thoughts of itself, that it feels it is nothing, Thou dost love to come and comfort, to dwell with it and revive it.

O my God! my creature nothingness humbles me; my

many transgressions humble me; my innate sinfulness humbles me; but this humbles me most of all, Thine infinite condescension, and the ineffable indwelling Thou dost vouchsafe. It is Thy Holiness, in Christ bearing our sin, Thy Holy Love bearing with our sin, and consenting to dwell in us; O God! it is this love that passeth knowledge that humbles me. I do beseech Thee, let it do its work, until self hides its head and flees away at the presence of Thy glory, and Thou alone art all.

Holy Lord God! I pray Thee to humble me. Didst Thou not of old meet Thy servants, and show Thyself unto them until they fell upon their faces and feared? Thou knowest, my God! I have no humility which I can bring Thee. In my blessed Saviour, who humbled Himself in the form of a servant, and unto the death of the cross, I hide myself. In Him, in His spirit and likeness, I would live before Thee. Work Thou it in me, by the Holy Spirit dwelling in me, and as I am dead to self in Him, and His cross makes me nothing, let Thy holy indwelling revive and quicken me. Amen.

1. Lowliness and holiness. Keep fast hold of the intimate connection. Lowliness is taking the place that becomes me; holiness, giving God the place that becomes Him. If I be nothing before Him, and God be all to me, I am in the sure path of holiness. Lowliness is holiness, because it gives all the glory to God.

2. 'Blessed are the poor in spirit, for theirs is the kingdom of heaven.' These first words of the Master when He opened His lips to proclaim the Kingdom, are often the last in the hearts of His disciples. 'The Kingdom is in the Holy Ghost:' to the poor in spirit, those who know they have nothing that is really spiritual, the Holy Spirit comes to be their life. The poor in spirit are the Kingdom of the Saints: in them the Holy Spirit reveals the King.

3. Many strive hard to be humble with God, but with men they maintain their rights, and nourish self. Remember that the great school of humility before God, is to accept the humbling of man. Christ sanctified Himself in accepting the humiliation and injustice which evil men laid upon Him.

4. Humility never sees its own beauty, because it refuses to look to itself: It only wonders at the condescension of the Holy God, and rejoices in the humility of Jesus, God's Holy One, our Holy One.

5. The link between holiness and humility is indwelling.

The Lofty One, whose name is Holy, dwells with the contrite one. And where He dwells is the Holy Place.

Fourteenth Day

HOLY IN CHRIST

The Holy One of God

'Therefore also that holy thing which shall be born of thee shall be called the Son of God.'—Luke i. 35.

'We have believed and know that Thou art the Holy One of God.'—John vi. 69.

'The holy one of the Lord'—only once (Ps. cvi. 16) the expression is found in the Old Testament. It is spoken of Aaron, in whom holiness, as far as it could then be revealed, had found its most complete embodiment. The title waited for its fulfilment in Him who alone, in His own person, could perfectly show forth the holiness of God on earth—Jesus the Son of the Father. In Him we see holiness, as Divine, as human, as our very own.

1. In Him we see wherein that Incomparable Excellence of the Divine Nature consists. 'Thou lovest righteousness, and hatest iniquity, therefore God, even Thy God, hath anointed Thee with the oil of gladness above Thy fellows.' God's infinite hatred of sin, and His maintenance of the Right, might appear to have little moral worth, as being a necessity of His nature. In the Son we see Divine Holiness tested. He is tried and tempted. He suffers, being tempted. He proves that Holiness has indeed a moral worth: it is ready to make any sacrifice, yea to give up life and cease to be, rather than consent to sin. In giving Himself to die, rather than yield to the temptation of sin; in giving Himself to die, that the Father's righteous judgment may be honoured; Jesus proved how Righteousness is an element of the Divine Holiness, and how the Holy One is sanctified in Righteousness.

But this is only one side of Holiness. The fire that consumes also purifies: it makes partakers of its own beautiful Light-nature all that is capable of assimilation. So Divine Holiness not only maintains its own purity; it communicates it too. Herein was Jesus indeed seen to be the Holy One of God, that He never said, 'Stand by, for I am holier than thou.' His holiness proved itself to be the very incarnation of Him who had spoken, 'Thus saith the High and Lofty One, whose Name is

76

Holy: I dwell in the High and Holy place, and with him who is of a contrite spirit.' In Him was seen the affinity holiness has for all that is lost and helpless and sinful. He proved that holiness is not only the energy which in holy anger separates itself from all that is impure, but which in holy love separates to itself even what is most sinful, to save and to bless. In Him we see how the Divine Holiness is the harmony of Infinite Righteousness with Infinite Love.

2. Such is the Divine aspect of the character of Christ, as He shows in human form what God's Holiness is. But there is another aspect, to us no less interesting and important. We not only want to know how God is holy, but how man must act to be holy as God is holy. Jesus came to teach us that it is possible to be men, and yet to have the life of God dwelling in us. We ordinarily think that the glory and the infinite Perfection of Deity are the proper setting in which the beauty of holiness is to be seen: Jesus proved the perfect adaptation and suitability of human nature for showing forth that which is the essential glory of Deity. He showed us how, in choosing and doing the will of God, and making it his own will, man may truly be holy as God is holy.

The value of this aspect of the Incarnation depends upon our realizing intensely the true humanity of our Lord. The awful separating and purifying process that is ever being carried on in the fiery furnace of the Divine Holiness, ever consuming and ever assimilating, we expect to see in Him in the struggles of a truly human will. Holiness, to be truly human, must not only be a gift, but an acquirement. Coming from God, it must be accepted and personally appropriated, in the voluntary surrender of all that is not in accordance with it. In Jesus, as He distinctly gave up His own will, and did and suffered the Father's will, we have the revelation of what human holiness is, and how truly man, through the unity of will, can be holy as God is holy.

3. But what avails that we have seen in Jesus that a man can be holy? His example were indeed a mockery if He show us not the way, and give us not the power, to become like Himself. To bring us this, was indeed the supreme object of the Incarnation. The Divine nature of Christ did not simply make His humanity partaker of its holiness, leaving Him still nothing more than an individual man. His Divinity gave the human holiness He wrought out, the holy human nature which He perfected, an infinite value and power of communication. With Him a new life,

the Eternal Life, was grafted into the stem of humanity. For all who believe in Him, He sanctified Himself, that they themselves might also be sanctified in truth. Because His death was the great triumph of His obedience to the will of the Father, it broke for ever the dominion of sin, it atoned for our guilt, and won for Him from the Father the power to make His people partakers of His own life and holiness. In His Resurrection and Ascension the power of the New Life, and its right to universal dominion, were made manifest, and He is now in full truth the Holy One of God, holding in Himself as Head the power of a Holiness, at once Divine and human, to communicate to every member of His body.

The Holy One of God! in a fulness of meaning that passeth knowledge, in spirit and in truth, Jesus now bears this title. He is now the One Holy One whom God sees, of such an infinite compass and power of holiness, that He can be holiness to each of His brethren. And even as He is to God the Holy One, in whom He delights, and for whose sake He delights in all who are in Him, so Christ may now be to us too the One Holy One in whom we delight, in whom the Holiness of God is become ours. 'We have believed and know that Thou art the Holy One of God,'—blessed they who can say this, and know themselves to be holy in Christ.

In speaking of the mystery of the Holy Trinity, we saw how Christ stands midway between the Father and the Spirit, as the point of union in which they meet. In the Son, 'the very image of His substance' (Heb. i. 3), we have the objective revelation of Deity, the Divine Holiness embodied and brought nigh. In the Holy Spirit we have the same revelation subjectively, the Divine Holiness entering our inmost being and revealing itself there. The work of the Holy Spirit is to reveal and glorify Christ as the Holy One of God, as He takes of His Holiness and makes it ours. He shows us how all is in Christ; how Christ is all for us; how we are in Christ; and how, as a living Saviour, Christ through His Spirit takes and keeps charge of us and our life of holiness. He makes Christ indeed to be to us the Holy One of God.

My Brother! wouldst thou be holy, wouldst thou know God's way of holiness—learn to know Christ as the Holy One of God. Thou art in Him, 'holy in Christ.' Thou hast been placed, by an act of Divine Power, in Christ, and that same Power keeps thee there, planted and rooted in that Divine fulness of life and holiness which there is in Him. His Holy Presence, and the power of His eternal life, surround thee: let the Holy Spirit reveal this to thee. The Holy Spirit is within thee as the power of Christ and His life. Secretly, silently, but mightily, if thou wilt look to the Father for His working, will He strengthen the faith that thou art in Christ, and that the Divine life, which thus encircles thee on every side, will enter in and take possession of thee. Study and pray to believe and realize that it is in Christ as the Holy One of God, in Christ in whom the Holiness of God is prepared for thee as a holy nature and holy living, that thou art, and that thou mayest abide.

And then remember, also, that this Christ is thy Saviour, the most patient and compassionate of teachers. Study holiness in the light of His countenance, looking up into His face. He came from heaven for the very purpose of making thee holy. His love and power are more than thy slowness and sinfulness. Do learn to think of holiness as the inheritance prepared for thee, as the power of a new life which Jesus waits and lives to dispense. Just think of it as all in Him, and of its possession as being dependent upon the possession of Himself. And as the disciples, though they scarce understood what they confessed, or knew whither the Lord was leading them, became His saints, His holy ones, in virtue of their intense attachment to Him, so wilt thou find that to love Jesus fervently, and obey Him simply, is the sure path to holiness and the fulness of the Holy Spirit.

Be ye holy, as I am holy

Most Holy Lord God! I do bless Thee that Thy beloved Son, whom Thou didst sanctify and send into the world, is now to us the Holy One of God. I beseech Thee that my inner life may so be enlightened by the Spirit that I may in faith fully know what this means.

May I know Him as the revelation of Thy Holiness, the incarnation in human nature, even unto the death, of Thine infinite and unconquerable hatred of sin, as of Thy amazing love to the sinner. May my soul be filled with great fear and trust of Thee.

May I know Him as the exhibition of the Holiness in which we are now to walk before Thee. He lived in Thy holy will. May I know Him as He wrought out that holiness, to be communicated to us in a new human nature, making it possible for us to live a holy life.

May I know Him as Thou hast placed me in Him in heaven, holy in Christ, and as I may abide in Him by faith.

May I know Him, as He dwells in me, the Holy One of God on the throne of my heart, breathing His Holy Spirit and maintaining His holy rule. So shall I live holy in Christ.

O my Father! it pleased Thee that in Thy Son should all the fulness dwell. In Him are hid all the treasures of wisdom and knowledge; in Him dwell the unsearchable riches of grace and holiness. I beseech Thee, reveal Him to me, reveal Him in me, that I may not have to satisfy myself with thoughts and desires, without the reality, but that in the power of an endless life I may know Him, and be known of Him, the Holy One of God. Amen.

1. In the holiness of Jesus we see what ours must be: righteousness, that hates sin and gives everything to have it destroyed; love, that seeks the sinner and gives everything to have him saved. 'Whosoever doeth not righteousness is not of God, neither he that loveth not his brother.'

2. It is a solemn thought that we may be studying earnestly to know what holiness is, and yet have little of it, because we have little of Jesus. It is a blessed thought that a man may directly be little occupied with the thought of holiness, and yet have much of it, because he is full of Jesus.

3. We need the whole of what God teaches in His Word in regard to holiness in all its different aspects. We need still more to be ever returning to the living centre where God imparts holiness. Jesus is the Holy One of God: to have Him truly, to love Him fervently, to trust and obey Him, to be in Him—this makes us holy.

4. Your holiness is thus treasured up in this Divine, Almighty, and most gentle Saviour—surely there need to be no fear that He will not be ready or able to make you holy.

5. With such a Sanctifier, how comes it that so many seekers after holiness fail so sadly, and know so little of the joy of a holy life?

I am sure it is with very many this one thing: they seek to grasp and hold this Christ in their own strength, and know not how it is the Holy Spirit within them who must be waited for to reveal this Divine Being, the Holy One of God, in their hearts.

Fifteenth Day

HOLY IN CHRIST

The Holy Spirit

'But this spake He of the Spirit, which they that believed on Him were to receive: for the Holy Spirit was not yet: because Jesus was not yet glorified.'—John vii. 39.

'The Comforter, even the Holy Spirit, whom the Father will send in my name, He shall teach you all things.'—John xiv. 26.

'God chose you to salvation in sanctification of the Spirit, and belief of the truth.'—2 Thess. ii. 13. (See 1 Pet. i. 2.)

It has sometimes been said, that while the Holiness of God stands out more prominently in the Old Testament, in the New it has to give way to the revelation of His love. The remark could hardly be made if it were fully realized that the Spirit is God, and that when He takes up the epithet Holy as His own proper name, it is to teach us that now the Holiness of God is to come nearer than ever, and to be specially revealed as the power that makes us holy. In the Holy Spirit, God the Holy One of Israel, and He who was the Holy One of God, come nigh for the fulfilment of the promise, 'I am the Lord that make you holy.' The unseen and unapproachable holiness of God had been revealed and brought near in the life of Christ Jesus; all that hindered our participation in it had been removed by His death. The name of Holy Spirit teaches us that it is specially the Spirit's work to impart it to us and make it our own.

Try and realize the meaning of this; the epithet that through the whole Old Testament has belonged to the Holy God, is now appropriated to that Spirit which is within you. The Holiness of God in Christ becomes holiness in you, because this Spirit is in you. The words, and the Divine realities the words express, Holy and Spirit, are now inseparably and eternally united. You can only have as much of the Spirit as you are willing

81

to have of holiness. You can only have as much holiness as you have of the indwelling Spirit.

There are some who pray for the Spirit because they long to have His light and joy and strength. And yet their prayers bring little increase of blessing or power. It is because they do not rightly know or desire Him as the Holy Spirit. His burning purity, His searching and convicting light, His making dead of the deeds of the body, of self with its will and its power, His leading into the fellowship of Jesus as He gave up His will and His life to the Father,—of all this they have not thought. The Spirit cannot work in power in them because they receive Him not as the Holy Spirit, in sanctification of the Spirit. At times, in seasons of revival, as among the Corinthians and Galatians, He may indeed come with His gifts and mighty workings, while His sanctifying power is but little manifest. (1 Cor. xiv. 4, xiii. 8, iii. 1–3; Gal. iii. 3, v. 15–26.) But unless that sanctifying power be acknowledged and accepted, His gifts will be lost. His gifts coming on us are but meant to prepare the way for the sanctifying power within us. We must take the lesson to heart; we can have as much of the Spirit as we are willing to have of His Holiness. Be full of the Spirit, must mean to us, Be fully holy.

The converse is equally true. We can only have so much holiness as we have of the Spirit. Some souls do very earnestly seek to be holy, but it is very much in their own strength. They will read books and listen to addresses most earnestly; they will use every effort to lay hold of every thought, and act out every advice. And yet they must confess that they are still very much strangers to the true, deep rest and joy and power of abiding in Christ, and being holy in Him. They sought for holiness more than for the Spirit. They must learn how even all the holiness which is so near and clear in Christ, is beyond our reach, except as the Holy Spirit dwells within and imparts it. They must learn to pray for Him and His mighty strengthening (Eph. iii. 16), to believe for Him (John iv. 14, vii. 37), in faith to yield to Him as indwelling (1 Cor. iii. 14, vi. 19). They must learn to cease from self-effort in thinking and believing, in willing and in running; to hope in God, and wait patiently for Him. He will by His Holy Spirit make us holy. Be holy means, Be filled with the Spirit.

If we inquire more closely how it is that this Holy Spirit makes holy, the answer is,—He reveals and imparts the Holiness of Christ. Scripture tells us: Christ is made unto us sanctification. He sanctified Himself for us, that we ourselves might also be sanctified in truth. We have been sanctified through the offering of the body of Jesus Christ once for all. We are sanctified in Christ Jesus. The whole living Christ is just a treasury of holiness for man. In His life on earth He exchanged the Divine Holiness He possessed into the current coin needed for this human earthly life, obedience to the Father, and humility, and love, and zeal. As God, He has a sufficiency of it for every moment of the life of every believer.

And yet, it is all beyond our reach, except as the Holy Spirit brings it to us and inwardly communicates it. But this is the very work for which He bears the Divine Name, the Holy Spirit, to glorify Jesus, the Holy One of God, within us, and so make us partakers of His Holiness. He does it by revealing Christ, so that we begin to see what is in Him. He does it by discovering the deep unholiness of our nature (Rom. vii. 14–23). He does it by mightily strengthening us to believe, to receive Jesus Himself as our life. He does it by leading us to utter despair of self, to absolute surrender of obedience to Jesus as Lord, to the assured confidence of faith in the power of an indwelling Christ. He does it by, in the secret silent depths of the heart and life, imparting the dispositions and graces of Christ, so that from the inner centre of our life, which has been renewed and sanctified in Christ, holiness should flow out and pervade all to the utmost circumference. Where the desire has once been awakened, and the delight in the law of God after the inward man been created, there, as the Spirit of this life in Christ Jesus, He makes free from the law of sin and death in the members, he leads into the glorious liberty of the sons of God. As God within us, He communicates what God in Christ has prepared.

And if we ask once more how the working of this Holy Spirit, who thus makes holy, is to be secured, the answer is very simple and clear. He is the Spirit of the Holy Father, and of Christ, the Holy One of God: from them He must be received. 'He showed me a river of water of life proceeding out of the throne of God and the Lamb.' Jesus speaks of 'the Holy Spirit, whom the Father will send in my Name.' He taught us to ask the Father. Paul prays for the Ephesians: 'I bow my knees to the Father, that He may grant unto you, according to the riches of His glory, that ye may be strengthened with might by His Spirit in the inner man.' It is as we look to God in His Holiness, and all its revelation from Creation downward, and see how the Spirit now flows out from the throne of His Holiness as the water of life, that our hope will be awakened that God will give Him to work mightily in us. And as we then see Jesus revealing that holiness in human nature, rending the veil in His atoning death, that the Spirit from the Holiest of all may come forth and, as the Holy Spirit, be His representative, making Him present within us, we shall become confident that faith in Jesus will bring the fulness of the Spirit. As He told us to ask the Father, He told us to believe in Himself. 'He that believeth in me, rivers of living water shall flow out of him.' Let us bow to the Father in the name of Christ, His Son; let us believe very simply in the Son as Him in whom we are well-pleasing to the Father, and through whom the Father's love and blessing reach us, and we may be sure the Spirit, who is already within us, will, as the Holy Spirit, do His work in ever-increasing power. The mystery of holiness is the mystery of the Trinity: as we bow to the Father, believing in the Son, the Holy Spirit will work. And we shall see the true meaning of what God spake in Israel: 'I am holy,' thus speaks the Father; 'Be holy,' as my Son and in my Son; 'I make holy,' through the Spirit of my Son dwelling in you. Let our souls worship and cry out, 'Holy, holy, holy is the Lord God of hosts.'

The Holy Spirit. All true knowledge of the Father in His adorable Holiness, and of the Son in His, which is meant to be ours, and all participation of it, depend upon our life in the Spirit, upon our knowing and owning Him as abiding in us as our Life. Oh, what can it be that, with such a Thrice Holy God, His Holiness does not more cover His Church and children? The Holy Spirit is among us, is in us: it must be we grieve and resist Him. If you would not do so, at once bow the knee to the Father, that He may grant you the Spirit's mighty workings in the inner man. Believe that the Holy Spirit, bearer to you of all the Holiness of God and of Jesus, is indeed in you. Let Him take the place of self, with its thoughts and efforts. Set your soul still before God in holy silence, for Him to give you wisdom; rest, in emptiness and poverty of spirit, in the faith that He will work in His own way. As Divine as is the holiness that Jesus brings, so Divine is the power in which the Holy Spirit communicates it. Yield yourself day by day in growing dependence and obedience, to wait on and be led of Him. Let the fear of the Holy One be on you: sanctify the Lord God in your heart: let Him be your fear and dread. Fear not only sin: fear above all self, as it thrusts itself in before God with its service. Let self die, in refusing and denying its work: let the Holy Spirit, in quietness, and dependence, in the surrender of obedience and trust, have the rule, the free disposal of every faculty. Wait for Him—He can, He will in power reveal and impart the Holiness of the Father and the Son. [7]

Be holy, as I am holy

Holy, holy, holy, Lord God of hosts! the whole earth is full of Thy glory! Let that glory fill the heart of Thy child, as he bows before Thee. I come now to drink of the river of the water of life that flows from under the throne of God and of the Lamb. Glory be to God and to the Lamb for the gift that hath not entered into the heart of man to conceive—the gift of the Holy indwelling Spirit.

O my Father! in the name of Jesus I ask Thee that I may be strengthened with might by Thy Spirit in the inner man. Teach me, I pray Thee, to believe that Thou hast given Him, to accept and expect Him to fill and rule my whole inner being. Teach me to give up to Him; not to will or to run, not to think or to work in my strength, but in quiet confidence to wait and to know that He works in me. Teach me what it is to have no confidence in the flesh, and to serve Thee in the Spirit. Teach me what it is in all things to be led by Thy Holy Spirit, the Spirit of Thy Holiness.

And grant, gracious Father, that through Him I may hear Thee speak and reveal Thyself to me in power: I am holy. May He glorify to me and in me, Jesus, in whom Thy command 'Be holy' hath been so blessedly fulfilled on my behalf. And let the Holy Spirit give me the anointing and the sealing which bring the perfect assurance that in Him Thy promise is being gloriously fulfilled, 'I make you holy.' Amen.

1. It it universally admitted that the Holy Spirit has not, in the teaching of the Church or the faith of believers, that place of honour and power, which becomes Him as the Revealer of the

---

[7] I cannot say how deeply I feel that one of the great wants of believers is that they do not know the Holy Spirit, who is within them, and thereby lose the blessed life He would work in them. If it please God, I hope that the next volume of this series may be on The Spirit of Christ. May the Father give me a message that shall help His children to know what the Holy Spirit can be to them.

Father and the Son. Seek a deep conviction that without the Holy Spirit the clearest teaching on holiness, the most fervent desires, the most blessed experiences even, will only be temporary, will produce no permanent result, will bring no abiding rest.

2. The Holy Spirit dwells within, and works within, in the hidden deep of your nature. Seek above everything the clear and habitual assurance that He is within you, doing His work.

3. To this end, deny self and its work in serving God. Your own power to think and pray and believe and strive—lay it all down expressly and distinctly in God's presence; claim, accept, and believe in the hidden workings of the indwelling Spirit.

4. As the Son ever spake of the Father, so the Spirit ever points to Christ. The soul that yields itself to the Spirit will of Him learn to know how Christ is our holiness, how we can always abide in Christ our Sanctification. What a vain effort it has often been without the Spirit! 'As the anointing taught you, ye abide in Him.'

5. In the temple of thine heart, beloved believer, there is a secret place, within the veil, where dwells, often all unknown, the Spirit of God. Do bow in deep reverence before the Father, and ask that He may work mightily. Expect the Spirit to do His work: He will make Thy inner man a fit home, Thy heart a throne, for Jesus, and reveal Him there.

Sixteenth Day

HOLY IN CHRIST

Holiness and Truth

'Make them holy in the Truth: Thy word is Truth.'—John xvii. 17.

'God chose you unto salvation in sanctification and belief of the Truth.'—2 Thess. ii. 12.

The chief means of sanctification that God uses is His word. And yet how much there is of reading and studying, of teaching and preaching the word, that has almost no effect in making men holy. It is not the word that sanctifies; it is God Himself who alone can sanctify. Nor is it simply through the word that God does it, but through the Truth which is in the word. As a means the word is of unspeakable value, as the vessel which contains the truth, if God use it; as a means it is of no value, if God does not use it. Let us strive to connect God's Holy Word with the Holy God Himself. God sanctifies in the Truth through His word.

Jesus had just said, 'The words which Thou gavest me, I have given them.' Let us try and realize what that means. Think of that great transaction in eternity: the Infinite Being, whom we call God, giving His words to His Son; in His words opening up His heart, communicating His mind and will, revealing Himself and all His purpose and love. In a Divine power and reality passing all conception, God gave Christ His words. In the same living power Christ gave them to His disciples, all full of a Divine life and energy to work in their hearts, as they were able to receive them. And just as in the words of a man on earth we expect to find all the wisdom or all the goodness there is in him, so the word of the Thrice Holy One is all alive with the Holiness of God. All the holy fire, alike of His burning zeal and His burning love, dwells in His words.

And yet men can handle these words, and study them, and speak them, and be entire strangers to their holiness, or their power to make holy. It is God Himself, the Holy One, who must make holy through the word. Every seed, in which the life of a tree is contained, has around it a husk or shell, which protects and hides the inner life. Only where the seed finds a place in congenial soil, and the husk is burst and removed, can the seed germinate and grow up. And it is only where there is a heart in harmony with God's Holiness, longing for it, yielding itself to it, that the word will really make holy. It is the heart that is not content with the word, but seeks the Living, Holy One in the word, to which He will reveal the truth, and in it Himself. It is the word given to us by Christ as God gave it Him, and received by us as it was by Him, to rule and fill our life, which has power to make holy.

But we must notice very specially how our Saviour says, Sanctify them, not in the word, but in the truth. Just as in man there is body, soul, and spirit, so in truth too. There is first word-truth; a man may have the correct form of words while he does not really apprehend the truth they contain. Then there is thought-truth; there may be a clear intellectual apprehension of truth without the experience of its power. The Bible speaks of truth as a living reality: this is the life-truth, in which the very Spirit of the truth we profess has entered and possessed our inner being. Christ calls Himself the Truth: He is said to be full of grace and truth. The Divine life and grace are in Him as an actually substantial existence and reality. He not only acts upon us by thoughts and motives, but communicates, as a reality, the eternal life He brought for us from the Father. The Holy Spirit is called the Spirit of Truth; what He imparts is all real and actual, the very substance of unseen things; He guides into the Truth, not thought-truth or doctrine only, but life-truth, the personal possession of the Truth as it is in Jesus. As the Spirit of Truth He is the Spirit of Holiness; the life of God, which is His Holiness, He brings to us as an actual possession.

It is now of this living Truth, which dwells in the word, as the seed-life dwells in the husk, that Jesus says, 'Make them holy in the Truth: Thy word is Truth.' He would have us mark the intimate connection, as well as the wide difference, between the word and the truth. The connection is one willed by God and meant to be inseparable. 'Thy word is truth;' with God they are one. But not with man. Just as there were men in close contact and continual intercourse with Jesus, to whom He was only a man, and nothing more, so there are Christians who know and understand the word, and yet are strangers to its true spiritual power. They have the letter but not the spirit; the Truth comes to them in word but not in power. The word does not make them holy, because they hold it not in Spirit and in Truth. To others, on the contrary, who know what it is to receive the truth in the love of it, who yield themselves, in all their dealings with the word, to the Spirit of Truth who dwells in it and in them too, the word comes indeed as Truth, as a Divine reality, communicating and working what it speaks of. And it is of such a use of the word that the Saviour says, 'Make them holy in the truth: Thy word is truth.' As the words, which God gave Him, were all in the power of the eternal Life and Love and Will of God, the revelation and communication of the Father's purpose, as God's word was Truth to Him and in Him, so it can be in us. And as we thus receive it, we are made holy in the Truth.

And what now are the lessons we have to learn here for the path of Holiness? The first is: Let us see to it that in all our intercourse with God's Blessed Word we rest content with nothing short of the experience of it, as truth of God, as spirit and as power. Jesus said, 'If ye abide in my word, ye shall know the truth.' No analysis can ever find or prove the life of a seed: plant it in its proper soil, and the growth will testify to the life. It is only as the word of God is received in the love of it, as it grows and works in us, that we can know its truth, can know that it is the Truth of God. It is as we live in the words of Jesus, in love and obedience, keeping and doing them, that the Truth from heaven, the Power of the Divine Life which there is in them, will unfold itself to us. Christ is the Truth; in Him the love and grace, the very life of God, has come to earth as a substantial existence, a Living, Mighty Power, something new that was never on earth before (John i. 17); let us yield ourselves to the Living Christ to possess us and to rule us as the Living Truth, then will God's word be Truth to us and in us.

The Spirit of Christ is the Spirit of Truth; that actual heavenly reality of Divine life and love in Christ, the Truth, has a Spirit, who comes to communicate and impart it. Let us beware of trying to study or understand or take possession of God's word without that Spirit through whom the word was spoken of old; we shall find only the husk, the truth or thought and sentiment, very beautiful perhaps, but with no power to make us holy. We must have the Spirit of the Truth within us. He will lead us into the Truth; when we are in the Truth, God makes us holy in it and by it. The Truth must be in us, and we in it. God desires truth in the inward parts: we must be of the people of whom Christ says, 'If ye were of the truth,' 'he that is of the truth knoweth me.' In the lower sphere of daily life and conduct, of thought and action, there must be an intense love of truth, and a willingness to sacrifice everything for it; in the spiritual life, a deep hungering to have all our religion every day, every moment, stand fully in the truth of God. It is to the simple, humble, childlike spirit that the truth of the word will be unsealed and revealed. In such the Spirit of truth comes to dwell. In such, as they daily wait before the Holy One in silence and emptiness, in reverence and holy fear, His Holy Spirit works and gives the truth within. In thus imparting Christ as revealed in the word, in His Divine life and love, as their own life, He makes them holy with the holiness of Christ.

There is another lesson. Listen to that prayer, the earthly echo of the prayer which He ever liveth to pray, 'Holy Father! make them holy in the truth.' Would you be holy, child of God? cast yourself into that mighty current of intercession ever flowing into, ever reaching, the Father's bosom. Let yourself be borne upon it until your whole soul cries, with the unutterable groanings, too deep and too intense for human speech, 'Holy Father! make me holy in the truth.' As you trust in Christ as the truth, the reality of what you long for, and in His all-prevailing intercession; as you wait for the Spirit within as the Spirit of truth; look up to the Father, and expect His own direct and almighty working to make you holy. The mystery of holiness is the mystery of the Triune One. The deeper entrance into the holy life rests in the fellowship of the Three in One. It is the Father who establishes us in Christ, who gives, in a daily fresh giving, the Holy Spirit; it is to the Father, the Holy Father, the soul must look up continually in the prayer, 'Make me holy in the truth.'

It has been well said that in the word Holy we have the central thought of the high-priestly prayer. As the Father's attribute (John xvii. 11), as the Son's work for Himself and us (ver. 19), as the direct work of the Father through the Spirit (vers. 17, 20), it is the revelation of the glory of God in Himself and in us. Let us enter into the Holiest of all, and as we bow with our Great High Priest, let the deep, unceasing cry go up for all the Church of God, 'Holy Father! make them holy in the truth: Thy word is truth.' The word in which God makes holy is summed up in this, Holy in Christ. May God make it truth in us!

Be ye holy, as I am holy

Blessed Father! to Israel Thou didst say, I the Lord am holy and make holy. But it is only in Thy beloved Son that the full glory of Thy Holiness, as making us holy, has been revealed. Thou art our Holy Father, who makest us holy in Thy truth.

We thank Thee that Thy Son hath given us the words Thou gavest Him, and that as He received them from Thee in life and power, we may receive them too. O Father! with our whole heart we do receive them; let the Spirit make them truth and life within us. So shall we know Thee as the Holy One, consuming the sin, renewing the sinner.

We bless Thee most for Thy Blessed Son, the Holy One of God, the Living Word in whom the Truth dwelleth. We thank Thee that in His never-ceasing intercession, this cry ever reacheth Thee, 'Father, sanctify them in Thy truth,' and that the answer is ever streaming forth from Thy glory. Holy Father! make us holy in Thy truth, in Thy wonderful revelation of Thyself in Him who is the truth. Let Thy Holy Spirit so have dominion in our hearts that Thy Holy Child Jesus, sanctifying Himself for us that we may be sanctified in the truth, may be to us the Way, the Truth, and the Life. May we know that we are in Him in Thy presence, and that Thy one word in answer to our prayer to make us holy is—Holy in Christ. Amen.

1. God is the God of truth—not truth in speaking only, or truth of doctrine—but truth of existence, or life in its Divine reality. And Christ is the truth; the actual embodiment of this Divine life. And there is a kingdom of truth, of Divine Spiritual realities, of which Christ is King. And of all this truth of God in Christ, the very essence is, the Spirit. He is the Spirit of truth: He leads us into it, so that we are of the truth and walk in it. Of the truth, the reality there is in God, Holiness, is the deepest root; the Spirit of truth is the Holy Spirit.

2. It is the work of the Father to make us holy in the truth: let us bow very low in childlike trust as we breathe the prayer: 'Holy Father! make us holy in the truth.' He will do it.

3. It is the intercession of the Son that asks and obtains this blessing: let us take our place in Him, and rejoice in the assurance of an answer.

4. It is the Spirit of truth through whom the Father does this work, so that we dwell in the truth, and the truth in us. Let

us yield very freely and very fully to the leading of the Spirit, in our intercourse with God's Word, that, as the Son prays, the Father may make us holy in the truth.

5. Let us, in the light of this work of the Three-One, never read the Word but with this aim: to be made holy in the truth by God.

Seventeenth Day

HOLY IN CHRIST

Holiness and Crucifixion

'For their sakes I sanctify myself, that they themselves also may be sanctified in truth.'—John xvii. 19.

'He said, Lo, I am come to do Thy will. In which will we have been sanctified through the offering of the body of Jesus once for all. For by one offering He hath perfected for ever them that are sanctified.'—Heb. x. 9, 10, 14.

It was in His High-priestly prayer, on His way to Gethsemane and Calvary, that Jesus thus spake to the Father: 'I sanctify myself.' He had not long before spoken of Himself as 'the Son whom the Father hath sanctified and sent into the world.' From the language of Holy Scripture we are familiar with the thought that, what God has sanctified, man has to sanctify too. The work of the Father, in sanctifying the Son, is the basis and groundwork of the work of the Son in sanctifying Himself. If His Holiness as man was to be a free and personal possession, accepted and assimilated in voluntary and conscious self-determination, it was not enough that the Father sanctify Him: He must sanctify Himself too.

This self-sanctifying of our Lord found place through His whole life, but culminates and comes out in special distinctness in His crucifixion. Wherein it consists is made clear by the words from the Epistle to the Hebrews. The Messiah spake: 'Lo, I come to do Thy will.' And then it is added, 'In the which will we have been sanctified through the offering of the body of Christ.' It was the offering of the body of Christ that was the will of God: in doing that will He sanctified us. It was of the doing that will in the offering His body that He spake, 'I sanctify myself, that they themselves also may be sanctified in truth.' The giving up of His will to God's will in the agony of Gethsemane, and then the doing of that will in the obedience unto death, this was Christ's sanctifying Himself and us too. Let us try and understand this.

The Holiness of God is revealed in His will. Holiness even in the Divine Being has no moral value except as it is freely

93

willed. In speaking of the Trinity, theologians have pointed out how, as the Father represents the absolute necessity of Everlasting Goodness, the Son proves its liberty: within the Divine Being it is willed in love. And this now was the work of the Son on earth, amid the trials and temptations of a human life, to accept and hold fast at any sacrifice, with His whole heart to will, the will of the Father. 'Though He was a Son, yet He learned obedience in that He suffered.' In Gethsemane the conflict between the will of human nature and the Divine will reached its height: it manifests itself in language which almost makes us tremble for His sinlessness, as He speaks of His will in antithesis to God's will. But the struggle is a victory, because in presence of the clearest consciousness of what it means to have His own will, He gives it up, and says, 'Thy will be done.' To enter into the will of God He gives up His very life. In His crucifixion He thus reveals the law of sanctification. Holiness is the full entrance of our will into God's will. Or rather, Holiness is the entrance of God's will to be the death of our will. The only end of our will and deliverance from it, is death to it under the righteous judgment of God. It was in the surrender to the death of the cross that Christ sanctified Himself, and sanctified us, that we also might be sanctified in truth.

And now, just as the Father sanctified Him, and He in virtue thereof appropriated it and sanctified Himself, so we, whom He has sanctified, have to appropriate it to ourselves. In no other way than crucifixion, the giving up of Himself to the death, could Christ realize the sanctification He had from the Father. And in no other way can we realize the sanctification we have in Him. His own and our sanctification bears the common stamp of the cross. We have seen before that obedience is the path to holiness. In Christ we see that the path to perfect holiness is perfect obedience. And that is obedience unto death, even to the giving up of life, even the death of the cross. As the sanctification which Christ wrought out for us, even unto the offering of His body, bears the death mark, we cannot partake of it, we cannot enter it, except as we die to self and its will. Crucifixion is the path to sanctification.

This lesson is in harmony with all we have seen. The first revelation of God's Holiness to Moses was accompanied with the command, Put off. God's praise, as Glorious in Holiness, Fearful in Praises, was sounded over the dead bodies of the Egyptians. When Moses on Sinai was commanded to sanctify the Mount, it was said, 'If any touch it, man or beast, it shall not live.' The Holiness of God is death to all that is in contact with sin. Only through death, through blood-shedding, was there access to the Holiest of all. Christ chose death, even death as a curse, that He might sanctify Himself for us, and open to us the path to Holiness, to the Holiest of all, to the Holy One. And so it is still. No man can see God and live. It is only in death, the death of self and of nature, that we can draw near and behold God. Christ led the way. No man can see God and live. 'Then let me die, Lord,' one has cried, 'but see Thee I must.' Yes, blessed be God, so real is our interest in Christ and our union to Him, that we may live in His death; as day by day self is kept in the place of death, the life and the holiness of Christ can be ours. [8]

And where is the place of death? And how can the crucifixion which leads to Holiness and to God be accomplished in us? Thank God! it is no work of our own, no weary process of self-crucifixion. The crucifixion that is to sanctify us is an accomplished fact. The cross bears the banner, 'It is finished.' On it Christ sanctified Himself for us, that we might be sanctified in truth. Our crucifixion, as our sanctification, is something that in Christ has been completely and perfectly finished. 'We have been sanctified through the offering of the body of Jesus Christ once for all.' 'By one offering He hath perfected for ever them that are sanctified.' In that fulness, which it is the Father's good pleasure should dwell in Christ, the crucifixion of our old man, of the flesh, of the world, of ourselves, is all a spiritual reality; he that desires and knows and accepts Christ, fully receives all this in Him. And as the Christ, who had previously been known more in His pardoning, quickening, and saving grace, is again sought after as a real deliverer from the power of sin, as a sanctifier, He comes and takes up the soul into the fellowship of the sacrifice of His will. 'He put away sin by the sacrifice of Himself,' must become true of us as it is of Him. He reveals how it is a part of His salvation to make us partakers of a will entirely given up to the will of God, of a life that had yielded itself to the death, and had then been given back from the dead by the power of God, a life of which the crucifixion of self-will was the spirit and the power. He reveals this, and the soul that sees it, and consents to it, and yields its will and its life, and believes in Jesus as its death and its life, and in His crucifixion as its possession and its

---

[8] See Note D.

95

inheritance, enters into the enjoyment and experience of it. The language is now, 'I died that I might live: I have been crucified with Christ, and it is no longer I that live, but Christ that liveth in me.' And the life it now lives is by the faith on the Son of God, the daily acceptance in faith of Him who lives within us in the power of a death that has been passed through and for ever finished.

'I sanctify myself for them, that they themselves also may be sanctified in truth.' 'I come to do Thy will, O God. In the which will,' the will of God accomplished by Christ, 'we have been sanctified through the one offering of the body of Christ.' Let us understand and hold it fast: Christ's giving up His will in Gethsemane and accepting God's will in dying; Christ's doing that will in the obedience to the death of the cross, this is His sanctifying Himself, and this is our being sanctified in truth. 'In the which will we have been sanctified.' The death to self, the utter and most absolute giving up of our own life, with its will and its power and its aims, to the cross, and into the crucifixion of Christ, the daily bearing the cross—not a cross on which we are yet to be crucified, but the cross of the crucified Christ in its power to kill and make dead—this is the secret of the life of holiness—this is true sanctification.

Believer! is this the holiness which you are seeking? Have you seen and consented that God alone is holy, that self is all unholy, and that there is no way to be made holy but for the fire of the Divine Holiness to come in and be the death of self? 'Always bearing about in the body the dying of Jesus, that the life also of Jesus may be manifested in our mortal body'—is the pathway for each one who seeks to be sanctified in truth, even as He sanctified Himself; sanctified just like Jesus.

He sanctified Himself for us, that we ourselves also might be sanctified in truth. Yes, our sanctification rests and roots in His, in Himself. And we are in Him. The secret roots of our being are planted into Jesus: deeper down than we can see or feel, there is He our Vine, bearing and quickening us. Let us by faith understand that, in a manner and a measure which are far beyond our comprehension, intensely Divine and real, we are in Him who sanctified Himself for us. Let us dwell there, where we have been placed of God. And let us bow our knees to the Father, that He would grant us to be mightily strengthened by His Spirit, that Christ as our Sanctification may dwell in our hearts, that the power of His death and His life may be revealed in us, and God's will be done in us as it was in Him.

Be holy, for I am holy

Holy Father! I do bless Thee for this precious blessed word, for this precious blessed work of Thy beloved Son. In His never-ceasing intercession Thou ever hearest the wonderful prayer, 'I sanctify myself for them, that they themselves also may be sanctified in truth.'

Blessed Father! I beseech Thee to strengthen me mightily by Thy Spirit, that in living faith I may be able to accept and live the holiness prepared for me in my Lord Jesus. Give me spiritual understanding to know what it means that He sanctified Himself, that my sanctification is secured in His, that as by faith I abide in Him, its power will cover my whole life. Let His sanctification indeed be the law as it is the life of mine. Let His surrender to Thy fatherly will, His continual dependence and obedience, be its root and its strength. Let His death to the world and to sin be its daily rule. Above all, let Himself, O my Father! let Himself, as sanctified for me, the living Jesus, be my only trust and stay. He sanctified Himself for me, that I myself also may be sanctified in truth.

Beloved Saviour! how shall I rightly bless and love and glorify Thee for this wondrous grace! Thou didst give Thyself, so that now I am holy in Thee. I give myself, that in Thee I myself may be made holy in truth. Amen. Lord Jesus! Amen.

1. 'If any man would come after me, let him deny himself, and take up his cross, and follow me.' Jesus means that our life shall be the exact counterpart of His, including even the crucifixion. The beginning of such a life is the denial of self, to give Christ its place. The Jews would not deny self, but 'denied the Holy One, and killed the Prince of Life.' The choice is still between Christ and self. Let us deny the unholy one, and give him to the death.

2. The steps in this path are these: First, the deliberate decision that self shall be given up to the death; then, the surrender to Christ crucified to make us partakers of His crucifixion; then, 'knowing that our old man is crucified,' the faith that says, 'I am crucified with Christ;' and then, the power to live as a crucified one, to glory in the cross of Christ.

3. This is God's way of holiness, a Divine mystery, which the Holy Spirit alone can daily maintain in us. Blessed be God, it is the life which a Christian can live, because Christ lives in us.

4. The central thought is: We are in Christ, who gave up His will and did the will of God. By the Holy Spirit the mind that was in Him is in us, the will of self is crucified, and we live in the will of God.

Eighteenth Day

HOLY IN CHRIST

Holiness and Faith

'That they may receive remission of sins, and an inheritance among them that are sanctified by faith in me.'—Acts xxvi. 18.

The more we study Scripture in the light of the Holy Spirit, or practise the Christian life in His power, the deeper becomes our conviction of the unique and central place faith has in God's plan of salvation. And we learn, too, to see that it is meet and right that it should be so: the very nature of things demands it. Because God is a Spiritual and Invisible Being, every revelation of Himself, whether in His works, His word, or His Son, calls for faith. Faith is the spiritual sense of the soul, being to it what the senses are to the body; by it alone we enter into communication and contact with God.

Faith is that meekness of soul which waits in stillness to hear, to understand, to accept what God says; to receive, to retain, to possess what God gives or works. By faith we allow, we welcome God Himself, the Living Person, to enter in to make His abode with us, to become our very life. However well we think we know it, we always have to learn the truth afresh, for a deeper and fuller application of it, that in the Christian life faith is the first thing, the one thing that pleases God, and brings blessing to us. And because Holiness is God's highest glory, and the highest blessing He has for us, it is especially in the life of holiness that we need to live by faith alone.

Our Lord speaks here of 'them that are sanctified by faith in me.' [9] He Himself is our Sanctification as He is our

---

[9] The best commentators connect the expression, 'by faith in me,' not with the word 'sanctified,' but with the whole clause, 'that by faith in me they may receive.' This will, however, in no way affect the application to the word sanctified. Thus read, the text tells us that the remission of sin, and the inheritance, and the sanctification which qualifies for the inheritance, are all received by faith.

Justification: for the one as for the other it is faith that God asks, and both are equally given at once. The participle used here is not the present, denoting a process or work that is being carried on, but the aorist, indicating an act done once for all. When we believe in Christ, we receive the whole Christ, our justification and our sanctification: we are at once accepted by God as righteous in Him, and as holy in Him. God counts and calls us, what we really are, sanctified ones in Christ. It is as we are led to see what God sees, as our faith grasps that the holy life of Christ is ours in actual possession, to be accepted and appropriated for daily use, that we shall really be able to live the life God calls us to, the life of holy ones in Christ Jesus. We shall then be in the right position in which what is called our progressive sanctification can be worked out. It will be, the acceptance and application in daily life of the power of a holy life which has been prepared in Jesus, which has in the union with Him become our present and permanent possession, and which works in us according to the measure of our faith. **10**

From this point of view it is evident that faith has a twofold operation. Faith is the evidence of things not seen, though now actually existing, the substance of things hoped for, but not yet present. It deals with the unseen present, as well as with the unseen future. As the evidence of things not seen, it rejoices in Christ our complete sanctification, as a present possession. Through faith I simply look to what Christ is, as revealed in the Word by the Holy Spirit. Claiming all He is as my own, I know that His Holiness, His holy nature and life, are mine; I am a holy one: by faith in Him I have been sanctified. This is the first aspect of sanctification: it looks to what is a complete and finished thing, an absolute reality. As the substance of things hoped for, this faith reaches out in the assurance of hope to the future, to things I do not yet see or experience, and claims, day by day, out of Christ our sanctification, what it needs for practical holiness, 'to be holy in all manner of living.' This is the second aspect of sanctification: I depend upon Jesus to supply, in personal experience, gradually and unceasingly, for the need of each moment, what has been treasured up in His fulness. 'Of God are ye in Christ Jesus, who of God is made unto us sanctification.' Under its first aspect faith says, I know I am in Him, and all His Holiness is mine; in its second aspect it speaks,

---

[10] See Note E.

100

I trust in Him for the grace and the strength I need each moment to live a holy life.

And yet, it need hardly be said, these two are one. It is one Jesus who is our sanctification, whether we look at it in the light of what He is made for us once for all, or what, as the fruit of that, He becomes to our experience day by day. And so it is one faith which, the more it studies and adores and rejoices in Jesus as made of God unto us sanctification, as Him in whom we have been sanctified, becomes the bolder to expect the fulfilment of every promise for daily life, and the stronger to claim the victory over every sin. Faith in Jesus is the secret of a holy life: all holy conduct, all really holy deeds, are the fruit of faith in Jesus as our holiness.

We know how faith acts, and what its great hindrances are, in the matter of justification. It is well that we remind ourselves that there are the same dangers in the exercise of sanctifying as of justifying faith. Faith in God stands opposed to trust in self: specially to its willing and working. Faith is hindered by every effort to do something ourselves. Faith looks to God working, and yields itself to His strength, as revealed in Christ through the Spirit; it allows God to work both to will and to do. Faith must work; without works it is dead, by works alone can it be perfected; in Jesus Christ, as Paul says, nothing avails but 'faith working by love.' But these works, which faith in God's working inspires and performs, are very different from the works in which a believer often puts forth his best efforts, only to find that he fails. The true life of holiness, the life of them who are sanctified in Christ, has its root and its strength in an abiding sense of utter impotence, in the deep restfulness which trusts to the working of a Divine power and life, in the entire personal surrender to the loving Saviour, in that faith which consents to be nothing, that He may be all. It may appear impossible to discern or describe the difference between the working that is of self and the working that is of Christ through faith: if we but know that there is such a difference, if we learn to distrust ourselves, and to count on Christ working, the Holy Spirit will lead us into this secret of the Lord too. Faith's works are Christ's works.

And as by effort, so faith is also hindered by the desire to see and feel. 'If thou believest, thou shalt see;' the Holy Spirit will seal our faith with a Divine experience; we shall see the glory of God. But this is His work: ours is, when all appears dark and cold, in the face of all that nature or experience testifies, still each moment to believe in Jesus as our all-sufficient sanctification, in whom we are perfected before God. Complaints as to want of feeling, as to weakness or deadness, seldom profit: it is the soul that refuses to occupy itself with itself, either with its own weakness or the strength of the enemy, but only looks to what Jesus is, and has promised to do, to whom progress in holiness will be a joyful march from victory to victory. 'The Lord Himself doth fight for you;' this thought, so often repeated in connection with Israel's possession of the promised land, is the food of faith: in conscious weakness, in presence of mighty enemies, it sings the conqueror's song. When God appears to be not doing what we trusted Him for, then is just the time for faith to glory in Him.

There is perhaps nothing that more reveals the true character of faith than joy and praise. You give a child the promise of a present to-morrow: at once it says, Thank you, and is glad. The joyful thanks are the proof of how really your promise has entered the heart. You are told by a friend of a rich legacy he has left you in his will: it may not come true for years, but even now it makes you glad. We have already seen what an element of holiness joy is: it is especially an element of holiness by faith. Each time I really see how beautiful and how perfect God's provision is, by which my holiness is in Jesus, and by which I am to allow Him to work in me, my heart ought to rise up in praise and thanks. Instead of allowing the thought that it is, after all, a life of such difficult attainment and such continual self-denial, this life of holiness through faith, we ought to praise Him exceedingly that He has made it possible and sure for us: we can be holy, because Jesus the Mighty and the Loving One is our holiness. Praise will express our faith; praise will prove it; praise will strengthen it. 'Then believed they His words; they sang His praise.' Praise will commit us to faith: we shall see that we have but one thing to do, to go on in a faith that ever trusts and ever praises. It is in a living, loving attachment to Jesus, that rejoices in Him, and praises Him continually for what He is to us, that faith proves itself, and receives the power of holiness.

'Sanctified by faith in me.' Yes, 'by faith in Me:' it is the personal living Jesus who offers Himself, Himself in all the riches of His Power and Love, as the object, the strength, the life of our faith. He tells us that if we would be holy, always and in everything holy, we must just see to one thing: to be always and altogether full of faith in Him. Faith is the eye of the soul: the power by which we discern the presence of the Unseen One, as

He comes to give Himself to us. Faith not only sees, but appropriates and assimilates: let us set our souls very still for the Holy Spirit who dwells in us, to quicken and strengthen that faith, for which He has been given us. Faith is surrender: yielding ourselves to Jesus to allow Him to do His work in us, giving up ourselves to Him to live out His life and work out His will in us, we shall find Him giving Himself entirely to us, and taking complete possession. So faith will be power: the power of obedience to do God's will: 'our most holy faith,' 'the faith delivered to the holy ones.' And we shall understand how simple, to the single-hearted, is the secret of holiness: just Jesus. We are in Him, our Sanctification: He personally is our Holiness; and the life of faith in Him, that receives and possesses Him, must necessarily be a life of holiness. Jesus says, 'Sanctified by faith in me.'

Be ye holy, as I am holy

Beloved Lord! again have I seen, with adoring wonder, what Thou art willing to be to me. It is in Thyself, and a life of living fellowship with Thyself, that I am to become holy. It is in the simple life of personal attachment, of trust and love, of surrender and consecration, that Thou dost become my all, and make me partaker of Thyself and Thy Holiness.

Blessed Lord Jesus! I do believe in Thee, help Thou mine unbelief. I confess what still remains of unbelief, and count on Thy presence to conquer and cast it out. My soul is opening up continually to see more how Thou Thyself art my Life and my Holiness. Thou art enlarging my heart to rejoice in Thyself as my all, and to be assured that Thou dost Thyself take possession and fill the temple of my being with Thy glory. Thou art teaching me to understand that, however feeble and human and disappointing experiences may be, Thy Holy Spirit is the strength of my faith, leading me on to grow up into a stronger and a larger confidence in Thee in whom I am holy. O my Saviour! I take Thy word this day, 'Sanctified by faith in me,' as a new revelation of Thy love and its purpose with me. In Thee Thyself is the Power of my holiness; in Thee is the Power of my faith. Blessed be Thy name that Thou hast given me too a place among them of whom Thou speakest: 'Sanctified by faith in me.' Amen.

1. Let us remember that it is not only the faith that is

dealing specially with Christ for sanctification, but all living faith, that has the power to sanctify. Anything that casts the soul wholly on Jesus, that calls forth intense and simple trust, be it the trial of faith, or the prayer of faith, or the work of faith, helps to make us holy, because it brings us into living contact with the Holy One.

2. It is only through the Holy Spirit that Christ and His Holiness are day by day revealed and made ours in actual possession. And so the faith which receives Him is of the Spirit too. Yield yourself in simplicity and trust to His working. Do not be afraid, as if you cannot believe: you have 'the Spirit of faith' within you: you have the power to believe. And you may ask God to strengthen you mightily by His Spirit in the inner man, for the faith that receives Christ in the indwelling that knows no break.

3. I have only so much of faith as I have of the Spirit. Is not this then what I most need—to live entirely under the influence of the Spirit?

4. Just as the eye in seeing is receptive, and yields to let the object placed before it make its impression, so faith is the impression God makes on the soul when He draws nigh. Was not the faith of Abraham the fruit of God's drawing near and speaking to him, the impression God made on him? Let us be still to gaze on the Divine mystery of Christ our holiness: His Presence, waited for and worshipped, will work the faith. That is, the Spirit that proceeds from Him into those who cling to Him, will be faith.

5. Holiness by faith in Jesus, not by effort of thine own,

Sin's dominion crushed and broken by the power of grace alone,—

God's own holiness within thee, His own beauty on thy brow,—

This shall be thy pilgrim brightness, this thy blessed portion now.

F. R. H.

Nineteenth Day

HOLY IN CHRIST

Holiness and Resurrection

'The Son of God, who was born of the seed of David according to the flesh, who was declared to be the Son of God with power, according to the Spirit of holiness, by the resurrection of the dead.'—Rom. i. 4.

These words speak of a twofold birth of Christ. According to the flesh, He was born of the seed of David. According to the Spirit, He was the first begotten from the dead. As He was a Son of David in virtue of His birth through the flesh, so He was declared to be the Son of God with power, in virtue of His resurrection-birth through the Spirit of holiness. As the life He received through His first birth was a life in and after the flesh with its weakness, so the new life He received in the resurrection was a life in the power of the Spirit of holiness.

The expression, the Spirit of holiness, is a peculiar one. It is not the ordinary word for God's Holiness that is here used as in Heb. xii. 10, describing holiness in the abstract as the attribute of an object, but another word (also used in 2 Cor. vii. 1 and 1 Thess. iii. 13) expressing the habit of holiness in its action—practical holiness or sanctity. [11] Paul used this word, because He wished to emphasize the thought, that Christ's resurrection was distinctly the result of that life of holiness and self-sanctifying which had culminated in His death. It was the spirit of the life of holiness which he had lived, in the power of which He was raised again. He teaches us that that life and death of self-sanctification, in which alone our sanctification stands, was the root and ground of His resurrection, and of its declaration that He was the Son of God with power, the first begotten from the dead. The resurrection was the fruit which that Life of Holiness bore.

And so the Life of Holiness becomes the property of all who are partakers of the resurrection. The Resurrection Life and the Spirit of Holiness are inseparable. Christ sanctified Himself in

---

[11] See Note F.

death, that we ourselves might be sanctified in truth: when in virtue of the Spirit of sanctity He was raised from the dead, that Spirit of holiness was proved to be the power of Resurrection Life, and the Resurrection Life to be a Life of Holiness.

As a believer you have part in this Resurrection Life. You have been 'begotten again by the resurrection of Jesus Christ from the dead.' You are 'risen with Christ.' You are commanded 'to reckon yourself to be alive unto God in Christ Jesus.' But the life can work in power only as you seek to know it, to yield to it, to let it have full possession and mastery. And if it is to do this, one of the most important things for you to realize is, that as it was in virtue of the Spirit of holiness that Christ was raised, so the Spirit of that same holiness must be in you the mark and the power of your life. Study to know and possess the Spirit of holiness as it was seen in the life of your Lord.

And wherein did it consist? Its secret was, we are told: 'Lo, I am come to do Thy will, O God.' 'In the which will,' as done by Christ, 'we have been sanctified by the one offering of the body of Jesus Christ.' This was Christ's sanctifying Himself, in life and in death; this was what the Spirit of holiness wrought in Him; this is what the same Spirit, the Spirit of the life in Christ Jesus, will work in us: a life in the will of God is a life of holiness. Seek earnestly to grasp this clearly. Christ came to reveal what true holiness would be in the conditions of human life and weakness. He came to work it out for you, that He might communicate it to you by His Spirit. Except you intelligently apprehend and heartily accept it, the Spirit cannot work it in you. Do seek with your whole heart to take hold of it: the will of God unhesitatingly accepted, is the power of holiness.

It is in this that any attempt to be holy as Christ is holy, with and in His Holiness, must have its starting-point. Many seek to take single portions of the life or image of Christ for imitation, and yet fail greatly in others. They have not seen that the self-denial, to which Jesus calls, really means the denial of self, in the full meaning of that word. In not one single thing is the will of self to be done: Jesus, as He did the will of the Father only, must rule, and not self. To 'stand perfect and complete in all the will of God' must be the purpose, the prayer, the expectation of the disciple. There need be no fear that it is not possible to know the will of the Father in everything. 'If any man will do, he shall know.' The Father will not keep the willing child in ignorance of His will. As the surrender to the Spirit of holiness, to Jesus and the dominion of His holy life, becomes more simple, sin and self-will will be discovered, the spiritual understanding will be opened up, and the law written in the inward parts become legible and intelligible. There need be no fear that it is not possible to do the will of the Father when it is known. When once the grief of failure and sin has driven the believer into the experience of Rom. vii., and the 'delight in the law of God after the inward man' has proved its earnestness in the cry, 'O wretched man that I am,' deliverance will come through Jesus Christ. The Spirit works not only to will but to do; where the believer could only complain, 'To perform that which is good, I find not,' He gives the strength and song, 'The law of the Spirit of life in Christ Jesus hath made me free from the law of sin and death.'

In this faith, that it is possible to know and do the will of God in all things, take over from Him, in whom alone you are holy, as your life-principle; 'I come to do Thy will, O God.' It is the principle of the resurrection life: without it Jesus had never been raised again. It is the principle of the new life in you. Accept it; study it; realize it; act it out. Many a believer has found that some simple words of dedication, expressive of the purpose in everything to do God's will, have been an entrance into the joy and power of the resurrection life previously unknown. The will of God is the complete expression of His moral perfection, His Divine Holiness. To take one's place in the centre of that will, to live it out, to be borne and sustained by it, was the power of that life of Jesus that could not be held of death, that could not but burst out in resurrection glory. What it was to Jesus it will be to us.

Holiness is Life: this is the simplest expression of the truth our text teaches. There can be no holiness until there be a new life implanted. The new life cannot grow and break forth in resurrection power, cannot bring forth fruit, but as it grows in holiness. As long as the believer is living the mixed life, part in the flesh and part in the spirit, with some of self and some of Christ, he seeks in vain for holiness. It is the New Life that is the holy life: the full apprehension of it in faith, the full surrender to it in conduct, will be the highway of holiness. Jesus lived and died and rose again to prepare for us a new nature, to be received day by day in the obedience of faith: we 'have put on the new man, which after God is created in righteousness and true holiness.' Let the inner life, hid with Christ in God, hid also deep in the recesses of our inmost being, be acknowledged, be waited on, be yielded to, it will work itself out in all the beauties of holiness.

There is more. This life is not like the life of nature, a blind, non-conscious principle, involuntarily working out its ideal in unresisting obedience to the law of its being. There is the Spirit of the life in Christ Jesus—the Spirit of holiness—the Holy Spirit dwelling in us as a Divine Person, entering into fellowship with us, and leading us into the fellowship of the Living Christ. It is this fills our life with hope and joy. The Risen Saviour breathed the Holy Spirit on His disciples: the Spirit brings the Risen One into the field, into our hearts, as a personal friend, as a Living Guide and Strengthener. The Spirit of holiness is the Spirit, the Presence, and the Power of the Living Christ. Jesus said of the Spirit, 'Ye know Him.' Is not our great need to know this Holy Spirit, the Spirit of Christ, of His Holiness and of ours? How can we 'walk after the Spirit' and follow His leading, if we know not Him and His voice and His way?

Let us learn one more lesson from our text. It is out of the grave of the flesh and the will of self that the Spirit of holiness breaks out in resurrection power. We must accept death to the flesh, death to self with its willing and working, as the birthplace of our experience of the power of the Spirit of holiness. In view of each struggle with sin, in each exercise of faith or prayer, we must enter into the death of Jesus, the death to self, and as those who say, 'we are not sufficient to think anything as of ourselves,' in quiet faith expect the Spirit of Christ to do His work. The Spirit will work, strengthening you mightily in the inner man, and building up within you an holy temple for the Lord. And the time will come, if it has not come to you yet, and it may be nearer than you dare hope, when the conscious indwelling of Christ in your heart by faith, the full revelation and enthronement of Him as ruler and keeper of heart and life, shall have become a personal experience. According to the Spirit of holiness, by the resurrection from the dead, will the Son of God be declared with power in the kingdom that is within you.

Be ye holy, for I am holy

Most Holy Lord God! we do bless Thee that Thou didst raise Thy Son from the dead and give Him glory, that our faith and hope might be in Thee. Thou didst make His resurrection the power of eternal life in us, and now, even as He was raised, so we may walk in newness of life. As the Spirit of holiness dwelt and wrought in Him, it dwells and works in us, and becomes in us the Spirit of life.

O God! we beseech Thee to perfect Thy work in Thy saints. Give them a deeper sense of the holy calling with which Thou hast called them in Christ, the Risen One. Give all to accept the Spirit of His life on earth, delight in the will of God, as the spirit of their life. May those who have never yet fully accepted this be brought to do it, and in faith of the power of the new life to say, I accept the will of God as my only law. May the Spirit of holiness be the spirit of their lives!

Father! we beseech Thee, let Christ thus, in ever increasing experience of His resurrection power, be revealed in our hearts as the Son of God, Lord and Ruler within us. Let His life within inspire all the outer life, so that in the home and society, in thought and speech and action, in religion and in business, His life may shine out from us in the beauty of holiness. Amen.

1. Scripture regards the resurrection in two different aspects. In one view, it is the title to the new life, the source of our justification. (Rom. iv. 25, 1 Cor. xv. 17.) In another it is our regeneration, the power of the new life working in us, the source of our sanctification. (Rom. vi. 4; 1 Pet. i. 3.) Pardon and holiness are inseparable; they have the same source, union with the Risen Living Christ.

2. The blessedness to the disciples of having a Risen Christ was this: He, whom they thought dead, came and revealed Himself to them. Christ lives to reveal Himself to thee and to me; wait on Him, trust Him for this. He will reveal Himself to thee as thy sanctification. See to it that thou hast Him in living possession, and thou hast His Holiness.

3. The life of Christ is the holiness of Christ. The reason we so often fail in the pursuit of holiness is that the old life, the flesh, in its own strength seeks for holiness as a beautiful garment to wear and enter heaven with. It is the daily death to self out of which the life of Christ rises up.

4. To die thus, to live thus in Christ, to be holy—how can we attain it? It all comes 'according to the Spirit of holiness.' Have the Holy Spirit within thee. Say daily, 'I believe in the Holy Ghost.'

5. Holy in Christ. When Christ lives in us, and His mind, as it found expression in His words and work on earth, enters and fills our will and personal consciousness, then our union with Him becomes what He meant it to be. It is the Spirit of His holy conduct, the Spirit of His sanctity, must be in us.

Twentieth Day

HOLY IN CHRIST

Holiness and Liberty

'Being made free from sin, ye became servants of righteousness: now present your members as servants of righteousness unto sanctification. Now being made free from sin, and become servants unto God, ye have your fruit unto sanctification, and the end eternal life.'—Rom. vi. 18, 19, 22.

'Our liberty which we have in Christ Jesus.'—Gal. ii. 4.

'With freedom did Christ set us free: stand fast therefore, and be not entangled again in a yoke of bondage.'—Gal. v. 1.

There is no possession more precious or priceless than liberty. There is nothing more inspiring and elevating; nothing, on the other hand, more depressing and degrading than slavery. It robs a man of what constitutes his manhood, the power of self-decision, self-action, of being and doing what he would.

Sin is slavery; the bondage to a foreign power that has obtained the mastery over us, and compels often a most reluctant service. The redemption of Christ restores our liberty and sets us free from the power of sin. If we are truly to live as redeemed ones, we need not only to look at the work Christ did to accomplish our redemption, but to accept and realize fully how complete, how sure, how absolute the liberty is wherewith He hath made us free. It is only as we 'stand fast in our liberty in Christ Jesus,' that we can have our fruit unto sanctification.

It is remarkable how seldom the word holy occurs in the great argument of the Epistle to the Romans, and how, where twice used in chap. vi. in the expression 'unto sanctification,' it is distinctly set forth as the aim and fruit to be reached through a life of righteousness. The twice repeated 'unto sanctification,' pointing to a result to be obtained, is preceded by a twice repeated 'being made free from sin and become servants of righteousness.' It teaches us how the liberty from the power of

111

sin and the surrender to the service of righteousness are not yet of themselves holiness, but the sure and only path by which it can be reached. A true insight and a full entering into our freedom from sin in Christ are indispensable to a life of holiness. It was when Israel was freed from Pharaoh that God began to reveal Himself as the Holy One: it is as we know ourselves 'freed from sin,' delivered from the hand of all our enemies, that we shall serve God in righteousness and holiness all the days of our life.

'Being made free from sin:' to understand this word aright, we must beware of a twofold error. We must neither narrow it down to less, nor import into it more, than the Holy Spirit means by it here. Paul is speaking neither of an imputation nor an experience. We must not limit it to being made free from the curse or punishment of sin. The context shows that he is speaking, not of our judicial standing, but of a spiritual reality, our being in living union with Christ in His death and resurrection, and so being entirely taken out from under the dominion or power of sin. 'Sin shall not have dominion over you.' Nor is he as yet speaking of an experience, that we feel that we are free from all sin. He speaks of the great objective fact, Christ's having finally delivered us from the power which sin had to compel us to do its will and its works, and urges us, in the faith of this glorious fact, boldly to refuse to listen to the bidding or temptation of sin. To know our liberty which we have in Christ, our freedom from sin's mastery and power, is the way to realize it as an experience.

In olden times, when Turks or Moors often made slaves of Christians, large sums were frequently paid for the ransom of those who were in bondage. But it happened more than once, away in the interior of the slave country, that the ransomed ones never got the tidings; the masters were only too glad to keep it from them. Others, again, got the tidings, but had grown too accustomed to their bondage to rouse themselves for the effort of reaching the coast. Slothfulness or hopelessness kept them in slavery; they could not believe that they would be able ever in safety to reach the land of liberty. The ransom had been paid; in truth they were free; and yet in their experience, by reason of ignorance or want of courage, they were still in bondage. Christ's redemption has so completely made an end of sin and the legal power it had over us,—for 'the strength of sin is the law,'—that in very deed, in the deepest reality, sin has no power to compel our obedience. It is only as we allow it again to reign, as we yield ourselves again as its servants, that it can exercise the mastery. Satan does his utmost to keep believers in ignorance of the completeness of this their freedom from his slavery. And because believers are so content with their own thoughts of what redemption means, and so little long and plead to see it and possess it in its fulness of deliverance and blessing, the experience of the extent to which the freedom from sin can be realized is so feeble. 'Where the Spirit of the Lord is, there is liberty.' It is by the Holy Spirit, His light and leading within, humbly watched for and yielded to, that this liberty becomes our possession.

In the sixth chapter Paul speaks of freedom from sin, in chap. vii. (vers. 3, 4, 6) of freedom from the law, as both being ours in Christ and union with Him. In chap. viii. (ver. 2) he speaks of this freedom as become ours in experience. He says, 'The law of the Spirit of life in Christ Jesus hath made me free from the law of sin and death.' The freedom which is ours in Christ, must become ours in personal appropriation and enjoyment through the Holy Spirit. The latter depends on the former: the fuller the faith, the clearer the insight, the more triumphant the glorying in Christ Jesus and the liberty with which He has made us free, the speedier and the fuller the entrance into the glorious liberty of the children of God. As the liberty is in Christ alone, so it is the Spirit of Christ alone that makes it ours in practical possession, and keeps us dwelling in it: 'the spirit of the life in Christ Jesus hath made me free from the law of sin and death.' 'Where the Spirit of the Lord is, there is liberty.' As the Spirit reveals Jesus to us as Lord and Master, the new Master, who alone has ought to say over us, and leads us to yield ourselves, to present our members, to surrender our whole life to the service of God in Christ, our faith in the freedom from sin becomes a consciousness and a realization. Believing in the completeness of the redemption, the captive goes forth as 'the Lord's freedman.' He knows now that sin has no longer power for one moment to command obedience. It may seek to assert its old right; it may speak in the tone of authority; it may frighten us into fear and submission; power it has none over us, except as we, forgetting our freedom, yield to its temptation, and ourselves give it power.

We are the Lord's freedmen. 'We have our liberty in Christ Jesus.' In Rom. vii. Paul describes the terrible struggles of the soul who still seeks to fulfil the law, but finds itself utterly helpless; sold under sin, a captive and a slave, without the liberty to do what the whole heart desires. But when the Spirit takes the place of the law, the complaint, 'O wretched man that I am,' is changed into the song of victory: 'I thank God, through Jesus Christ, the law of the Spirit of life hath made me free.'

What numberless complaints of insufficient strength to do God's will, of unsuccessful effort and disappointed hopes, of continual failure, re-echo in a thousand different forms the complaint of the captive, 'O wretched man that I am!' Thank God! there is deliverance. 'With freedom did Christ set us free! Stand fast therefore, and be not entangled again in a yoke of bondage.' Satan is ever seeking to lay on us again the yoke either of sin or the law, to beget again the spirit of bondage, as if sin or the law with their demands somehow had power over us. It is not so: be not entangled; stand fast in the liberty with which Christ has made you free. Let us listen to the message: 'Being made free from sin, ye became servants unto righteousness; now yield your members servants to righteousness unto sanctification.' 'Having been made free from sin, and having been enslaved unto God, ye have your fruit unto sanctification.' To be holy, you must be free, perfectly free; free for Jesus to rule you, to lead you; free for the Holy Spirit to dispose of you, to breathe in you, to work His secret, gentle, but mighty work, so that you may grow up unto all the liberty Jesus has won for you. The temple could not be sanctified by the indwelling of God, except as it was free from every other master and every other use, to be for Him and His service alone. The inner temple of our heart cannot be truly and fully sanctified, except as we are free from every other master and power, from every yoke of bondage, or fear, or doubt, to let His Spirit lead us into the perfect liberty which has its fruit in true holiness.

Being made free from sin, having become servants unto righteousness, ye have your fruit unto holiness, and the end life everlasting. Freedom, Righteousness, Holiness—these are the steps on the way to the coming glory. The more deeply we enter by faith into our liberty, which we have in Christ, the more joyfully and confidently we present our members to God as instruments of righteousness. The God is the Father whose will we delight to do, whose service is perfect liberty. The Redeemer is the Master, to whom love binds us in willing obedience. The liberty is not lawlessness: 'we are delivered from our enemies, that we may serve Him in righteousness and holiness all the days of our life.' [12]

The liberty is the condition of the righteousness; and this again of the holiness. The doing of God's will leads up into that fellowship, that heart sympathy with God Himself, out of which comes that reflection of the Divine Presence, which is Holiness. Being made free from sin, being made the slaves of righteousness and of God, we have our fruit unto holiness, and the end—the fruit of holiness becomes, when ripe, the seed of—everlasting life.

Be ye holy, as I am holy

Most glorious God! I pray Thee to open my eyes to this wonderful liberty with which Christ has made me free. May I enter fully into Thy word, that sin shall have no dominion over me because I am not under the law but under grace. May I know my liberty which I have in Christ Jesus, and stand fast in it.

Father! Thy service is perfect liberty: reveal this too to me. Thou art the infinitely Free, and Thy will knows no limits but what its own perfection has placed. And Thou invitest us into Thy will, that we may be free as Thou art. O my God! show me the beauty of Thy will, as it frees me from self and from sin, and let it be my only blessedness. Let the service of righteousness so be a joy and a strength to me, having its fruit unto sanctification, leading me into Thy Holiness.

Blessed Lord Jesus! my Deliverer and my Liberty, I belong to Thee. I give myself to Thy will, to know no will but Thine. Master! Thee and Thee alone would I serve. I have my liberty in Thee! be Thou my Keeper. I cannot stand for one moment out of Thee. In Thee I can stand fast: in Thee I put my trust.

Most Holy God! as Thy free, obedient, loving child, Thou wilt make me holy. Amen.

1. Liberty is the power to carry out unhindered the impulse of our nature. In Christ the child of God is free from every power that could hinder his acting out the law of his new nature.

2. This liberty is of faith (Gal. v. 5, 6). By faith in Christ I enter into it, and stand in it.

---

[12] See Note G.

3. This liberty is of the Holy Spirit. 'Where the Spirit of the Lord is, there is liberty.' 'If ye be led of the Spirit, ye are not under the law.' A heart filled with the Spirit is made free indeed. But we are not made free that we may do our own will. No, made free to follow the leading of the Holy Spirit. 'Where the Spirit is, there is liberty.'

4. This liberty is in love. 'Ye were called for freedom; only use not your freedom for an occasion to the flesh, but through love be servants, one to another.' The freedom with which the Son makes free is a freedom to become like Himself, to love and to serve. 'Though I was free from all men, I brought myself under bondage to all, that I might gain the more.' This is the liberty of love.

5. 'Being made free from sin, ye became servants of righteousness unto sanctification.' 'Let my people go, that they may serve me.' It is only the man that doeth righteousness that can become holy.

6. This liberty is a thing of joy and singing.

7. This liberty is the groundwork of holiness. The Redeemer who makes free is God the Holy One. As the Holy Spirit He leads into the full possession of it. To be so free from everything that God can take complete possession, is to be holy.

Twenty-first Day

HOLY IN CHRIST

Holiness and Happiness

'The kingdom of God is joy in the Holy Ghost.'—Rom. xiv. 17.

'The disciples were filled with joy and the Holy Ghost.'—Acts xiii. 52.

'Then Nehemiah said, This day is holy unto the Lord: neither be ye sorry, for the joy of the Lord is your strength. So the Levites stilled the people, saying, Hold your peace; for the day is holy; neither be ye grieved. And all the people went their way to make great mirth, because they had understood the words.'—Neh. viii. 10–12.

The deep significance of joy in the Christian life is hardly understood. It is too often regarded as something secondary; whereas its presence is essential as the proof that God does indeed satisfy us, and that His service is our delight. In our domestic life we do not feel satisfied if all the proprieties of deportment are observed, and each does his duty to the other; true love makes us happy in each other; as love gives out its warmth of affection, gladness is the sunshine that fills the home with its brightness. Even in suffering or poverty, the members of a loving family are a joy to each other. Without this gladness, especially, there is no true obedience on the part of the children. It is not the mere fulfilment of a command, or performance of a service, that a parent looks to; it is the willing, joyful alacrity with which it is done that makes it pleasing.

It is just so in the intercourse of God's children with their Father. Even in the effort after a life of consecration and gospel obedience, we are continually in danger of coming under the law again, with its, Thou shalt. The consequence always is failure. The law only worketh wrath; it gives neither life nor strength. It is only as long as we are standing in the joy of our Lord, in the joy of our deliverance from sin, in the joy of His love, and what He is for us, in the joy of His presence, that we have the power to serve

117

and obey. It is only when made free from every master, from sin and self and the law, and only when rejoicing in this liberty, that we have the power to render service that is satisfying either to God or to ourselves. 'I will see you again,' Jesus said, 'and your heart shall rejoice, and your joy shall no man take from you.' Joy is the evidence and the condition of the abiding personal presence of Jesus.

If holiness be the beauty and the glory of the life of faith, it is manifest that here especially the element of joy may not be wanting. We have already seen how the first mention of God as the Holy One was in the song of praise on the shore of the Red Sea; how Hannah and Mary in their moments of inspiration praised God as the Holy One; how the name of the Thrice Holy in heaven comes to us in the song of the seraphs; and how before the throne both the living creatures and the conquering multitude who sing the song of the Lamb, adore God as the Holy One. We are to 'worship Him in the beauty of holiness,' 'to sing praise at the remembrance of His Holiness;' it is only in the spirit of worship and praise and joy that we fully can know God as holy. Much more, it is only under the inspiration of adoring love and joy that we can ourselves be made holy. It is as we cease from all fear and anxiety, from all strain and effort, and rest with singing in what Jesus is in His finished work as our sanctification, as we rest and rejoice in Him, that we shall be made partakers of His Holiness. It is the day of rest, is the day that God has blessed, the day of blessing and gladness; and it is the day He blessed that is His holy day. Holiness and blessedness are inseparable.

But is not this at variance with the teaching of Scripture and the experience of the saints? Are not suffering and sorrow among God's chosen means of sanctification? Are not the promises to the broken in heart, the poor in spirit, and the mourner? Are not self-denial and the forsaking of all we have, the crucifixion with Christ and the dying daily, the path to holiness? and is not all this more matter of sorrow and pain than of joy and gladness?

The answer will be found in the right apprehension of the life of faith. Faith lifts above, and gives possession of, what is the very opposite of what we feel or experience. In the Christian life there is always a paradox: what appear irreconcilable opposites are found side by side at the same moment. Paul expresses it in the words, 'As dying, and, behold, we live; as sorrowful, yet always rejoicing; as poor, yet making many rich; as having

118

nothing, yet possessing all things.' And elsewhere thus, 'When I am weak, then am I strong.' The apparent contradiction has its reconciliation, not only in the union of the two lives, the human and the Divine, in the person of each believer, but specially in our being, at one and the same moment, partakers of the death and the resurrection of Christ. Christ's death was one of pain and suffering, a real and terrible death, a rending asunder of the bonds that united soul and body, spirit and flesh. The power of that death works in us: we must let it work mightily if we are to live holy; for in that death He sanctified Himself, that we ourselves might be sanctified in truth. Our holiness is, like His, in the death to our own will, and to all our own life. But—this we must seek to grasp—we do not approach death from the side from which Christ met it, as an enemy to be conquered, as a suffering to be borne, before the new life can be entered on. No, the believer who knows what Christ is as the Risen One, approaches death, the crucifixion of self and the flesh and the world, from the resurrection side, the place of victory, in the power of the Living Christ. When we were baptized into Christ, we were baptized into His death and resurrection as ours; and Christ Himself, the Risen Living Lord, leads us triumphantly into the experience of the power of His death. And so, to the believer who truly lives by faith, and seeks not in his own strugglings to crucify and mortify the flesh, but knows the living Lord, the deep resurrection joy never for a moment forsakes Him, but is his strength for what may appear to others to be only painful sacrifice and cross-bearing. He says with Paul, 'I glory in the cross through which I have been crucified.' He never, as so many do, asks Paul's question, 'Who shall deliver me from the body of this death?' without sounding the joyful and triumphant answer as a present experience, 'I thank God, through Jesus Christ our Lord.' 'Thanks be to God, which always leadeth us in triumph in Christ.' It is the joy of a Present Saviour, of the experience of a perfect salvation, the joy of a resurrection life, which alone gives the power to enter deeply and fully into the death that Christ died, and yield our will and our life to be wholly sanctified to God. In the joy of that life, from which the power of the death is never absent, it is possible to say with the Apostle each moment, 'As dying, and, behold, we live; as sorrowful, yet always rejoicing.'

Let us seek to learn the two lessons: Holiness is essential to true happiness; happiness essential to true holiness. Holiness is essential to true happiness. If you would have joy, the fulness of joy, an abiding joy which nothing can take away, be holy as God is holy. Holiness is blessedness. Nothing can darken or interrupt our joy but sin. Whatever be our trial or temptation, the joy of Jesus of which Peter says, 'in whom ye now rejoice with joy unspeakable,' can more than compensate and outweigh. If we lose our joy, it must be sin. It may be an actual transgression, or an unconscious following of self or the world; it may be the stain on conscience of something doubtful, or it may be unbelief that would live by sight, and thinks more of itself and its joy than of the Lord alone: whatever it be, nothing can take away our joy but sin. If we would live lives of joy, assuring God and man and ourselves that our Lord is everything, is more than all to us, oh, let us be holy! Let us glory in Him who is our holiness: in His presence is fulness of joy. Let us live in the Kingdom which is joy in the Holy Ghost; the Spirit of holiness is the Spirit of joy, because He is the Spirit of God. It is the saints, God's holy ones, who will shout for joy.

And happiness is essential to true holiness. If you would be a holy Christian, you must be a happy Christian. Jesus was anointed by God with 'the oil of gladness,' that He might give us 'the oil of joy.' In all our efforts after holiness, the wheels will move heavily if there be not the oil of joy; this alone removes all strain and friction, and makes the onward progress easy and delightful. Study to understand the Divine worth of joy. It is the evidence of your being in the Father's presence, and dwelling in His love. It is the proof of your being consciously free from the law and the strain of the spirit of bondage. It is the token of your freedom from care and responsibility, because you are rejoicing in Christ Jesus as your Sanctification, your Keeper, and your Strength. It is the secret of spiritual health and strength, filling all your service with the childlike happy assurance that the Father asks nothing that He does not give strength for, and that He accepts all that is done, however feebly, in this spirit. True happiness is always self-forgetful: it loses itself in the object of its joy. As the joy of the Holy Ghost fills us, and we rejoice in God the Holy One, through our Lord Jesus Christ, as we lose ourselves in the adoration and worship of the Thrice Holy, we become holy. This is, even here in the wilderness, 'the Highway of Holiness: the ransomed of the Lord shall come with singing; the redeemed shall walk there; everlasting joy shall be upon their heads; they shall obtain joy and gladness.'

Do all God's children understand this? that holiness is just another name, the true name, that God gives for happiness; that it is indeed unutterable blessedness to know that God does make us holy, that our holiness is in Christ, that Christ's Holy Spirit is within us. There is nothing so attractive as joy: have believers understood it that this is the joy of the Lord—to be holy? Or is not the idea of strain, and sacrifice, and sighing, of difficulty and distance so prominent, that the thought of being holy has hardly ever made the heart glad? If it has been so, let it be so no longer. 'Thou shalt glory in the Holy One of Israel:' let us claim this promise. Let the believing assurance that our Loving Father, and our Beloved Lord Jesus, and the Holy Spirit, who in dove-like gentleness rests within us, have engaged to do the work, and are doing it, fill us with gladness. Let us not seek our joy in what we see in ourselves of holiness: let us rejoice in the Holiness of God in Christ as ours; let us rejoice in the Holy One of Israel. So shall our joy be unspeakable and unceasing; so shall we give Him the glory.

Be ye holy, as I am holy

Most Blessed God! I beseech Thee to reveal to me and to all Thy children the secret of rejoicing in Thee, the Holy One of Israel.

Thou seest how much of the service of Thine own dear children is still in the spirit of bondage, and how many have never yet believed that the Highway of Holiness is one on which they may walk with singing, and shall obtain joy and gladness. O Father! teach Thy children to rejoice in Thee.

I ask Thee especially to teach us that, in deep poverty of spirit, in humility and contrition and utter emptiness, in the consciousness that there is no holiness in us, we can sing all the day of Thy Holiness as ours, of Thy glory which Thou layest upon us, and which yet all the time is Thine alone. O Father! open wide to Thy children the blessed mystery of the Kingdom, even the faith which sees all in Christ and nothing in itself; which indeed has and rejoices in all in Him; which never has or rejoices in ought in itself.

Blessed God, in Thy Word Thou hast said, 'The meek shall increase their joy in the Lord, and the poor among men shall rejoice in the Holy One of Israel.' Oh, give us, by Thy Holy Spirit, in meekness and poverty of spirit, to live so in Christ, that His

Holiness may be our ever-increasing joy, and that in Thyself, the Holy One of Israel, we may rejoice all the day. And may all see in us what blessedness it is to live as God's holy ones. Amen.

1. The great hindrance to joy in God is expecting to find something in ourselves to rejoice over. At the commencement of this pursuit of holiness we always expect to see a great change wrought in ourselves. As we are led deeper into what faith, and the faith-life is, we understand how, though we do not see the change as we expected, we may yet rejoice with joy unspeakable in what Jesus is. This is the secret of holiness.

2. Joy must be cultivated. To rejoice is a command more frequently given than we know. It is part of the obedience of faith, to rejoice when we do not feel like doing so. Faith rejoices and sings, because God is holy.

3. 'Filled with joy and the Holy Ghost,' 'The Kingdom is joy in the Holy Ghost.' The Holy Spirit, the Blessed Spirit of Jesus is within thee, a very fountain of living water, of joy and gladness. Oh, seek to know Him, who dwells in thee, to work all that Jesus has for thee: He will be in thee the Spirit of faith and of joy.

4. Love and joy ever keep company. Love, denying and forgetting itself for the brethren and the lost, living in them, finds the joy of God. 'The kingdom of God is joy in the Holy Ghost.'

Twenty-second Day

HOLY IN CHRIST

In Christ our Sanctification

'Of God are ye in Christ Jesus, who was made unto us wisdom from God, both righteousness and sanctification and redemption; that, according as it is written, He that glorieth, let him glory in the Lord.'—1 Cor. i. 30, 31.

These words lead us on now to the very centre of God's revelation of the way of holiness. We know the steps of the road leading hither. He is holy, and holiness is His. He makes holy by coming near. His presence is holiness. In Christ's life, the holiness that had only been revealed in symbol, and as a promise of good things to come, had really taken possession of a human will, and been made one with true human nature. In His death every obstacle had been removed that could prevent the transmission of that holy nature to us: Christ had truly become our sanctification. In the Holy Spirit the actual communication of that holiness took place. And now we want to understand what the work is the Holy Spirit does, and how He communicates this holy nature to us: what our relation is to Christ as our sanctification, and what the position we have to take up toward Him, that in its fulness and its power it may do its work for us.

The Divine answer to this question is, 'Of God are ye in Christ.' The one thing we need to apprehend is, what this our position and life in Christ is, and how that position and life may on our part be accepted and maintained. Of this we may be sure, that it is not something that is high and beyond our reach. There need be no exhausting effort or hopeless sighing, 'Who shall ascend into heaven, that is, to bring Christ down from above?' It is a life that is meant for the sinful and the weary, for the unworthy and the impotent. It is a life that is the gift of the Father's love, and that He Himself will reveal in each one who comes in childlike trust to Him. It is a life that is meant for our every-day life, that in every varying circumstance and situation will make and keep us holy.

'Of God are ye in Christ.' Ere our Blessed Lord left the world, He spake: Lo! I am with you alway, even to the end of the

123

world. And it is written of Him: 'He that descended is the same that ascended far above all the heavens, that He might fill all things.' 'The Church is His body, the fulness of Him that filleth all in all.' In the Holy Spirit the Lord Jesus is with His people here on earth. Though unseen, and not in the flesh, His Personal Presence is as real on earth as when He walked with His disciples. In regeneration the believer is taken out of his old place 'in the flesh;' he is no longer in the flesh, but in the spirit (Rom. viii. 9); he is really and actually in Christ. The living Christ is around him by His holy Presence. Wherever and whatever he be, however ignorant of his position or however unfaithful to it, there he is in Christ. By an act of Divine and omnipotent grace, he has been planted into Christ, encircled on every side by the Power and the Love of Him who filleth all things, whose fulness specially dwells in His body here below, the Church.

And how can one who is longing to know Christ fully as his sanctification, come to live out what God means and has provided in this—'in Christ'? The first thing that must be remembered is that it is a thing of faith and not of feeling. The promise of the indwelling and the quickening of the Holy One is to the humble and contrite. Just when I feel most deeply that I am not holy, and can do nothing to make myself holy, when I feel ashamed of myself, just then is the time to turn from self and very quietly to say: I am in Christ. Here He is all around me. Like the air that surrounds me, like the light that shines on me, here is my Lord Jesus with me in His hidden but Divine and most real presence. My faith must in quiet rest and trust bow before the Father, of whom and by whose Mighty Grace I am in Christ: He will reveal it to me with ever-growing clearness and power. He does it as I believe, and in believing open my whole soul to receive what is implied in it: the sense of sinfulness and unholiness must become the strength of my trust and dependence. In such faith I abide in Christ.

But because it is of faith, therefore it is of the Holy Spirit. Of God are ye in Christ. It is not as if God placed and planted us in Christ, and left it to us now to maintain the union. No, God is the Eternal One, the God of the everlasting life, who works every moment in a power that does not for one moment cease. What God gives, He continues with a never-ceasing giving. It is He who by the Holy Spirit makes this life in Christ a blessed reality in our consciousness. 'We have received the Spirit of God that we might know the things that are freely given us of God.' Faith is not only dependent on God for the gift it is to accept, but for the power to accept. Faith not only needs the Son as its filling and its food; it needs the Spirit as its power to receive and hold. And so the blessed possession of all that it means to be in Christ our sanctification comes as we learn to bow before God in believing prayer for the mighty workings of the Spirit, and in the deep childlike trust that He will reveal and glorify in us this Christ our sanctification in whom we are.

And how will the Spirit reveal this Christ in whom we are? It will specially be as the Living One, the Personal Friend and Master. Christ is not only our Example and our Ideal. His life is not only an atmosphere and an inspiration, as we speak of a man who mightily influences us by his writings. Christ is not only a treasury and a fulness of grace and power, into which the Spirit is to lead us. But Christ is the Living Saviour, with a heart that beats with a love that is most tenderly human, and yet Divine. It is in this love He comes near, and into this love He receives us, when the Father plants us into Him. In the power of a personal love He wishes to exercise influence, and to attach us to Himself. In that love of His we have the guarantee that His Holiness will enter us; in that love the great power by which it enters. As the Spirit reveals to us where we are dwelling, in Christ and His love, and that this Christ is a living Lord and Saviour, there wakens within us the enthusiasm of a personal attachment, and the devotion of a loving allegiance, that make us wholly His. And it becomes possible for us to believe that we can be holy: we feel sure that in the path of holiness we can go from strength to strength.

Such believing insight into our relation to Christ as being in Him, and such personal attachment to Him who has received us into His love and keeps us abiding there, becomes the spring of a new obedience. The will of God comes to us in the light of Christ's life and His love—each command first fulfilled by Him, and then passed on to us as the sure and most blessed help to more perfect fellowship with the Father and His Holiness. Christ becomes Lord and King in the soul, in the power of the Holy Spirit, guiding the will into all the perfect will of God, and proving Himself to be its sanctification, as He crowns its obedience with ever larger inflow of the Presence and the Holiness of God.

Is there any dear child of God at all disposed to lose heart as he thinks of what manner of man he ought to be in all holy living, let me call him to take courage. Could God have devised anything more wonderful or beautiful for such sinful, impotent creatures? Just think, Christ, God's own Son, made to be sanctification to you. The Mighty, Loving, Holy Christ, sanctified through suffering that He might have sympathy with you, given to make you holy. What more could you desire? Yes, there is more: 'Of God you are in Him.' Whether you understand it or not, however feebly you realize it, there it is, a thing most Divinely true and real. You are in Christ, by an act of God's own Mighty Power. And there, in Christ, God Himself longs to establish and confirm you to the end. And you have, greatest wonder of all, the Holy Spirit within you to teach you to know, and believe, and receive, all that there is in Christ for you. And if you will but confess that there is in you no wisdom or power for holiness, none at all, and allow Christ, 'the Wisdom of God and the Power of God,' by the Holy Spirit within you, to lead you on, and prove how completely, how faithfully, how mightily, He can be your sanctification, He will do it most gloriously.

O my brother! come and consent more fully to God's way of holiness. Let Christ be your sanctification. Not a distant Christ to whom you look, but a Christ very near, all around you, in whom you are. Not a Christ after the flesh, a Christ of the past, but a present Christ in the power of the Holy Ghost. Not a Christ whom you can know by your wisdom, but the Christ of God, who is a Spirit, and whom the Spirit within you, as you die to the flesh and self, will reveal in power. Not a Christ such as your little thoughts can frame a conception of, but a Christ according to the greatness of the heart and the love of God. Oh, come and accept this Christ, and rejoice in Him! Be content now to leave all your feebleness, and foolishness, and faithlessness to Him, in the quiet confidence that He will do for you more than you can think. And so let it henceforth be, as it is written, He that glorieth, let him glory in the Lord.

Be ye holy, as I am holy

Most Blessed Father! I bow in speechless adoration before the holy mystery of Thy Divine Love....

Oh, forgive me, that I have known and believed it so little as it is worthy of being known and believed.

Accept my praise for what I have seen and tasted of its

Divine blessedness. Accept, Lord God! of the praise of a glad and loving heart that only knows that it never can praise Thee aright.

And hear my prayer, O my Father! that in the power of Thy Holy Spirit, who dwells in me, I may each day accept and live out fully what Thou hast given me in Christ my sanctification. May the unsearchable riches there are in Him be the daily supply for my every need. May His Holiness, His delight in Thy will, indeed become mine. Teach me, above all, how this can most surely be, because I am, through the work of Thine Almighty Quickening Power, in Him, kept there by Thyself. My Father! my faith cries out: I can be holy, blessed be my Lord Jesus!

In this faith I yield myself to Thee, Lord Jesus, my King and Master, to do Thy will alone. In everything I do, great or small, I would act as one sanctified in Jesus, united to God's will in Him. It is Thou alone canst teach me to do this, canst give me strength to perform it. But I trust in Thee—art Thou not Christ my sanctification? Blessed Lord! I do trust Thee. Amen.

1. Christ, as He lived and died on earth, is our sanctification. His life, the Spirit of His life, is what constitutes our holiness. To be in perfect harmony with Christ, to have His mind, is to be holy.

2. Christ's Holiness had two sides. God sanctified Him by His Spirit: Christ sanctified Himself by following the leading of the Spirit, by giving up His will to God in everything. So God has made us holy in Christ; and so we follow after and perfect holiness by yielding ourselves to God's Spirit, by giving up our will and living in the will of God.

3. It is well that we take in every aspect of what God has revealed of holiness in His word. But let us never weary ourselves by seeking to grasp all completely. Let us even return to the simplicity that is in Jesus. To bow at His feet, to believe that He knows all we need, and has it all, and loves to give it all, is rest. And holiness is resting in Jesus the rest of God. Let all our thoughts be gathered up into this one: Jesus, Blessed Jesus.

4. This holy life in Christ is for to-day, when you read this. For to-day He is made of God unto you sanctification: to-day He will indeed be your holiness. Believe in Him for it; trust Him, praise Him. And remember: you are in Him.

Twenty-third Day

HOLY IN CHRIST

Holiness and the Body

'The temple of God is holy, which temple ye are. The body is for the Lord, and the Lord for the body. Know ye not that your body is the temple of the Holy Ghost which is in you; therefore glorify God in your body.'—1 Cor. iii. 16, vi. 13, 19.

'She that is unmarried is careful for the things of the Lord, that she may be holy both in body and spirit.'—1 Cor. vii. 34.

'Present your bodies a living sacrifice, holy, acceptable to God.'—Rom. xii. 1.

Coming into the world, our Blessed Lord spake: 'A body didst Thou prepare for me; lo, I come to do Thy will, O God.' Leaving this world again, it was in His own body that He bore our sins upon the tree. So it was in the body, no less than in soul and spirit, that He did the will of God. And therefore it is said, 'By which will we have been sanctified through the offering of the body of Jesus Christ once for all.'

When praying for the Thessalonians and their sanctification, Paul says, 'And the God of peace Himself sanctify you wholly; and may your spirit and soul and body be preserved entire, without blame, at the coming of our Lord Jesus Christ.' Of himself he had spoken as 'always bearing about in the body the dying of Jesus, that the life also of Jesus may be manifested in our body. For we which live are always delivered unto death for Jesus' sake, that the life also of Jesus may be manifested in our mortal flesh.' His earnest expectation and hope was, 'that Christ be magnified in my body, whether by life or by death.' The relation between body and spirit is so intimate, the power of sin in the spirit comes so much through the body, the body is so distinctly the object both of Christ's redemption and the Holy Spirit's renewal, that our study of holiness will be seriously defective if we do not take in the teaching of Scripture on holiness in the body.

It has been well said that the body is, to the soul and spirit

128

dwelling and acting within it, like the walls of the city. Through them the enemy enters in. In time of war, everything yields to the defence of the walls. It is often because the believer does not know the importance of keeping the walls defended, keeping the body sanctified, that he fails in having the soul and spirit preserved blameless. Or it is because he does not understand that the guarding and sanctifying of the body in all its parts must be as distinctly a work of faith, and as directly through the mighty power of Jesus and the indwelling of the Spirit, as the renewing of the inner life, that progress in holiness is so feeble. The rule of the city we entrust to Jesus: but the defence of the walls we keep in our own hands; the King does not keep us as we expected, and we cannot discover the secret of failure. It is the God of peace Himself, who sanctifies wholly, who must preserve spirit and soul and body entire and without blame. The tabernacle with its wood, the temple with its stone, were as holy as all included within their walls: God's holy ones need the body to be holy.

To realize the full meaning of this, let us remember how it was through the body sin entered. 'The woman saw that the tree was good for food,' this was the temptation in the flesh; through this the soul was reached, 'it was a delight to the eyes;' through the soul it then passed into the spirit, 'and to be desired to make one wise.' In John's description of what is in the world (1 John ii. 15), we find the same threefold division, 'the lust of the flesh, the lust of the eyes, and the pride of life.' And the three temptations of Jesus by Satan correspond exactly: he first sought to reach Him through the body, in the suggestion to satisfy His hunger by making bread; the second (see Luke iv.) appealed to the soul, in the vision of the kingdoms of this world and their glory; the third to the spirit, in the call to assert and prove His Divine Sonship by casting Himself down. Even to the Son of God the first temptation came, as to Adam and all in the world, as lust of the flesh, the desire to gratify the natural and lawful appetite of hunger. We cannot note too carefully that it was on a question of eating what appeared good for food that man's first sin was committed, and that that same question of eating to satisfy hunger was the battleground on which the Redeemer's first encounter with Satan took place. It is on the question of eating and drinking what is good and lawful that more Christians than are aware of it are foiled by Satan. To have every appetite of the body under the rule and regulation of the Holy Spirit appears to some needless, to others too difficult. And yet it must be, if the body is to be holy, as God's temple, and we are to glorify Him in our body and our spirit. The first approaches of sin are made through the body: in the body the complete victory will be gained.

What Scripture teaches as to the intimacy of the connection between the body and spirit, physiology confirms. What appear at first merely physical transgressions leave a stain and have a degrading influence on the soul, and through it drag down the spirit. And on the other side, spiritual sins, sins of thought and imagination and disposition, pass through the soul into the body, fix themselves in the nervous constitution, and express themselves even in the countenance and the habits or tendencies of the body. Sin must be combated not only in the region of the spirit: if we are to perfect holiness, we must cleanse ourselves from all defilement of flesh and spirit. 'If through the Spirit ye do make dead the deeds of the body, ye shall live.' If we are indeed to be cleansed from sin and made holy unto God, the body, as the outworks, must very specially be secured from the power of Satan and of sin.

And how is this to be done? God has made very special provision for this. Holy Scripture speaks so explicitly of the Holy Spirit, the Spirit that communicates holiness, in connection with the body. At first sight it looks as if the word, your bodies, were simply used as equivalent to, your persons, yourselves. But as the deeper insight into the power of sin in the body, and the need of a deliverance specially there, quickens our perception, we see what is meant by the body being the temple of the Holy Spirit. We notice how very specially it is of sins in the body that Paul speaks as defiling God's holy temple; and how it is through the power of the Holy Ghost in the body that he would have us glorify God. 'Know ye not that your body is the temple of the Holy Ghost: glorify God therefore, in the power of the Holy Spirit, in your body.' The Holy Spirit must not only exercise a restraining and regulating influence on the appetites of the body and their gratification, so that they be in moderation and temperance,—this is only the negative side,—but there must be a positively spiritual element, making the exercise of natural functions a service of holy joy and liberty to the glory of God; no longer a threatened hindrance to the life of obedience and fellowship, but a means of grace, a real help to the spiritual life.

It is only in a body that is full of the holy life, very entirely possessed of God's Spirit, that this will be the case.

And how can this be obtained? In the true Christian life, self-denial is the path to enjoyment, renunciation to possession, death to life. As long as there is ought that we think we have liberty and power to use or enjoy aright, if we but do so in moderation, we have not yet seen or confessed our own unholiness, or the need of the entire renewing of the Holy Spirit. It is not enough to say, 'Every creature of God is good, if it be received with thanksgiving;' we must remember the addition, 'for it is sanctified by the word and by prayer.' This sanctifying of every creature and its use is a thing as real and solemn as the sanctifying of ourselves. And this will only be where, if need be, we sacrifice the gift and the liberty to use it, until God gives us the power truly to use it to His glory alone. Of one of the most sacred of Divine institutions, marriage, Paul, who so denounces those who would forbid to marry, says distinctly that there may be cases in which a voluntary celibacy may be the surest and acceptable way of being 'holy both in body and spirit.' When to be holy as God is holy indeed becomes the great desire and aim of life, everything will be cherished or given up as it promotes the chief end. The actual and active presence of the Holy Spirit in the life of the body will be the fire that is kept burning continually on the altar.

And how is this to be attained? Of the body as of the spirit it is God, God in Christ, who is our Keeper and our Sanctifier. The guarding of the walls of the city must be entrusted to Him who rules within. 'I am persuaded that He is able to guard my deposit,' to keep that which I have committed to Him, must become as definitely true of the body, and of each of its functions of which we are conscious that it is the occasion of doubt or of stumbling, as it has been of the soul we entrusted to Him for salvation. A fixed deposit in a bank is money given away out of my hands to be kept there: the body or any part of it that needs to be made holy must be a deposit with Jesus. Faith must trust His acceptance and guarding of it; prayer and praise must daily afresh renew the assurance, must confirm the committal of the deposit, and maintain the fellowship with Jesus. Abiding thus in Him and His Holiness, we shall receive, in a life of trust and joy, the power to prove, even in the body, how fully and wholly we are in Him who is made unto us sanctification, how real and true the Holiness of God is in His people.

131

Be ye holy, as I am holy

Blessed Lord! who art my sanctification, I come to Thee now with a very special request. O Thou who didst in Thine own body bear our sins on the tree, and of whom it is written, 'We have been sanctified through the offering of the body of Jesus Christ once for all,' be pleased to reveal to me how my body may to the full experience the power of Thy wonderful redemption. I do desire in soul and body to be holy to the Lord.

Lord! I have too little understood that my body is the temple of the Holy Ghost, that there is nothing in it that can be matter of indifference, that its every state and function is to be holiness to the Lord. And where I saw that this should be so, I have still sought myself to guard from the enemy's approaches these the walls of the city. I forgot how this part of my being too could alone be kept and sanctified by faith, by Thy taking and keeping charge of what faith entrusted to Thee.

Lord Jesus! I come now to surrender this body with all its needs into Thy hands. In weariness and nervousness, in excitement and enjoyment, in hunger and want, in health and plenty, O my holy Saviour, let my body be in Thy keeping every moment. Thou callest us, 'being made free from sin, to present our members as servants of righteousness unto sanctification.' Saviour! in the faith of the freedom from sin which I have in Thee, I present every member of my body to Thee: I believe the Spirit of life in Thee makes me free from the law of sin in my members. Whether living or dying, be Thou magnified in my body. Amen.

1. In the tabernacle and temple, the material part was to be in harmony with, and the embodiment of, the holiness that dwelt within. It was therefore all made according to the pattern shown in the mount. In the two last chapters of Exodus, we have eighteen times 'as the Lord commanded.' Everything, even in the exterior, was the embodiment of the will of God. Even so our body, as God's temple, must in everything be regulated by God's word, quickened and sanctified by the Holy Spirit.

2. As part of this holiness in the body, Scripture mentions dress. Speaking of the 'outward adorning of plaiting the hair, of wearing jewels, or the putting on of apparel,' as inconsistent with 'the apparel of a meek and quiet spirit,' Peter says, 'After this manner aforetime the holy women, who hoped in God, adorned

132

themselves.' Holiness was seen in their dressing; their body was the temple of the Holy Spirit.

3. 'If ye through the Spirit do make dead the deeds of the body, ye shall live.' His quickening energy must reign through the whole. We are so accustomed to connect the spiritual with the ideal and invisible, that it will need time and thought and faith to realize how the physical and the sensible influence our spiritual life, and must be under the mastery and inspiration of God's Spirit. Even Paul says, 'I buffet my body, and bring it into bondage, lest I myself should be rejected.'

4. If God actually breathed His Spirit into the body of Adam formed out of the ground, let it not be thought strange that the Holy Spirit should now animate our bodies too with His sanctifying energy.

5. 'Corporeality is the end of the ways of God.' This deep saying of an old divine reminds us of a much neglected truth. The great work of God's Spirit is to ally Himself with matter, and form it into a spiritual body for a dwelling for God. In our body the Holy Spirit will do it, if He gets complete possession.

6. It is on this truth of the Holy Spirit's power in the body that what is called Faith-healing rests. Through all ages, in times of special spiritual quickening, God has given it to some to see how Christ would make, even here, the body partaker of the life and power of the Spirit. To those who do see it, the link between Holiness and Healing is a very close and blessed one, as the Lord Jesus takes possession of the body for Himself.

Twenty-fourth Day

HOLY IN CHRIST

Holiness and Cleansing

'Having therefore these promises, beloved, let us cleanse ourselves from all defilement of flesh and spirit, perfecting holiness in the fear of God.'—2 Cor. vii. 1.

That holiness is more than cleansing, and must be preceded by it, is taught us in more than one passage of the New Testament. 'Christ loved the Church, and gave Himself up for it, that He might sanctify it, having cleansed it by the washing of water with the word.' 'If a man cleanse himself from these, he shall be a vessel sanctified.' The cleansing is the negative side, the being separate and not touching the unclean thing, the removal of impurity; the sanctifying is the positive union and fellowship with God, and the participation of the graces of the Divine life and holiness (2 Cor. vi. 17, 18). So we read too of the altar, that God spake to Moses: 'Thou shalt cleanse the altar, when thou makest atonement for it, and thou shalt anoint it, to sanctify it' (Ex. xxix. 36). Cleansing must ever prepare the way, and ought always to lead on to holiness.

Paul speaks of a twofold defilement, of flesh and spirit, from which we must cleanse ourselves. The connection between the two is so close, that in every sin both are partakers. The lowest and most carnal form of sin will enter the spirit, and, dragging it down into partnership in crime, will defile and degrade it. And so will all defilement of spirit in course of time show its power in the flesh. Still we may speak of the two classes of sins as they owe their origin more directly to the flesh or the spirit.

'Let us cleanse ourselves from all defilement of flesh.' The functions of our body may be classed under the three heads of the nourishment, the propagation, and the protection of our life. Through the first the world daily solicits our appetite with its food and drink. As the fruit good for food was the temptation that overcame Eve, so the pleasures of eating and drinking are among the earliest forms of defilement of the flesh. Closely connected with this is what we named second, and which is in

134

Scripture specially connected with the word flesh. We know how in Paradise the sinful eating was at once followed by the awakening of sinful lust and of shame. In his First Epistle to the Corinthians, Paul closely connects the two (1 Cor. vi. 13, 15), as he also links drunkenness and impurity (1 Cor. vi. 9, 10). Then comes the third form in which the vitality of the body displays itself: the instinct of self-preservation, setting itself against everything that interferes with our pleasures and comfort. What is called temper, with its fruits of anger and strife, has its roots in the physical constitution, and is one among the sins of the flesh. From all this, the Christian, who would be holy, must most determinedly cleanse himself. He must yield himself to the searching of God's Spirit, to be taught what there is in the flesh that is not in harmony with the temperance and self-control demanded both by the law of nature and the law of the Spirit. He must believe, what Paul felt that the Corinthians so emphatically needed to be taught, that the Holy Spirit dwells in the body, making its members the members of Christ, and in this faith put off the works of the flesh; he must cleanse himself from all defilement of flesh.

'And of spirit.' As the source of all defilement of the flesh is self-gratification, so self-seeking is at the root of all defilement of the spirit. In relation to God, it manifests itself in idolatry, be it in the worship of other gods after our own heart, the love of the world more than God, or the doing our will rather than His. In relation to our fellow-men it shows itself in envy, hatred, and want of love, cold neglect or harsh judging of others. In relation to ourselves it is seen as pride, ambition, or envy, the disposition that makes self the centre round which all must move, and by which all must be judged.

For the discovery of such defilement of spirit, no less than of the sins of the flesh, the believer needs the light of the Holy Spirit; that the uncleanness may indeed be cleansed out and cast away for ever. Even unconscious sin, if we are not earnestly willing to have it shown to us, will most effectually prevent our progress in the path of holiness.

'Beloved! let us cleanse ourselves.' The cleansing is sometimes spoken of as the work of God (Acts xv. 9; 1 John i. 9); sometimes as that of Christ (John xv. 3; Eph. v. 26; Tit. ii. 14). Here we are commanded to cleanse ourselves. God does His work in us by the Holy Spirit; the Holy Spirit does His work by stirring us up and enabling us to do. The Spirit is the strength of the new life; in that strength we must set ourselves determinedly to cast out whatever is unclean. 'Come out, and be ye separate, and touch not the unclean thing.' It is not only the doing what is sinful, it is not only the willing of it, that the Christian must avoid, but even the touching it: the involuntary contact with it must be so unbearable as to force the cry, O wretched man that I am! and to lead on to the deliverance which the Spirit of the life of Christ does bring.

And how is this cleansing to be done? When Hezekiah called the priests to sanctify the temple that had been defiled, we read (2 Chron. xxix.), 'The priests went in unto the inner part of the house of the Lord to cleanse it, and brought out all the uncleanness that they found.' Only then could the sin-offering of atonement and the burnt-offering of consecration, with the thankofferings, be brought, and God's service be restored. Even thus must all that is unclean be looked out, and brought out, and utterly cast out. However deeply rooted the sin may appear, rooted in constitution and habit, we must cleanse ourselves of it if we would be holy. 'If we walk in the light, as He is in the light, the blood of Jesus Christ cleanseth from all sin.' As we bring out every sin from the inner part of the house into the light of God and walk in the light, the precious blood that justifies will work mightily to cleanse too: the blood brings into living contact with the life and the love of God. Let us come into the light with the sin: the blood will prove its mighty power. Let us cleanse ourselves in yielding ourselves to the light to reveal and condemn, to the blood to cleanse and sanctify.

'Let us cleanse ourselves, perfecting holiness in the fear of the Lord.' We read in Hebrews (x. 14), 'Christ hath perfected forever them that are sanctified.' As we have so often seen that what God has made holy man must make holy too, as he accepts and appropriates the holiness God has bestowed, so here with the perfection which the saints have in Christ. We must perfect holiness: holiness must be carried out into the whole of life, and carried on even to its end. As God's holy ones, we must go on to perfection, perfecting holiness. Do not let us be afraid of the word. Our Blessed Lord used it when He gave us the command, 'Be ye perfect, even as your Father in heaven is perfect.' A child striving after the perfection in knowledge of his profession, which he hopes to attain when he has finished school, is told by his teacher that the way to the perfection he hopes for at the end of his course is to seek to be perfect in the lessons of each day. To be perfect in the small portion of the work that each hour brings, is the path to the perfection that will crown the whole. The Master calls us to a perfection like that of the Father: He hath already perfected us in Himself: He holds out the prospect of perfection ever growing. His word calls us here day by day to be perfecting holiness. Let us seek in each duty to be whole-hearted and entire. Let us, as teachable scholars, in every act of worship or obedience, in every temptation and trial, do the very best which God's Spirit can enable us to do. 'Let patience have its perfect work, that ye may be perfect and entire, lacking in nothing.' 'The God of peace make you perfect in every good work to do His will.'

'Having therefore these promises, beloved, let us cleanse ourselves from all defilement of flesh and spirit, perfecting holiness in the fear of God.' It is faith that gives the courage and the power to cleanse from all defilement, perfecting holiness in the fear of God. It is as the promises of the Divine love and indwelling (2 Cor. vi 16–18) are made ours by the Holy spirit, that we shall share the victory which overcometh the world, even our faith. In the path along which we have already come, from the rest in Paradise down through Holy Scripture, we have seen the wondrous revelation of these promises in ever-growing splendour. That God the Holy One will make us holy; that God the Holy One will dwell with the lowly; that God in His Holy One has come to be our holiness; that God has planted us in Christ that He may be our sanctification; that God, who chose us in sanctification of the Spirit, has given us the Holy Spirit in our hearts, and now watches over us in His love to work out through Him His purposes and to perfect our holiness: such are the promises that have been set before us. 'Having therefore these promises, beloved, let us cleanse ourselves from all filthiness of flesh and spirit, perfecting holiness in the fear of God.'

Beloved brother! see here again God's way of holiness. Arise and step on to it in the faith of the promise, fully persuaded that what He hath promised He is mighty to perform. Bring out of the inner part of the house all uncleanness; bring it into the light of God; confess it and cast it at His feet, who takes it away, and cleanses you in His blood. Yield yourself in faith to perfect, in Christ your Strength, the Holiness to which you are called. As your Father in heaven is perfect, give yourself to Him as a little child to be perfect too in your daily lessons and your daily walk. Believe that your surrender is accepted: that the charge committed to Him is undertaken. And give glory to Him who is able to do above what you can ask or think.

Be ye holy, as I am holy

Holy Lord Jesus! Thou didst give Thyself for us, that, having cleansed us for Thyself as Thine own, Thou mightest sanctify us and present us to Thyself a glorious Church, not having spot or wrinkle or any such thing. Blessed be Thy Name for the wonderful love. Blessed be Thy Name for the wonderful cleansing. Through the washing by the word and the washing in the blood, Thou hast made us clean every whit. And as we walk in the light, Thou cleansest every moment.

With these promises, in the power of Thy word and blood, Thou callest us to cleanse ourselves from all defilement of flesh and spirit. Blessed Lord! graciously reveal in Thy Holy Light all that is defilement, even its most secret working. Let me live as one who is to be presented to Thee without spot or wrinkle or any such thing—cleansed with a Divine cleansing, because Thou gavest Thyself to do it. Under the living power of Thy word and blood, applied by the Holy Spirit, let my way be clean, and my hands clean, my lips clean, and my heart clean. Cleanse me thoroughly, that I may walk with Thee in white here on earth, keeping my garments unspotted and undefiled. For Thy great love's sake, my Blessed Lord. Amen.

1. Cleansing has almost always one aim: a cleansed vessel is fit for use. Spiritual work done for God, with the honest desire that He may through His Spirit use us, will give urgency to our desire for cleansing. A vessel not cleansed cannot be used: is not this the reason that there are some workers God cannot bless?

2. All defilement: one stain defiles. 'Let us cleanse ourselves from all defilement.'

3. No cleansing without Light. Open the heart for the Light to shine in.

4. No cleansing like fire. Give the defilement over to the fire of His Holiness, the fire that consumes and purifies. Give it into the death of Jesus, to Jesus Himself.

5. 'Perfecting holiness in the fear of God:' it is a solemn work. Rejoice with trembling—work out your salvation with fear and trembling.

6. 'Having these promises,' it is a blessed work to cleanse ourselves—entering into the promises, the purity, the love of our Lord. The fear of God need never hinder the faith in Him. And true faith will never hinder the practical work of cleansing.

7. If we walk in the light, the blood cleanseth. The light reveals; we confess and forsake, and accept the blood; so we cleanse ourselves. Let there be a very determined purpose to be clean from all defilement, everything that our Father considers a stain.

Twenty-fifth Day

HOLY IN CHRIST

Holy and Blameless

'Ye are witnesses, and God also, how holily and justly and unblameably we behaved ourselves among you that believe.— The Lord make you to increase and abound in love one toward another, and toward all men, to the end He may stablish your hearts unblameable in holiness before our God and Father at the coming of our Lord Jesus with all His holy ones.'—1 Thess. ii. 10, iii. 12, 13.

'He chose us in Him before the foundation of the world, that we should be holy and without blemish before Him in love.'—Eph. i. 4.

There are two Greek words, signifying nearly the same, used frequently along with the word holy, and following it, to express what the result and effect of holiness will be as manifested in the visible life. The one is translated without blemish, spotless, and is that also used of our Lord and His sacrifice, the Lamb without blemish (Heb. ix. 14; 1 Pet. i. 19). It is then used of God's children with holy—holy and without blemish (Eph. i. 4, 5, 27; Col. i. 22; Phil. ii. 15; Jude 24; 2 Pet. iii. 14). The other is without blame, faultless (as in Luke i. 6; Phil ii. 15, iii. 6), and is also found in conjunction with holy (1 Thess. ii. 10, iii. 13, v. 23). In answer to the question as to whether this blamelessness has reference to God's estimate of the saints or men's, Scripture clearly connects it with both. In some passages (Eph. i. 4, v. 27; Col. i. 22; 1 Thess. iii. 15; 2 Pet. iii. 14) the words 'before Him,' 'to Himself,' 'before our God and Father,' indicate that the first thought is of the spotlessness and faultlessness in the presence of a Holy God, which is held out to us as His purpose and our privilege. In others (such as Phil. ii. 15; 1 Thess. ii. 10), the blamelessness in the sight of men stands in the foreground. In each case the word may be considered to include both aspects: without blemish and without blame must stand the double test of the judgment of God and man too.

And what is now the special lesson which this linking

together of these two words in Scripture, and the exposition of holy by the addition of blameless, is meant to teach us? A lesson of deep importance. In the pursuit of holiness, the believer, the more clearly he realizes what a deep spiritual blessing it is, to be found only in separation from the world, and direct fellowship with God, to be possessed fully only through a real Divine indwelling, may be in danger of looking too exclusively to the Divine side of the blessing, in its heavenly and supernatural aspect. He may forget how repentance and obedience, as the path leading up to holiness, must cover every, even the minutest detail of daily life. He may not understand how faithfulness to the leadings of the Spirit, in such measure as we have Him already, faithfulness to His faintest whisper in reference to ordinary conduct, is essential to all fuller experience of His power and work as the Spirit of holiness. He may, above all, not have learnt how, not only obedience to what he knows to be God's will, but a very tender and willing teachableness to receive all that the Spirit has to show him of his imperfections and the Father's perfect will concerning him, is the only condition on which the Holiness of God can be more fully revealed to us and in us. And so, while most intent on trying to discover the secret of true and full holiness from the Divine side, he may be tolerating faults which all around him can notice, or remaining,—and that not without sin, because it comes from the want of perfect teachableness,— ignorant of graces and beauties of holiness with which the Father would have had him adorn the doctrine of holiness before men. He may seek to live a very holy, and yet think little of a perfectly blameless life.

There have been such saints, holy but hard, holy but distant, holy but sharp in their judgments of others; holy, but men around said, unloving and selfish; the half-heathen Samaritan more kind and self-sacrificing than the holy Levite and priest. If this be true, it is not the teaching of Holy Scripture that is to blame. In linking holy and without blemish (or without blame) so closely, the Holy Spirit would have led us to seek for the embodiment of holiness as a spiritual power in the blamelessness of practice and of daily life. Let every believer who rejoices in God's declaration that he is holy in Christ seek also to perfect holiness, reach out after nothing less than to be 'unblameable in holiness.'

That this blamelessness has very special reference to our intercourse with our fellow-men we see from the way in which it is linked with love. So in Eph. i. 4, 'That we should be holy and without blemish before Him in love.' But specially in that remarkable passage: 'The Lord make you to increase and abound in love toward one another, and toward all men, to the end He may establish your hearts unblameable in holiness.' The holiness and the blamelessness, the positive hidden Divine life-principle, and the external and human life-practice—both are to find their strength, by which we are to be established in them, in our abounding and ever-flowing love.

Holiness and lovingness—it is of deep importance that these words should be inseparably linked in our minds, as their reality in our lives. We have seen, in the study of the holiness of God, how love is the element in which it dwells and works, drawing to itself and making like itself all that it can get possession of. Of the fire of Divine holiness love is the beautiful flame, reaching out to communicate itself and assimilate to itself all it can lay hold of. In God's children true holiness is the same; the Divine fire burns to bring into its own blessedness all that comes within its reach. When Jesus sanctified Himself that we might be sanctified in truth, that was nothing but love giving itself to the death that the sinful might share His holiness. Selfishness and holiness are irreconcilable. Ignorance may think of sanctity as a beautiful garment with which to adorn itself before God, while underneath there is a selfish pride saying, 'I am holier than thou,' and quite content that the other should want what it boasts of. True holiness, on the contrary, is the expulsion and the death of selfishness, taking possession of heart and life to be the ministers of that fire of love that consumes itself, to reach and purify and save others. Holiness is love. Abounding love is what Paul prays for as the condition of unblameable holiness. It is as the Lord makes us to increase and abound in love, that He can establish our hearts unblameable in holiness.

The Apostle speaks of a twofold love, 'love toward each other, and toward all men.' Love to the brethren was what our Lord Himself enjoined as the chief mark of discipleship. And He prayed the Father for it as the chief proof to the world of the truth of His Divine mission. It is in the holiness of love, in a loving holiness, that the unity of the body will be proved and promoted, and prepared for the fuller workings of the Holy Spirit. In the Epistles to the Corinthians and Galatians, division and distance among believers are named as the sure proof of the life of self and the flesh. Oh, let us, if we would be holy, begin by being very gentle, and patient, and forgiving, and kind, and generous in our intercourse with all the Father's children. Let us study the Divine image of the love that seeketh not its own, and pray unceasingly that the Lord may make us to abound in love to each other. The holiest will be the humblest and most self-forgetting, the gentlest and most self-denying, the kindest and most thoughtful of others for Jesus' sake. 'Put on therefore, as God's elect, holy and beloved, a heart of compassion, kindness, humility, meekness, long-suffering' (Col. iii. 12, 13).

And then the love toward all men. A love proved in the conduct and intercourse of daily life. A love that not only avoids anger and evil temper and harsh judgments, but exhibits the more positive virtue of active devotion to the welfare and interests of all. A charitable love that cares for the bodies as well as the souls. A love that not only is ready to help when it is called, but that really gives itself up to self-denial and self-sacrifice to seek out and relieve the needs of the most wretched and unworthy. A love that does indeed take Christ's love, that brought Him from heaven and led Him to choose the cross, as the only law and measure for its conduct, and makes everything subordinate to the Godlike blessedness of giving, of doing good, of embracing and saving the needy and lost. Thus abounding in love, we shall be unblameable in holiness.

It is in Christ we are holy; of God we are in Christ, who is made of God unto us sanctification: it is in this faith that Paul prays that the Lord, our Lord Jesus, may make us increase and abound in love. The Father is the fountain, He is the channel; the Holy Spirit is the living stream. And He is our Life, through the Spirit. It is by faith in Him, by abiding in Him and in His love, by allowing, in close union with Him, the Spirit to shed abroad the love of God, that we shall receive the answer to our prayer, and shall by Himself be established unblameable in holiness. Let it be with us a prayer of faith that changes into praise: Blessed be the Lord, who will make us increase and abound in love, and will establish us unblameable in holiness before our God and Father, at the coming of our Lord Jesus with His holy ones.

Be ye holy, as I am holy

Most Gracious God and Father! again do I thank Thee for that wondrous salvation, through sanctification of the Spirit, which has made us holy in Christ. And I thank Thee that the Spirit can so make us partakers of the life of Christ, that we too may be unblameable in holiness. And that it is the Lord Himself who makes us to increase and abound in love, to the end our hearts may be so established; that the abounding love and the unblameable holiness are both from Him.

Blessed Lord and Saviour! I come now to claim and take as my own, what Thou art able to do for me. I am holy only in Thee; in Thee I am holy. In Thee there is for me the power to abound in love. O Thou, in whom the fulness of God's love abides, and in whom I abide, the Lord, my Lord, make me to abound in love. In union with Thee, in the life of faith in which Thou livest in me, it can be and it shall be. By the teaching of Thy Holy Spirit lead me in all the footsteps of Thy self-denying love, that I too may be consumed in blessing others.

And thus, Lord! mightily establish my heart to be unblameable in holiness. Let self perish at Thy presence. Let Thy Holiness, giving itself to make the sinner holy, take entire possession, until my heart and life are sanctified wholly, and my whole spirit and soul and body be preserved blameless unto Thy coming. Amen.

1. Let us pray very earnestly that our interest in the study of holiness may not be a thing of the intellect or the emotions, but of the will and the life, seen of all men in the daily walk and conversation. 'Abounding in love,' 'unblameable in holiness,' will give favour with God and man.

2. 'God is Love;' Creation is the outflow of love. Redemption is the sacrifice and the triumph of love. Holiness is the fire of love. The beauty of the life of Jesus is love. All we enjoy of the Divine we owe to love. Our holiness is not God's, is not Christ's, if we do not love.

3. 'Love seeketh not its own.' 'Love never faileth.' 'Love is the fulfilling of the law.' 'The greatest of these is love.' 'The end of the commandment is love.' To love God and man is to be holy. In the intercourse of daily life, holiness can have its simple and sweet beginnings and its exercise; so, in its highest attainment, holiness is love made perfect.

4. Faith has all its worth from love, from the love of God, whence it draws and drinks, and the love to God and man which streams out of it. Let us be strong in faith, then shall we abound in love.

5. 'The love of God hath been shed abroad in our hearts by the Holy Ghost which was given unto us.' Let this be our confidence.

Twenty-sixth Day

HOLY IN CHRIST

Holiness and the Will of God

'This is the will of God, even your sanctification.'—1 Thess. iv. 3.

'Lo, I am come to do Thy will. By which will we have been sanctified, through the offering of the body of Jesus Christ once for all.'—Heb. x. 9, 10.

In the will of God we have the union of His Wisdom and Power. The Wisdom decides and declares what is to be: the Power secures the performance. The declarative will is only one side; its complement, the executive will, is the living energy in which everything good has its origin and existence. So long as we only look at the will of God in the former light, as law, we feel it a burden, because we have not the power to perform—it is too high for us. When faith looks to the Power that works in God's will, and carries it out, it has the courage to accept it and fulfil it, because it knows God Himself is working it out. The surrender in faith to the Divine will as Wisdom thus becomes the pathway to the experience of it as a Power. 'He doeth according to His will,' is then the language not only of forced submission, but of joyful expectation.

'This is the will of God, your sanctification.' In the ordinary acceptation of these words, they simply mean that among many other things that God has willed, sanctification is one; it is something in accordance with His will. This thought contains teaching of great value. God very distinctly and definitely has willed your sanctification: your sanctification has its source and certainty in its being God's will. We are 'elect in sanctification of the Spirit,' 'chosen to be holy;' the purpose of God's will from eternity, and His will now, is our sanctification. We have only to think of what we said of God's will being a Divine power that works out what His wisdom has chosen, to see what strength this truth will give to our faith that we shall be holy: God wills it, and will work it out for all and in all who do not resist it, but yield themselves to its power. Seek your sanctification, not only in the

146

will of God, as a declaration of what He wants you to be, but as a revelation of what He Himself will work out in you.

There is, however, another most precious thought suggested. If our sanctification be God's will, its central thought and its contents, every part of that will must bear upon it, and the sure entrance to sanctification will be the hearty acceptance of the will of God in all things. To be one with God's will is to be holy. Let him who would be holy take his place here and 'stand in all the will of God.' He will there meet God Himself, and be made partaker of His Holiness, because His will works out its purpose in power to each one who yields himself to it. Everything in a life of holiness depends upon our being in the right relation to the will of God.

There are many Christians to whom it appears impossible to think of their accepting all the will of God, or of their being one with it. They look upon the will of God in its thousand commands, and its numberless providential orderings. They have sometimes found it so hard to obey one single command, or to give up willingly to some light disappointment. They imagine that they would need to be a thousandfold holier and stronger in grace, before venturing to say that they do accept all God's will, whether to do or to bear. They cannot understand that all the difficulty comes from their not occupying the right standpoint. They are looking at God's will as at variance with their natural will, and they feel that that natural will will never delight in all God's will. They forget that the new man has a renewed will. This new will delights in the will of God, because it is born of it. This new will sees the beauty and the glory of God's will, and is in harmony with it. If they are indeed God's children, the very first impulse of the spirit of a child is surely to do the will of the Father in heaven. And they have but to yield themselves heartily and wholly to this spirit of sonship, and they need not fear to accept God's will as theirs.

The mistake they make is a very serious one. Instead of living by faith they judge by feeling, in which the old nature speaks and rules. It tells them that God's will is often a burden too hard to be borne, and that they never can have the strength to do it. Faith speaks differently. It reminds us that God is Love, and that His will is nothing but Love revealed. It asks if we do not know that there is nothing more perfect or beautiful in heaven or earth than the will of God. It shows us how in our conversion we have already professed to accept God as Father and Lord. It assures us, above all, that if we will but definitely and trustingly give ourselves to that will which is Love, it will as Love fill our hearts and make us delight in it, and so become the power that enables us joyfully to do and to bear. Faith reveals to us that the will of God is the power of His love, working out its plan in Divine beauty in each one who wholly yields to it.

And which shall we now choose? And where shall we take our place? Shall we attempt to accept Christ as a Saviour without accepting His will? Shall we profess to be the Father's children, and yet spend our life in debating how much of His will we shall perform? Shall we be content to go on from day to day with the painful consciousness that our will is not in harmony with God's will? Or shall we not at once and for ever give up our will as sinful to His,—to that Will which He has already written on our heart? This is a thing that is possible. It can be done. In a simple, definite transaction with God, we can say that we do accept His holy will to be ours. Faith knows that God will not pass such a surrender unnoticed, but accept it. In the trust that He now takes us up into His will, and undertakes to breathe it into us, with the love and the power to perform it—in this faith let us enter into God's will, and begin a new life; standing in, abiding in the very centre of this most holy will.

Such an acceptance of God's will prepares the believer, through the Holy Spirit, to recognise and know that will in whatever form it comes. The great difference between the carnal and the spiritual Christian is that the latter acknowledges God, under whatever low and poor and human appearances He manifests Himself. When God comes in trials which can be traced to no hand but His, he says, 'Thy will be done.' When trials come through the weakness of men or his own folly, when circumstances appear unfavourable to his religious progress, and temptations threaten to be too much for him and to overcome him, he learns first of all to see God in everything, and still to say, 'Thy will be done.' He knows that a child of God cannot possibly be in any situation without the will of His Heavenly Father, even when that will has been to leave him to his own wilfulness for a time, or to suffer the consequences of his own or others' sin. He sees this, and in accepting his circumstances as the will of God to try and prove him, he is in the right position for now knowing and doing what is right. Seeing and honouring God's will thus in everything, he learns always to abide in that will.

He does so also by doing that will. As his spiritual

discernment grows to say of whatever happens, 'All things are of God,' so he grows too in wisdom and spiritual understanding to know the will of God as it is to be done. In the indications of conscience and of Providence, in the teaching of the word and the Spirit, he learns to see how God's will has reference to every part and duty of life, and it becomes his joy, in all things, to live, 'doing the will of God from the heart, as unto the Lord and not unto men.' 'Labouring fervently in prayer to stand complete and fully assured in all the will of God,' he finds how blessedly the Father has accepted his surrender, and supplies all the light and strength that is needed that His will may be done by him on earth as it is in heaven.

Let me ask every reader to say to a Holy God, whether he has indeed given himself to Him to be made holy? Whether he has accepted, and entered into, and is living in, the good and perfect will of God? The question is not, whether, when affliction comes, he accepts the inevitable and submits to a will he cannot resist. But whether he has chosen the will of God as his chief good, and has taken the life-principle of Christ to be his: 'I delight to do Thy will, O God.' This was the holiness of Christ, in which He sanctified Himself and us, the doing God's will. 'In which will we have been sanctified.' It is this will of God which is our sanctification.

Brother! are you in earnest to be holy? wholly possessed of God? Here is the path. I plead with you not to be afraid or to hold back. You have taken God to be your God; have you really taken His will to be your will? Oh, think of the privilege, the blessedness, of having one will with God! and fear not to surrender yourself to it most unreservedly. The will of God is, in every part of it, and in all its Divine power, your sanctification.

Be ye holy, as I am holy

Blessed Father! I come to say that I see that Thy will is my sanctification, and there alone I would seek it. Graciously grant that, by Thy Holy Spirit which dwelleth in me, the glory of that will, and the blessedness of abiding in it, may be fully revealed to me.

Teach me to know it as the Will of Love, purposing always what is the very best and most blest for Thy child. Teach me to know it as the Will of Omnipotence, able to work out its every counsel in me. Teach me to know it in Christ, fulfilled perfectly on my behalf. Teach me to know it as what the Spirit wills and works in each one who yields to Him.

O my Father! I acknowledge Thy claim to have Thy will alone done, and am here for it to do with me as Thou pleasest. With my whole heart I enter into it, to be one with it for ever. Thy Holy Spirit can maintain this oneness without interruption. I trust Thee, my Father, step by step, to let the light of Thy will shine in my heart and on my path, through that Spirit.

May this be the holiness in which I live, that I forget and lose self in pleasing and honouring Thee. Amen.

1. Make it a study, in meditation and prayer and worship, to get a full impression of the Majesty, the Perfection, the Glory of the Will of God, with the privilege and possibility of living in it.

2. Study it, too, as the expression of an infinite Love and Fatherliness; its every manifestation full of loving-kindness. Every providence is God's will; whatever happens, meet God in it in humble worship. Every precept is God's will; meet God in it with loving obedience. Every promise is God's will; meet God in it with full trust. A life in the will of God is rest and strength and blessing.

3. And forget not, above all, to believe in its Omnipotent Power. He worketh all things after the counsel of His will. In nature and those who resist Him, without their consent. In His children, according to their faith, and as far as they will it. Do believe that the will of God will work out its counsel in you, as you trust it to do so.

4. This will is Infinite Benevolence and Beneficence revealed in the self-sacrifice of Jesus. Live for others: so can you become an instrument for the Divine will to use (Matt. xviii. 14; John vi. 39, 40). Yield yourselves to this redeeming will of God, that it may get full possession, and work out through you too its saving purpose.

5. Christ is just the embodiment of God's will: He is, God's will done. Abide in Him, by abiding in, by doing heartily and always, the will of God. A Christian is, like Christ, a man given up to the Will of God.

Twenty-seventh Day

HOLY IN CHRIST

Holiness and Service

'If a man therefore cleanse himself from these, he shall be a vessel unto honour, sanctified, meet for the Master's use, prepared unto every good work.'—2 Tim. ii. 21.

'A holy priesthood, to offer up spiritual sacrifices. A holy nation, that ye may show forth the excellences of Him who called you out of darkness into His marvellous light.'—1 Pet. ii. 5, 9.

Through the whole of Scripture we have seen that whatever God sanctifies is to be used in the service of His Holiness. His Holiness is an infinite energy that only finds its rest in making holy: to the revelation of what He is in Himself, 'I the Lord am holy,' God continually adds the declaration of what He does, 'I am the Lord that make holy.' Holiness is a burning fire that extends itself, that seeks to consume what is unholy, and to communicate its own blessedness to all that will receive it. Holiness and selfishness, holiness and inactivity, holiness and sloth, holiness and helplessness, are utterly irreconcilable. Whatever we read of as holy, was taken into the service of the Holiness of God.

Let us just look back on the revelation of what is holy in Scripture. The seventh day was made holy, that in it God might make His people holy. The tabernacle was holy, to serve as a dwelling for the Holy One, as the centre whence His Holiness might manifest itself to the people. The altar was most holy, that it might sanctify the gifts laid on it. The priests with their garments, the house with its furniture and vessels, the sacrifices and the blood,—whatever bore the name of holy had a use and a purpose. Of Israel, whom God redeemed from Egypt that they might be a holy nation, God said, 'Let my people go, that they may serve me.' The holy angels, the holy prophets and apostles, the holy Scriptures,—all bore the title as having been sanctified for the service of God. Our Lord speaks of Himself 'as the Son, whom the Father sanctified and sent into the world.' And when

He says, 'I sanctify myself,' He adds at once the purpose: it is in the service of the Father and His redeemed ones,—'that they themselves may be sanctified in truth.' And can it be thought possible, now that God, in Christ the Holy One, and in the Holy Spirit, is accomplishing His purpose, and gathering a people of saints, 'holy ones,' 'made holy in Christ,' that now holiness and service would be put asunder? Impossible! Here first we shall fully realize how essential they are to each other. Let us try and grasp their mutual relation. We are only made holy that we may serve. We can only serve as we are holy.

Holiness is essential to effectual service. In the Old Testament we see degrees of holiness, not only in the holy places, but as much in the holy persons. In the nation, the Levites, the priests, and then the High Priest, there is an advance from step to step: as in each succeeding stage the circle narrows, and the service is more direct and entire, so the holiness required is higher and more distinct. It is even so in this more spiritual dispensation: the more of holiness, the greater the fitness for service; the more there is of true holiness, the more there is of God, and the more true and deep is the entrance He has had into the soul. The hold He has on the soul to use it in His service is more complete.

In the Church of Christ there is a vast amount of work done which yields very little fruit. Many throw themselves into work in whom there is but little true holiness, little of the Holy Spirit. They often work most diligently, and, as far as human influence is concerned, most successfully. And yet true spiritual results in the building up of a holy temple in the Lord are but few. The Lord cannot work in them, because He has not the mastery of their inner life. His personal indwelling and fellowship, the rest of His Holy Presence, His Holiness reigning and ruling in the heart and life,—to all these they are comparative strangers. It has been rightly said that work is the cure for spiritual poverty and disease; to some believers who had been seeking holiness apart from service, the call to work has been an unspeakable blessing. But to many it has only been an additional blind to cover up the terrible want of heart-holiness and heart-fellowship with the living God. They have thrown themselves into work more earnestly than ever, and yet have not in their heart the rest-giving and refreshing witness that their work is acceptable and accepted.

My brother! listen to the message. 'If a man cleanse

himself, he shall be a vessel unto honour, sanctified, meet for the Master's use, prepared unto every good work.' You cannot have the law of service more clearly or beautifully laid down. A vessel of honour, one whom the King will delight to honour, must be a vessel cleansed from all defilement of flesh and spirit. Then only can it be a sanctified vessel, possessed and indwelt by God's Holy Spirit. So it becomes meet for the Master's use. He can use it, and work in it, and wield it. And so, clean and holy, and yielded into the Master's hands, we are Divinely prepared for every good work. Holiness is essential to service. If service is to be acceptable to God, and effectual for its work on souls, and to be a joy and a strength to ourselves, we must be holy. The will of God must first live in us, if it is to be done by us.

How many faithful workers there are, mourning the want of power; longing and praying for it, and yet not obtaining it! They have spent their strength more in the outer court of work and service, than in the inner life of fellowship and faith. They truly have never understood that only as the Master gets possession of them, as the Holy Spirit has them at His disposal, can He use them, can they have true power. They often long and cry for what they call a baptism of power. They forget that the way to have God's power in us is for ourselves to be in His power. Put yourself into the power of God; let His holy will live in you; live in it and in obedience to it, as one who has no power to dispose of himself; let the Holy Spirit dwell within, as in His Holy Temple, revealing the Holy One on the throne, ruling all; He will without fail use you as a vessel of honour, sanctified and meet for the Master's use. Holiness is essential to effectual service.

And service is no less essential to true holiness. We have repeated it so often: Holiness is an energy, an intense energy of desire and self-sacrifice, to make others partakers of its own purity and perfection. Christ sacrificed Himself—wherein did that sacrifice consist, and what was its aim? He sanctified Himself that we might be sanctified too. A holiness that is selfish is a delusion. True holiness, God's holiness in us, works itself out in love, in seeking and loving the unholy, that they may become holy too. Self-sacrificing love is of the very essence of holiness. The Holy One of Israel is its Redeemer. The Holy One of God is the dying Saviour. The Holy Spirit of God makes holy. There is no holiness in God but what is most actively engaged in loving and saving and blessing. It must be so in us too. Let every thought of holiness, every act of faith or prayer, every effort in

153

pursuit of it, be animated by the desire and the surrender to the Holiness of God for use in the attaining of its object. Let your whole life be one distinctly and definitely given up to God for His use and service. Your circumstances may appear to be unfavourable. God may appear to keep the door closed against your working for Him in the way you would wish; your sense of unfitness may be painful. Still, let it be a matter settled between God and the soul, that your longing for holiness is that you may be fitter for Him to use, and that what He has given you of His Holiness in Christ and the Spirit is all at His disposal, waiting to be used. Be ready for Him to use; live out, in a daily life of humble, self-denying, loving service of others, what grace you have received. You will find that in the union and interchange of worship and work, God's Holiness will rest upon you.

'The Father sanctified the Son, and sent Him into the world.' The world is the place for the sanctified one, to be its light, its salt, its life. We are 'sanctified in Christ Jesus,' and sent into the world too. Oh, let us not fear to accept our position—our double position; in the world, and in Christ! In the world, with its sin and sorrow, with its thousands of needs touching us at every point, and its millions of souls all waiting for us. And in Christ too. For the sake of that world we 'have been sanctified in Christ,' we are 'holy in Christ,' we have 'the spirit of sanctification' dwelling in us. As a holy salt in a sinful world, let us give ourselves to our holy calling. Let us come nearer and nearer to God who has called us. Let us root deeper and deeper in Christ our sanctification, in whom we are of God. Let us enter more firmly and more fully into that faith in Him in whom we are, by which our whole life will be covered and taken up in His. Let us beseech the Father to teach us that His Holy Spirit does dwell in us every moment, making, if we live by faith, Christ with His Holiness, our home, our abode, our sure defence, and our infinite supply. As He which hath called us is holy, let us be holy in His own Son, through His own Spirit, and the fire of His Holy Love will work through us its work of judging and condemning, of saving and sanctifying. A sanctified soul God will use to save.

Be ye holy, as I am holy

Blessed Master! I thank Thee for being anew reminded of the purpose of Thy Redeeming Love. Thou gavest Thyself that

Thou mightest cleanse for Thyself a people of Thine own, zealous in good works. Thou wouldest make of each of us a vessel of honour, cleansed and sanctified, meet for Thy use, and prepared for every good work.

Blessed Lord! write the lessons of Thy word deep in my heart. Teach me and all Thy people that if we would work for Thee, if we would have Thee work in us, and use us, we must be very holy, holy as God is holy. And that if we would be holy, we must be serving Thee. It is Thy own Spirit, by which Thou dost sanctify us to use us, and dost sanctify in using. To be entirely possessed of Thee is the path to sanctity and service both.

Most Holy Saviour! we are in Thee as our sanctification: in Thee we would abide. In the rest of a faith that trusts Thee for all, in the power of a surrender that would have no will but Thine, in a love that would lose itself to be wholly Thine, Blessed Jesus, we do abide in Thee. In Thee we are holy: in Thee we shall bear much fruit.

Oh, be pleased to perfect Thine own work in us! Amen.

1. It is difficult to make it clear in words how growth in holiness will simply reveal itself as an increasing simplicity and self-forgetfulness, accompanied by the restful and most blessed assurance that God has complete possession of us and will use us. We pass from the stage in which work presses as an obligation; it becomes the joy of fruit-bearing; faith's assurance that He is working out His will through us.

2. It has sometimes been said that people might be better employed in working for God than attending Holiness Conventions. This is surely a misunderstanding. It was before the throne of the Thrice Holy One, and as he heard the Seraphim sing of God's Holiness, that the prophet said, 'Here am I, send me.' As the mission of Moses, and Isaiah, and the Son, whom the Father sanctified and sent, each had its origin in the revelation of God's Holiness, our missions will receive new power as they are more directly born out of the worship of God as the Holy One, and baptized into the Spirit of Holiness.

3. Let every worker take time to hear God's double call. If you would work, be very holy. If you would be holy, give yourself to God to use in His work.

4. Note the connection between 'sanctified' and 'meet for the Master's use.' True holiness is being possessed of God; true service being used of God. How much service there is in which

we are the chief agents, and ask God to help and to bless us. True service is being yielded up to the Master for Him to use. Then the Holy Ghost is the Agent, and we are the Instruments of His will. Such service is Holiness.

5. 'I sanctify Myself, that they also:' a reference to others is the root principle of all true holiness.

Twenty-eighth Day

HOLY IN CHRIST

The Way into the Holiest

*'Having therefore, brethren, boldness to enter into the
Holiest by the blood of Jesus, by the way which He dedicated, a
new and living way, through the veil, that is to say, His flesh:
and having a great Priest over the house of God; let us draw
near with a true heart, in fulness of faith.'—Heb. x. 19–22.*

When the High Priest once a year entered into the second
tabernacle within the veil, it was, we are told in the Epistle to the
Hebrews, 'the Holy Ghost signifying that the way into the Holiest
of all was not yet made manifest.' When Christ died, the veil was
rent; all who were serving in the holy place had free access at
once into the Most Holy; the way into the Holiest of all was
opened up. When the Epistle passes over to its practical
application (x. 19), all its teaching is summed up in the words:
'Having therefore, brethren, boldness to enter into the Holiest,
let us draw near.' Christ's redemption has opened the way to the
Holiest of all: our acceptance of it must lead to nothing less than
our drawing near and entering in. The words of our text suggest
to us four very precious thoughts in regard to the place of access,
the right of access, the way of access, the power of access.

The place of access. Whither are we invited to draw nigh?
'Having boldness to enter into the Holiest.' The priests in Israel
might enter the holy place, but were always kept excluded from
the Holiest, God's immediate presence. The rent veil proclaimed
liberty of access into that Presence. It is there that believers as a
royal priesthood are now to live and walk. Within the veil, in the
very Holiest of all, in the same place, the heavenlies, in which
God dwells, in God's very Presence, is to be our abode—our
home. Some speak as if the, 'Let us draw near,' meant prayer,
and that in our special approach to God in acts of worship we
enter the Holiest. No; great as this privilege is, God has meant
something for us infinitely greater. We are to draw near, and
dwell always, to live our life and do our work within the sphere,
the atmosphere, of the inner sanctuary. It is God's Presence
makes holy ground; God's immediate Presence in Christ makes

157

any place the Holiest of all: and this is it into which we are to draw nigh, and in which we are to abide. There is not a single moment of the day, there is not a circumstance or surrounding, in which the believer may not be kept dwelling in the secret place of the Most High. As by faith he enters into the completeness of his reconciliation with God, and the reality of his oneness with Christ, as he thus, abiding in Christ, yields to the Holy Spirit to reveal within the Presence of the Holy One, the Holiest of all is around him, he is indeed in it. With an uninterrupted access he draws near. [13]

The right of access. The thought comes up, and the question is asked: Is this not simply an ideal? can it be a reality, an experience in daily life to those who know how sinful their nature is? Blessed be God! it is meant to be. It is possible, because our right of access rests not in what we are, but in the blood of Jesus. 'Having boldness to enter into the Holiest by the blood of Jesus, let us draw near.' In the Passover we saw how redemption, and the holiness it aimed at, were dependent on the blood. In the sanctuary, God's dwelling, we know how in each part, the court, the holy place, the Most Holy, the sprinkling of blood was what alone secured access to God. And now that the blood of Jesus has been shed—oh! in what Divine power, what intense reality, what everlasting efficacy, we now have access into the Holiest of all, the Most Holy of God's heart and His love! We are indeed brought nigh by the blood. We have boldness to enter by the blood. 'The worshippers, being once cleansed, have no more conscience of sins.' Walking in the light, the blood of Jesus cleanses in the power of an endless life, with a cleansing that never ceases. No consciousness of unworthiness or remaining sinfulness need hinder the boldness of access: the liberty to draw near rests in the never-failing, ever-acting, ever-living efficacy of the Precious Blood. It is possible for a believer to dwell in the Holiest of all.

The way of access. It is often thought that what is said of the new and living way, dedicated for us by Jesus, means nothing different from the boldness through His blood. This is not the case. The words mean a great deal more. 'Having boldness by the

---

[13]   So near, so very near to God,
              I cannot nearer be;
          For in the person of His Son,
              I am as near as He.

158

blood of Jesus, let us draw near by the way which He dedicated for us.' That is, He opened for us a way to walk in, as He walked in it, 'a new and living way, through the veil, that is to say, His flesh.' The way in which Christ walked when He gave His blood, is the very same in which we must walk too. That way is the way of the Cross. There must not only be faith in Christ's sacrifice, but fellowship with Him in it. That way led to the rending of the veil of the flesh, and so through the rent veil of the flesh, in to God. And was the veil of Christ's holy flesh rent that the veil of our sinful flesh might be spared? Verily, no. He meant us to walk in the very same way in which He did, following closely after Himself. He dedicated for us a new and living way through the veil, that is, His flesh. As we go in through the rent veil of His flesh, we find in it at once the need and the power for our flesh being rent too: following Jesus ever means conformity to Jesus. It is Jesus with the rent flesh, in whom we are, in whom we walk. [14] There is no way to God but through the rending of the flesh. In acceptance of Christ's life and death by faith as the power that works in us, in the power of the Spirit which makes us truly one with Christ, we all follow Christ as He passes on through the rent veil, that is, His flesh, and become partakers with Him of His crucifixion and death. The way of the cross, 'by which I have been crucified,' is the way through the rent veil. Man's destiny, fellowship with God in the power of the Holy Spirit, is only reached through the sacrifice of the flesh.

And here we find now the solution of a great mystery—why so many Christians remain standing afar off, and never enter this Holiest of all; why the holiness of God's Presence is so little seen on them. They thought that it was only in Christ that the flesh needed to be rent, not in themselves. They thought that the liberty they had in the blood was the new and living way. They knew not that the way into true and full holiness, into the Holiest of all, that the full entrance into the fellowship of the holiness of the Great High Priest, was only to be reached through the rent veil of the flesh, through conformity to the death of Jesus. This is in very deed the way He dedicated for us. He is Himself the way;

---

[14] 'Christ suffered, that He might bring us to God, being put to death in the flesh, but quickened in the Spirit.' 'Forasmuch then as Christ suffered in the flesh, arm ye yourselves also with the same mind.' The flesh and the Spirit are antagonistic: as the flesh dies, the Spirit lives.

into His self-denial, His self-sacrifice, His crucifixion, He takes up all who long to be holy with His Holiness, holy as He is holy.

The power of access. Does any one shrink back from entering the very Holiest for fear of this rending of the flesh, because he doubts whether he could bear it, whether he could indeed walk in such a path? Let him listen once more. Hear what follows: 'And having a Great Priest over the House of God, let us draw near.' We have not only the Holiest of all inviting us, and the blood giving us boldness, and the way through the rent veil consecrated for us, but the Great Priest over the House of God, the Blessed Living Saviour, to draw, to help, and to welcome us. He is our Aaron. On His heart we see our name, because He only lives to think of us, and pray for us. On His forehead we see God's name, 'Holy to the Lord,' because in His Holiness the sins of our holy things are covered. In Him we are accepted and sanctified; God receives us as holy ones. In the power of His love and His Spirit, in the power of Him the Holy One, in the joy of drawing nearer to Him and being drawn by Him, we gladly accept the way He has dedicated, and walk in His holy footsteps of self-denial and self-sacrifice. We see how the flesh is the thick veil that separates from the Holy One who is a Spirit, and it becomes an unceasing and most fervent prayer, that the crucifixion of the flesh may, in the power of the Holy Spirit, be in us a blessed reality. With the glory of the Holiest of all shining out on us through the opened veil, and the Precious Blood speaking so loudly of boldness of access, and the Great Priest beckoning us with His loving Presence to draw near and be blessed,—with all this, we dare no longer fear, but choose the way of the rent veil as the path we love to tread, and give ourselves to enter in and dwell within the veil, in the very Holiest of all.

And so our life here will be the earnest of the glory that is to come, as it is written—note how we have the four great thoughts of our text over again—'These are they which came out of great tribulation,' that is, by the way of the rent flesh; 'and they washed their robes, and made them white in the blood of the Lamb,' their boldness through the blood; 'therefore are they before the throne of God,' their dwelling in the Holiest of all; 'the Lamb, which is in the midst of the throne, shall be their Shepherd,' the Great Priest still the Shepherd, Jesus Himself their all in all.

Brother! do you see what holiness is, and how it is to be found? It is not something wrought in yourself. It is not something put on you from without. Holiness is the Presence of God resting on you. Holiness comes as you consciously abide in that Presence, doing all your work, and living all your life as a sacrifice to Him, acceptable through Jesus Christ, sanctified by the Holy Ghost. Oh, be no longer fearful, as if this life were not for you! Look to Jesus; having a Great Priest over the House of God, let us draw near. Be occupied with Jesus. Our Brother has charge of the Temple; He has liberty to show us all, to lead us into the secret of the Father's presence. The entire management of the Temple has been given into His hands with this very purpose, that all the feeble and doubting ones might come with confidence. Only trust yourself to Jesus, to His leading and keeping. Only trust Jesus, God's Holy One, your Holy One; it is His delight to reveal to you what He has purchased with His blood. Trust Him to teach you the ordinances of the sanctuary. 'That thou mayest know how thou oughtest to behave thyself in the House of God,' He has been given. Having a Great Priest, let us enter in, let us dwell in the Holiest of all. In the power of the blood, in the power of the new and living way, in the power of the Living Jesus, let the Holiest of all, the Presence of God, be the home of our soul. You are 'Holy in Christ;' in Christ you are in God's Holy Presence and Love; just stay there.

Be holy, for I am holy

Most Holy God! how shall I praise Thee for the liberty to enter into the Holiest of all, and dwell there? And for the precious Blood, that brings us nigh? And for the new and living way, through the rent veil of that flesh which had separated us from Thee, in which my flesh now too has been crucified? And for the Great Priest over the House of God, our Living Lord Jesus, with Whom and in Whom we appear before Thee? Glory be to Thy Holy Name for this wonderful and most complete redemption.

I beseech Thee, O my God! give me, and all Thy children, some right sense of how really and surely we may live each day, may spend our whole life, within the veil, in Thine own Immediate Presence. Give us the spirit of revelation, I pray Thee, that we may see how, through the rent veil, the glory of Thy Presence streameth forth from the Most Holy into the holy place; how, in the pouring out of the Holy Spirit, the kingdom of heaven

161

came to earth, and all who yield themselves to that Spirit may know that in Christ they are indeed so near, so very near to Thee. O Blessed Father! let Thy Spirit teach us that this indeed is the holy life: a life in Christ the Holy One, always in the Light and the Presence of Thy Holy Majesty.

Most Holy God! I draw nigh. In the power of the Holy Spirit I enter in. I am now in the Holiest of all. And here I would abide in Jesus, my Great Priest—here, in the Holiest of all. Amen.

1. To abide in Christ is to dwell in the Holiest of all. Christ is not only the Sacrifice, and the Way, and the Great Priest, but also Himself the Temple. 'The Lamb is the Temple.' As the Holy Spirit reveals my union to Christ more clearly, and heart and will lose themselves in Him, I dwell in the Holy Presence, which is the Holiest of all. You are 'holy in Christ'—draw near, enter in with boldness, and take possession—have no home but in the Holiest of all.

2. 'Christ loved the Church, and gave Himself for it, that He might sanctify it.' He gave Himself! Have you caught the force of that word? Because He would have no one else do it, because none could do it; to sanctify His Church, He gave Himself to do it. And so it is His own special beloved work to sanctify the Church He loved. Just accept Himself to do it. He can and will make you holy, that He may present you to Himself glorious, without spot or wrinkle. Let that word Himself live in you. The whole life and walk in the House of God is in His charge. Having a Great Priest, let us draw near.

3. This entrance into the Holiest of all—an ever fresh and ever deeper entrance—is, at the same time, an ever blessed resting in the Father's Presence. Faith in the blood, following in the way of the rent flesh, and fellowship with the Living Jesus, are the three chief steps.

4. Enter into the Holiest of all, and dwell there. It will enter into thee, and transform thee, and dwell in thee. And thy heart will be the Holiest of all, in which He dwells.

5. Have we not at times been lifted, by an effort of thought and will, or in the fellowship of the saints, into what seemed the Holiest of all, and speedily felt that the flesh had entered there too? It was because we entered not by the new way of life—the way through death to life—the way of the rent veil of the flesh. O our crucified Lord! teach us what this means; give it us; be it Thyself to us.

162

6. Let me remember that my access into the Holiest is as a Priest. Let me dwell before the Lord all the day as an Intercessor, offering, unceasingly, pleadings which are acceptable in Christ. May God's Church be like her of whom it is written, 'She departed not from the temple, but served God with fastings and prayers night and day.' It is for this we have access to the Holiest of all.

Twenty-ninth Day

HOLY IN CHRIST

Holiness and Chastisement

'He chasteneth us for our profit, that we may be partakers of His holiness. Follow after sanctification, without which no man shall see the Lord.'—Heb. xii. 10, 14.

There is perhaps no part of God's word which sheds such Divine light upon suffering as the Epistle to the Hebrews. It does this because it teaches us what suffering was to the Son of God. It perfected His humanity. It so fitted Him for His work as the Compassionate High Priest. It proved that He, who had fulfilled God's will in suffering obedience, was indeed worthy to be its executor in glory, and to sit down on the right hand of the Majesty on high. 'It became God, in bringing many sons unto glory, to make the Author of their salvation perfect through sufferings.' 'Though He was a Son, yet learned He obedience by the things which He suffered, and having been made perfect, became the Author of eternal salvation to all them that obey Him.' As He said Himself of His suffering, 'I sanctify myself,' so we see here that His sufferings were indeed to Him the pathway to perfection and holiness.

What Christ was and won was all for us. The power which suffering was proved to have in Him to work out perfection, the power which He imparted to it in sanctifying Himself through suffering, is the power of the new life that comes from Him to us. In the light of His example we can see, in the faith of His power we too can prove, that suffering is to God's child the token of the Father's love, and the channel of His richest blessing. To such faith the apparent mystery of suffering is seen to be nothing but a Divine need—the light affliction that works out—yea, works out and actually effects the exceeding weight of glory. We agree not only to what is written, 'It became Him to make the Author of salvation perfect through suffering,' but understand somewhat how Divinely becoming and meet it is that we too should be sanctified by suffering.

'He chasteneth us for our profit, that we should be made partakers of His holiness.' Of all the precious words Holy

164

Scripture has for the sorrowful, there is hardly one that leads us more directly and more deeply into the fulness of blessing that suffering is meant to bring. It is His Holiness, God's own Holiness, we are to be made partakers of. The Epistle had spoken very clearly of our sanctification from its Divine side, as wrought out for us, and to be wrought in us, by Jesus Himself. 'He which sanctifieth and they which are sanctified are all of one.' 'We have been sanctified by the one offering of Christ.' In our text we have the other side, the progressive work by which we are personally to accept and voluntarily to appropriate this Divine Holiness. In view of all there is in us that is at variance with God's will, and that must be discovered and broken down, before we understand what it is to give up our will and delight in God's; in view of the personal fellowship of suffering which alone can lead to the full appreciation of what Jesus bore and did for us; in view, too, of the full personal entrance into and satisfaction with the love of God as our sufficient portion; chastisement and suffering are indispensable elements in God's work of making holy. In these three aspects we shall see how what the Son needed is what we need, how what was of such unspeakable value to the Son will to us be no less rich in blessing.

Chastisement leads to the acceptance of God's will. We have seen how God's will is our sanctification; how it is in the will of God Christ has sanctified us; yea more, how He found the power to sanctify us in sanctifying Himself by the entire surrender of His will to God. His 'I delight to do Thy will' derived its worth from His continual 'Not my will.' And wherever God comes with chastisement or suffering, the very first object He has in view is, to ask and to work in us union with His own blessed will, that through it we may have union with Himself and His love. He comes in some one single point in which His will crosses our most cherished affection or desire, and asks the surrender of what we will to what He wills. When this is done willingly and lovingly, He leads the soul on to see how the claim for the sacrifice in the individual matter is the assertion of a principle— that in everything His will is to be our one desire. Happy the soul to whom affliction is not a series of single acts of conflict and submission to single acts of His will, but an entrance into the school where we prove and approve all the good and perfect and acceptable will of God.

It has sometimes appeared, even to God's children, as if affliction were not a blessing: it so rouses the evil nature, and calls forth all the opposition of the heart against God's will, that it has brought the loss of the peace and the piety that once appeared to reign. Even in such cases it is working out God's purpose. 'That He might humble thee, to prove thee, to know what was in thine heart,' is still His object in leading into the wilderness. To an extent we are not aware of, our religion is often selfish and superficial: when we accept the teaching of chastisement in discovering the self-will and love of the world which still prevails, we have learnt one of its first and most needful lessons.

This lesson has special difficulty when the trial does not come direct from God, but through men or circumstances. In looking at second causes, and in seeking for their removal, in the feeling of indignation or of grief, we often entirely forget to see God's will in everything His Providence allows. As long as we do so, the chastisement is fruitless; and perhaps only hardens the more. If, in our study of the pathway of Holiness, there has been awakened in us the desire to accept and adore, and stand complete in, all the will of God, let us in the very first place seek to recognise that will in everything that comes on us. The sin of him who vexes us is not God's will. But it is God's will that we should be in that position of difficulty to be tried and tested. Let our first thought be: this position of difficulty is my Father's will for me: I accept that will as my place now where He sees it fit to try me. Such acceptance of the trial is the way to turn it into blessing. It will lead on to an ever clearer abiding in all the will of God all the day.

Chastisement leads to the fellowship of God's Son. The will of God out of Christ is a law we cannot fulfil. The will of God in Christ is a life that fills us. He came in the name of our fallen humanity, and accepted all God's will as it rested on us, both in the demands of the law, and in the consequences which sin had brought upon man. He gave Himself entirely to God's will, whatever it cost Him. And so He paved for us a way through suffering, not only through it in the sense of past it and out of it, but by means and in virtue of it, into the love and glory of the Father. And it is in the power which Christ gives in fellowship with Himself that we too can love the way of the Cross, as the best and most blessed way to the Crown. Scripture says that the will of God is our sanctification, and also that Christ is our Sanctification. It is only in Christ that we have the power to love and rejoice in the will of God. In Him we have the power. He

166

became our Sanctification once for all by delighting to do that will; He becomes our Sanctification in personal experience, by teaching us to delight to do it. He learned to do it; He could not become perfect in doing it otherwise than by suffering. In suffering He draws nigh; He makes our suffering the fellowship of His suffering; and in it makes Himself, who was perfected through suffering, our Sanctification.

O ye suffering ones! all ye whom the Father is chastening! come and see Jesus suffering, giving up His will, being made perfect, sanctifying Himself. His suffering is the secret of His Holiness, of His Glory, of His Life. Will you not thank God for anything that can admit you into the nearer fellowship of your blessed Lord? Shall we not accept every trial, great or small, as the call of His love to be one with Himself in living only for God's will. This is Holiness, to be one with Jesus as He does the will of God, to abide in Jesus who was made perfect through suffering.

Chastisement leads to the enjoyment of God's love. Many a father has been surprised as he made his first experience of how a child, after being punished in love, began to cling to him more tenderly than before. Even so, while to those who live at a distance from their Father, the misery in this world appears to be the one thing that shakes their faith in God's Love, it is just through suffering that His children learn to know the Reality of that Love. The chastening is so distinctly a father's prerogative; it leads so directly to the confession of its needfulness and its lovingness; it wakens so powerfully the longing for pardon and comfort and deliverance, that it does indeed become, strange though this may seem, one of the surest guides into the deeper experience of the Divine Love. Chastening is the school in which the blessed lesson is learnt that the will of God is all Love, and that Holiness is the fire of Love, consuming that it may purify, destroying the dross only that it may assimilate into its own perfect purity all that yields itself to the wondrous change.

'We know and have believed the love which God hath in us. God is love: and he that abideth in love abideth in God, and God in Him.' Man's destiny is fellowship with God, the fellowship, the mutual indwelling of love. It is only by faith that this Love of God can be known. And faith can only grow by exercise, can only thrive in trial: when visible things fail, its energy is roused to yield itself to be possessed by the Invisible, by the Divine. Chastisement is the nurse of faith; one of its chosen attendants, to lead deeper into the Love of God. This is the new and living way, the way of the rent flesh in fellowship with Jesus leading up into the Holiest of all. There it is seen how the Justice that will not spare the child, and the Love that sustains and sanctifies it, are both one in the Holiness of God.

o ye chastened saints! who are so specially being led in the way that goes through the rent veil of the flesh, you have boldness to enter in. Draw near; come and dwell in the Holiest of all. Make your abode in the Holiest of all: there you are made partakers of His Holiness. Chastisement is bringing your heart into unity with God's Will, God's Son, God's Love. Abide in God's Will. Abide in God's Son. Abide in God's Love. Dwell, within the veil, in the Holiest of all.

Be ye holy, as I am holy

Most Holy God! once again I bless Thee for the wondrous revelation of Thy Holiness. Not only have I heard Thee speak, 'I am holy,' but Thou hast invited me to fellowship with Thyself: 'Be holy, as I am holy.' Blessed be Thy name! I have heard more even: 'I make holy,' is Thy word of promise, pledging Thine own Power to work out the purpose of Thy Love. I do thank Thee for what Thou hast revealed in Thy Son, in Thy Spirit, in Thy Word, of the path of Holiness. But how shall I bless Thee for the lesson of this day, that there is not a loss or sorrow, not a pain or care, not a temptation or trial, but Thy love also means it, and makes it, to be a help in working out the holiness of Thy people. Through each Thou drawest to Thyself, that they may taste how, in accepting Thy Will of Love, there is blessing and deliverance.

Blessed Father! Thou knowest how often I have looked upon the circumstances and the difficulties of this life as hindrances. Oh, let them all, in the light of Thy holy purpose to make us partakers of Thy Holiness, in the light of Thy Will and Thy Love, from this hour be helps. Let, above all, the path of Thy Blessed Son, proving how suffering is the discipline of a Father's love, and surrender the secret of holiness, and sacrifice the entrance to the Holiest of all, be so revealed that in the power of His Spirit and His grace that path may become mine. Let even chastening, even the least, be from Thine own hand, making me partaker of Thy Holiness. Amen.

1. How wonderful the revelation in the Epistle to the Hebrews of the holiness and the holy making power of suffering,

as seen in the Son of God! 'He learned obedience by the things which He suffered.' 'It became God to make the Author of our salvation perfect through suffering, for both He that sanctifieth and they who are sanctified are all of one.' 'In that He Himself hath suffered, He is able to succour.' 'We behold Jesus, because of the suffering of death, crowned with glory and honour.' Suffering is the way of the rent veil, the new and living way Jesus walked in and opened for us. Let all sufferers study this. Let all who are 'holy in Christ' here learn to know the Christ in whom they are holy, and the way in which He sanctified Himself and sanctifies us.

2. If we begin by realizing the sympathy of Jesus with us in our suffering, it will lead us on to what is more: sympathy with Jesus in His suffering, fellowship with Him to suffer even as He did.

3. Let suffering and holiness be inseparably linked, as in God's mind and in Christ's person, so in your life through the Spirit. 'It became God to make Him perfect through suffering; for both He that sanctifieth and they who are sanctified are all of one.' Let every trial, small or great, be the touch of God's hand, laying hold on you, to lead you to holiness. Give yourself into that hand.

4. 'Insomuch as ye are partakers of Christ's sufferings, rejoice; for the Spirit of glory and of God resteth on you.'

Thirtieth Day

HOLY IN CHRIST

The Unction from the Holy One

'And ye have an anointing from the Holy One, and ye know all things. And as for you, the anointing which ye received of Him abideth in you, and ye need not that any one teach you; but as His anointing teacheth you concerning all things, and is true, and is no lie, and even as it taught you, ye abide in Him.'—1 John ii. 20, 27.

In the revelation by Moses of God's Holiness and His way of making holy, the priests, and specially the high priests, were the chief expression of God's Holiness in man. In the priests themselves, the holy anointing oil was the one great symbol of the grace that made holy. Moses was to make an holy anointing oil: 'And thou shalt take of the anointing oil, and sprinkle it upon Aaron and upon his sons, and he shall be hallowed, and his sons with him.' 'This shall be an holy anointing oil unto me. Upon man's flesh shall it not be poured; neither shall ye make any other like it; it is holy, it shall be holy unto you' (Exod. xxix. 21, xxx. 25–32). With this the priests, and specially the high priests, were to be anointed and consecrated: 'He that is the high priest among you, upon whose head the anointing oil was poured, shall not go out of the holy place, nor profane the holy place of his God; for the crown of the anointing oil of his God is upon him' (Lev. xxi. 10, 12). And even so it is said of David, as type of the Messiah, 'Our king is of the Holy One of Israel. I have found David, my servant; with my holy oil have I anointed him.'

We know how the Hebrew name Messiah, and the Greek Christ, has reference to this. So, in the passage just quoted, the Hebrew is, 'with my holy oil I have messiahed him.' And so in a passage like Acts x. 38: 'Concerning Jesus of Nazareth, whom God christed with the Holy Ghost and with power.' Or Ps. xlv.: 'God hath messiahed thee with the oil of gladness above thy fellows;' in Heb. i. 9, 'Thy God hath christed thee with the oil of gladness.' And so (as one of our Reformed Catechisms, the Heidelberg, has it, in answer to the question, Why art thou called a Christian?) we are called Christians, because we are fellow-partakers with Him of His christing, His anointing. This is the anointing of which John speaks, the chrisma or christing of the Holy One. The Holy Spirit is the holy anointing which every believer receives: what God did to His Son to make Him the Christ, He does to me to make me a Christian. 'Ye have the anointing of the Holy One.'

1. Ye have an anointing from the Holy One. It is as the Holy One that the Father gives the anointing: that wherewith He anoints is called the oil of holiness, the Holy Spirit. Holiness is indeed a Divine ointment. Just as there is nothing so subtle and penetrating as the odour with which the ointment fills a house, so holiness is an indescribable, all-pervading breath of heavenliness which pervades the man on whom the anointing rests. Holiness does not consist in certain actions: this is righteousness. Holiness is the unseen and yet manifest presence of the Holy One resting on His anointed. Direct from the Holy One, the anointing is alone received, or rather, only in the abiding fellowship with Him in Christ, who is the Holy One of God.

And who receives it? Only he who has given himself entirely to be holy as God is holy. It was the priest, who was separated to be holy to the Lord, who received the anointing: upon other men's flesh it was not to be poured. How many would fain have the precious ointment for the sake of its perfume to themselves! No, only he who is wholly consecrated to the service of the Holy One, to the work of the sanctuary, may receive it. If any one had said: I would fain have the anointing, but not be made a priest; I am not ready to go and always be at the call of sinners seeking their God, he could have no share in it. Holiness is the energy that only lives to make holy, and to bless in so doing: the anointing of the Holy One is for the priest, the servant of God Most High. It is only in the intensity of a soul truly roused and given up to God's glory, God's kingdom, God's work, that holiness becomes a reality. The holy garments were only prepared for priests and their service. In all our seekings after holiness, let us remember this. As we beware of the error of thinking that work for Christ will make holy, let us also watch against the other, the straining after holiness without work. It is the priest who is set apart for the service of the holy place and the Holy One, it is the believer who is ready to live and die that the Holiness of God may triumph among men around him, who will receive the anointing.

2. 'The anointing teacheth you.' The new man is created in knowledge, as well as in righteousness and holiness. Christ is made to us wisdom, as well as righteousness and sanctification. God's service and our holiness are above all to be a free and full, an intelligent and most willing, approval of His blessed will. And so the anointing, to fit us for the service of the sanctuary, teaches us to know all things. Just as the perfume of the ointment is the most subtle essence, something that has never yet been found or felt, except as it is smelt, so the spiritual faculty which the anointing gives is the most subtle there can be. It makes 'quick of scent in the fear of the Lord:' it teaches us by a Divine instinct, by which the anointed one recognises what has the heavenly fragrance in it, and what is of earth. It is the anointing that makes the Word and the name of Jesus in the Word to be indeed as ointment poured forth.

The great mark of the anointing is thus, teachableness. It is the great mark of Christ, the Holy One of God, the Anointed One, that He listens: 'I speak not of myself; as I hear, so I speak.' And so it is of the Holy Spirit too: 'He shall not speak out of Himself: whatsoever He shall hear, that shall He speak.' It cannot be otherwise: one anointed with the anointing of this Christ, with this Holy Spirit, will be teachable, will listen to be taught. 'The anointing teacheth.' 'And ye need not that any one teach you: but the anointing teacheth you concerning all things.' 'They shall be all taught of God,' includes every believer. The secret of true holiness is a very direct and personal relation to the Holy One: all the teaching through the word or men made entirely dependent on and subordinate to the personal teaching of the Holy Ghost. The teaching comes through the anointing. Not, in the first place, in the thoughts or feelings, but in that all-pervading fragrance which comes from the fresh oil having penetrated the whole inner man.

3. 'And the anointing abideth in you.' 'In you.' In the spiritual life it is of deep importance ever to maintain the harmony between the objective and the subjective: God in Christ above me, God in the Spirit within me. In us, not as in a locality, but in us, as one with us, entering into the most secret part of our being, and pervading all, dwelling in our very body, the anointing abideth in us, forming part of our very selves. And this just in proportion as we know it and yield ourselves to it, as we wait and are still to let the secret fragrance permeate our whole being. And this, again, not interruptedly, but as a continuous and unvarying

experience. Above circumstances and feelings, 'the anointing abideth.' Not, indeed, as a fixed state or as something in our own possession; but, according to the law of the new life, in the dependence of faith on the Holy One, and in the fellowship of Jesus. 'I am anointed with fresh oil,'—this is the objective side; every new morning the believer waits for the renewal of the Divine gift from the Father. 'The anointing abideth in you,'—this is the subjective side; the holy life, the life of faith and fellowship, the anointing, is always, from moment to moment, a spiritual reality. The holy anointing oil, always fresh, the anointing abiding always, is the secret of holiness.

4. 'And even as it taught you, ye abide in Him.' Here we have again the Holy Trinity: the Holy One, from whom the holy anointing comes; the Holy Spirit, who is Himself the anointing; and Christ, the Holy One of God, in whom the anointing teaches us to abide. In Christ the unseen holiness of God was set before us, and brought nigh: it became human, vested in a human nature, that it might be communicated to us. Within us dwells and works the Holy Spirit, drawing us out to the Christ of God, uniting us in heart and will to Him, revealing Him, forming Him within us, so that His likeness and mind are embodied in us. It is thus we abide in Christ: the holy anointing of the Holy One teacheth it to us. It is this that is the test of the true anointing: abiding in Christ, as He meant it, becomes truth in us. Here is the life of holiness as the Thrice Holy gives it: the Father, the first, the Holy One, making holy; the Son, the second, His Holy One, in whom we are; the Spirit, the third, who dwells in us, and through whom we abide in Christ, and Christ in us. Thus it is that the Thrice Holy makes us holy.

Let us study the Divine anointing. It comes from the Holy One. There is no other like it. It is God's way of making us holy— His holy priests. It is God's way of making us partakers of holiness in Christ. The anointing, received of Him day by day, abiding in us, teaching us all things, especially teaching us to abide in Christ, must be on us every day. Its subtle, all-pervading power must go through our whole life: the odour of the ointment must fill the house. Blessed be God, it can do so! The anointing that abideth makes the abiding in Christ a reality and a certainty; and God Himself, the Holy One, makes the abiding anointing a reality and a certainty too. To His Holy Name be the praise!

Be holy, for I am holy

O Thou, who art the Holy One, I come to Thee now for the renewed anointing. O Father! this is the one gift Thy child may most surely count on—the gift of Thy Holy Spirit. Grant me now to sing, 'Thou anointest my head;' 'I am anointed with fresh oil.'

I desire to confess with deep shame that Thy Spirit has been sorely grieved and dishonoured. How often the fleshly mind has usurped His place in Thy worship! How much the fleshly will has sought to do His work! O my Father! let Thy light shine through me to convince me very deeply of this. Let Thy judgment come on all that there is of human willing and running.

Blessed Father! grant me, according to the riches of Thy glory, even now to be strengthened with might by Thy Spirit in the inner man. Strengthen my faith to believe in Christ for a full share in His anointing. Oh, teach me day by day to wait for and receive the anointing with fresh oil!

O my Father! draw me and all Thy children to see that for the abiding in Christ we need the abiding anointing. Father! we would walk humbly, in the dependence of faith, counting upon the inner and ever-abiding anointing. May we so be a sweet savour of Christ to all. Amen.

1. I think I know now the reason why at times we fail in the abiding. We think and read, we listen and pray, we try to believe and strive to look to Jesus only, and yet we fail. What was wanting was this: 'His anointing teacheth you; even as it taught you, ye abide in him;' so far, and no farther.

2. The washing always precedes the anointing: we cannot have the anointing if we fail in the cleansing. When cleansed and anointed we are fit for use.

3. Would you have the abiding anointing? Yield yourself wholly to be sanctified and made meet for the Master's use: dwell in the Holiest of all, in God's presence: accept every chastisement as a fellowship in the way of the rent flesh: be sure the anointing will flow in union with Jesus. 'It is like the precious ointment upon the head of Aaron, that went down to the skirts of his garments.'

4. The anointing is the Divine eye-salve, opening the eyes of the heart to know Jesus. So it teaches to abide in Him. I am sure most Christians have no conception of the danger and deceitfulness of a thought religion, with sweet and precious

thoughts coming to us in books and preaching, and little power. The teaching of the Holy Spirit is in the heart first; man's teaching in the mind. Let all our thinking ever lead us to cease from thought, and to open the heart and will to the Spirit to teach there in His own Divine way, deeper than thought and feeling. Unseen, within the veil, the Holy Spirit abideth. Be silent and still, believe and expect, and cling to Jesus.

5. Oh that God would visit His Church, and teach His children what it is to wait for, and receive, and walk in the full anointing, the anointing that abideth and teacheth to abide! Oh that the truth of the personal leading of the Holy Spirit in every believer were restored in the Church! He is doing it; He will do it.

Thirty-first Day

HOLY IN CHRIST

Holiness and Heaven

'Seeing that all these things shall be dissolved, what manner of men ought ye to be in all holy living and godliness?'—2 Pet. iii. 11.

'Follow after the sanctification without which no man shall see the Lord.'—Heb. xii. 14.

'He that is holy, let him be made holy still…. The grace of the Lord Jesus be with the holy ones. Amen.'—Rev. xxii. 11, 21.

O my brother, we are on our way to see God. We have been invited to meet the Holy One face to face. The infinite mystery of holiness, the glory of the Invisible God, before which the seraphim veil their faces, is to be unveiled, to be revealed to us. And that not as a thing we are to look upon and to study. But we are to see the Thrice Holy One, the Living God Himself. God, the Holy One, will show Himself to us: we are to see God. Oh, the infinite grace, the inconceivable blessedness! we are to see God.

We are to see God, the Holy One. And all our schooling here in the life of holiness is simply the preparation for that meeting and that vision. 'Blessed are the pure in heart, for they shall see God.' 'Follow after the sanctification, without which no man shall see the Lord.' Since the time when God said to Israel, 'Be ye holy, as I am holy,' Holiness was revealed as the only meeting-place between God and His people. To be holy was to be the common ground on which they were to stand with Him; the one attribute in which they were to be like God; the one thing that was to prepare them for the glorious time when He would no longer need to keep them away, but would admit them to the full fellowship of His glory, to have the word fulfilled in them: 'He that is holy, let him be made yet more holy.'

In his second epistle, Peter reminds believers that the coming of the day of the Lord is to be preceded and accompanied by the most tremendous catastrophe—the dissolution of the heavens and the earth. He makes it a plea with them to give diligence that they may be found without spot and blameless in His sight. And he asks them to think and say, under the deep sense of what the coming of the day of God would be and would bring, what the life of those ought to be who look for such things: 'What manner of person ought ye to be in all holy living and godliness?' Holiness must be its one, its universal characteristic. At the close of our meditations on God's call to Holiness, we may take Peter's question, and in the light of all that God has revealed of His Holiness, and all that waits still to be revealed, ask ourselves, 'What manner of men ought we to be in all holy living and godliness?'

Note first the meaning of the question. In the original Greek, the words living and godliness are plural. Alford says, 'In holy behaviours and pieties; the plurals mark the holy behaviour and piety in all its forms and examples.' Peter would plead for a life of holiness pervading the whole man: our behaviours towards men, and our pieties towards God. True holiness cannot be found in anything less. Holiness must be the one, the universal characteristic of our Christian life. In God we have seen that holiness is the central attribute, the comprehensive expression for Divine perfection, the attribute of all the attributes, the all-including epithet by which He Himself, as Redeemer and Father, His Son and His Spirit, His Day, His House, His Law, His Servants, His People, His Name, are marked and known. Always and in everything, in Judgment as in Mercy, in His Exaltation and His Condescension, in His Hiddenness and His Revelation, always and in everything, God is the Holy One. And the Word would teach us that the reign of Holiness, to be true and pleasing to God, must be supreme, must be in all holy living and godliness. There must not be a moment of the day, nor a relation in life; there must be nothing in the outer conduct, nor in the inmost recesses of the heart; there must be nothing belonging to us, whether in worship or in business, that is not holy. The Holiness of Jesus, the Holiness which comes of the Spirit's anointing, must cover and pervade all. Nothing, nothing may be excluded, if we are to be holy; it must be as Peter said when he spoke of God's call—holy in all manner of living; it must be as he says here—'in all holy living and godliness.' To use the significant language of the Holy Spirit: Everything must be done, 'worthily of the holy ones,' 'as becometh holy ones' (Rom. xvi. 3; Eph. v. 3).

Note, too, the force of the question. Peter says, 'Wherefore, beloved, seeing that ye look for these things.' Yes, let us think what that means. We have been studying, down through the course of Revelation, the wondrous grace and patience with which God has made known and made partaker of His holiness, all in preparation for what is to come. We have heard God, the Holy One, calling us, pleading with us, commanding us to be holy, as He is holy. And we expect to meet Him, and to dwell through eternity in His Light, holy as He is holy. It is not a dream; it is a living reality; we are looking forward to it, as the only one thing that makes life worth living. We are looking forward to Love to welcome us, as with the confidence of childlike love we come as His holy ones to cry, Holy Father!

We have learnt to know Jesus, the Holy One of God, our Sanctification. We are living in Him, day by day, as those who are holy in Christ Jesus. We are drawing on His Holiness without ceasing. We are walking in that will of God which He did, and which He enables us to do. And we are looking forward to meet Him with great joy, 'when He shall come to be glorified in the holy ones, and to be admired in all them that believe.' We have within us the Holy Spirit, the Holiness of God in Christ come down to be at home within us, as the earnest of our inheritance. He, the Spirit of Holiness, is secretly transforming us within, sanctifying our spirit, soul, and body, to be blameless at His coming, and making us meet for the inheritance of the holy ones in light. We are looking forward to the time when He shall have completed His work, when the body of Christ shall be perfected, and the bride, all filled and streaming with the life and glory of the Spirit within her, shall be set with Him on His throne, even as He sat with the Father on His throne. We hope through eternity to worship and adore the mystery of the Thrice Holy One. Even here it fills our souls with trembling joy and wonder: when God's work of making holy is complete, how we shall join in the song, 'Holy, Holy, Holy, Lord God Almighty, which wast, and art, and art to come!'

In preparation for all this the most wonderful events are to take place. The Lord Jesus Himself is to appear, the power of sin and the world is to be destroyed; this visible system of things is to be broken up; the power of the Spirit is to triumph through all creation; there is to be a new heaven and a new earth, wherein dwelleth righteousness. And holiness is then to be unfolded in ever-growing blessedness and glory in the fellowship of the Thrice Holy: 'He that is holy, let him be holy yet more.' Surely it but needs the question to be put for each believer to feel and acknowledge its force: 'Wherefore, beloved, seeing that ye look for these things, what manner of men ought ye to be in all holy living and godliness?'

And note now the need and the point of the question. 'What manner of persons ought ye to be?' But is such a question needed? Can it be that God's holy ones, made holy in Christ Jesus, with the very spirit of holiness dwelling with them, on the way to meet the Holy One in His Glory and Love, can it be that they need the question? Alas! alas! it was so in the time of Peter; it is but too much so in our days too. Alas! how many Christians there are to whom the very word Holy, though it be the name by which the Father, in His New Testament, loves to call His children more than any other, is strange and unintelligible. And again, alas! for how many Christians there are for whom, when the word is heard, it has but little attraction, because it has never yet been shown to them as a life that is indeed possible, and unutterably blessed. And yet again, alas! for how many are there not, even workers in the Master's service, to whom the 'all holy living and godliness' is yet a secret and a burden, because they have not yet consented to give up all, both their will and their work, for the Holy One to take and fill with His Holy Spirit. And yet once more, alas! as the cry comes, even from those who do know the power of a holy life, lamenting their unfaithfulness and unbelief, as they see how much richer their entrance into the Holy Life might have been, and how much fuller the blessing they still feel so feeble to communicate to others. Oh, the question is needed! Shall not each of us take it, and keep it, and answer it by the Holy Spirit through whom it came, and then pass it on to our brethren, that we and they may help each other in faith, and live in joy and hope to give the answer our God would have?

'Seeing that these things are, then, all to be dissolved, what manner of persons ought we to be in all holy living and godliness?' Brethren! the time is short. The world is passing away. The heathen are perishing. Christians are sleeping. Satan is active and mighty. God's holy ones are the hope of the Church and the world. It is they their Lord can use. 'What manner of persons shall we be in all holy living and godliness!' Shall we not seek to be such as the Father commands, 'Holy, as He is holy'? Shall we not yield ourselves afresh and undividedly to Him who is our Sanctification, and to His Blessed Spirit, to make us holy in all behaviours and pieties? Oh! shall we not, in thought of the love of our Lord Jesus, in thought of the coming glory, in view of the coming end, of the need of the Church and the world, give ourselves to be holy as He is holy, that we may have power to bless each believer we meet with the message of what God will do, and that in concert with them we may be a light and a blessing to this perishing world?

I close with the closing words of God's Blessed Book, 'He which testifieth these things saith, Yea, I come quickly. Amen: Come, Lord Jesus. The grace of the Lord Jesus be with the holy ones. Amen.'

Be ye holy, as I am holy

Most Holy God! who hast called us to be holy, we have heard Thy voice asking, What manner of persons we ought to be in all holy living and godliness? With our whole soul we answer in deep contrition and humility: Holy Father! we ought to be so different from what we have been. In faith and love, in zeal and devotion, in Christlike humility and holiness, O Father! we have not been, before Thee and the world, what we ought to be, what we could be. Holy Father! we now pray for all who unite with us in this prayer, and implore of Thee to grant a great revival of True Holiness in us and in all Thy Church. Visit, we beseech Thee, visit all ministers of Thy word, that in view of Thy coming they may take up and sound abroad the question, What manner of persons ought ye to be? Lay upon them, and all Thy people, such a burden under surrounding unholiness and worldliness, that they may not cease to cry to Thee. Grant them such a vision of the highway of holiness, the new and living way in Christ, that they may preach Christ our Sanctification in the power and the joy of the Holy Ghost, with the confident and triumphant voice of witnesses who rejoice in what Thou dost for them. O God! roll away the reproach of Thy people, that their profession does not make them humbler or holier, more loving, and more heavenly than others.

O Holy God! give Thou Thyself the answer to Thy question, and teach us and the world what manner of persons Thy people can be, in the day of Thy power, in the beauty of holiness. We bow our knee to Thee, O Father, that Thou wouldst grant us, according to the riches of Thy glory, to be mightily strengthened in the inner man by the Spirit of Holiness. Amen.

1. What manner of men ought ye to be in all the holy living? This is a question God has written down for us. Might it not help us if we were to write down the answer, and say how holy we think we ought to be? The clearer and more distinct our views are of what God wishes, of what He has made possible, of what in reality ought to be, the more definite our acts of confession, of surrender, and of faith can become.

2. Let every believer, who longs to be holy, join in the daily prayer that God would visit His people with a great outpouring of the Spirit of Holiness. Pray without ceasing that every believer may live as a holy one.

3. 'Seeing that ye look for these things.' Our life depends, in more than one sense, upon what we look at. 'We look not at the things which are seen.' It is only as we look at the Invisible and Spiritual, and come under its power, that we shall be what we ought to be in all holy living and godliness.

4. Holy in Christ. Let this be our parting word. However strong the branch becomes, however far away it reaches round the home, out of sight of the vine, all its beauty and all its fruitfulness ever depend upon that one point of contact where it grows out of the vine. So be it with us too. All the outer circumference of my life has its centre in the ego—the living, conscious I myself, in which my being roots. And this I is rooted in Christ. Down in the depths of my inner life, there is Christ holding, bearing, guiding, quickening me into holiness and fruitfulness. In Him I am, In Him I will abide. His will and commands will I keep; His Love and Power will I trust. And I will daily seek to praise God that I am Holy in Christ.

NOTES

NOTE A

Holiness as Proprietorship

In a little book—Holiness, as understood by the Writers of the Bible; A Bible Study by Joseph Agar Beet—the thought that by Holiness is meant our relation to God, and the claim He has upon us, has been very carefully worked out. Holy ground was such because 'it stood in special relation to Himself.' The first-born 'were to stand in a special relation to God as His property.' So with the entire nation; when God declares that they shall be holy, He means 'that they shall render to Him the devotion He requires.' 'All holy objects stand in a special relation to God as His property.' The priests are said to sanctify themselves; they did this 'by formally placing themselves at God's disposal, or by separating themselves from whatever was inconsistent with the service of God.' 'When God declares He is holy, the word must represent the same idea in the hundreds of passages in which it is predicated of men and things.' 'Holiness is God's claim to the ownership of men and things; and the objects claimed were called holy. Now, God's claim was a new and wondrous revelation of His nature. To Aaron God was now the Great Being who had claimed from him a lifelong and exclusive service. This claim was a new era, not only in his everyday life, but in his conception of God. Consequently the word holy, which expressed Aaron's relation to God, was suitably used to express God's relation to Aaron. In other words, to Aaron and Israel God was holy in the sense that He claimed the exclusive ownership of the entire nation. When men yielded to God the devotion He claimed, they were said to sanctify God.' 'Jehovah and Israel stood in special relation to each other; therefore Jehovah was the Holy One of Israel, and Israel was Holy to Jehovah. This mutual relation rested upon God's claim that Israel should specially be His; and this claim implied that in a special manner He would belong to Israel. This claim was a manifestation of the nature of God.' 'The peculiar relation arises from God's own claim, in consequence of which they stand in a new and solemn relation to

182

Him. This may be called objective holiness. This is the most common sense of the word. In this sense God sanctified these objects for Himself. But since some of these objects were intelligent beings, and the others were in control of such, the word sanctify denotes these ones' formal surrender of themselves and their possessions to God. This may be called subjective holiness. From the word holy predicated of God, we learn that God's claim was not merely occasional, but an outflow of His Essence. As the one Being who claims unlimited and absolute ownership and supreme devotion, God is the Holy One.'

In the New Testament the Spirit of God claims the epithet holy 'as being in a very special manner the source and influence of which God is the one and only aim.' Here 'our conception of the holiness of God increases with our increasing perception of the greatness of His claim upon us, and that this claim springs from the very essence of God. In the incarnate Son of God we see the full development and realization of the Biblical idea of holiness. We find Him standing in a special relation to God, and living a life of which the one and only aim is to advance the purposes of God.' We see in Him 'holiness in its highest degree, i.e. the highest conceivable devotion to God and to the advancement of His kingdom.' 'In virtue of His intelligent, hearty, continued appropriation of the Father's purpose, and in virtue of its realization in all the details of the Saviour's life, He was called the Holy One of God.'

'The word saint is very appropriate as a designation of the followers of Christ; for it declares what God requires them to be. By calling His people saints, God declares His will that we live a life of which He is the one and only aim. This is the objective holiness of the Church of Christ. In some passages holiness is set before the people of God as a standard for their attainment. In these passages holy denotes a realization in man of God's purpose that he live a life of which God is the one and only aim. This is the subjective holiness of God's people.

'Holiness is God's claim that His creatures use all their powers and opportunities to work out His purposes. Holiness, thus understood, is an attribute of God. For His claim springs from His nature, even from that love which is the very essence of God. His love to us moves Him to claim our devotion; for only by absolute devotion to Him can we attain our highest happiness.'

'Though without purity we cannot be subjectively holy, yet holiness is much more than purity. Purity is a mere negative excellence; holiness implies the most intense mental and bodily activity of which we are capable. For it is the employment of all our powers and opportunities to advance God's purposes.'

The question 'How we become holy,' is answered thus: 'Our devotion to God is a result of inward spiritual contact with Him who once lived a human life on earth, and now lives a glorified human life on the throne, simply and only to work out the Father's purposes. We live for God because Christ does so, and because Christ lives in us, and we in Him: the Spirit of Christ is the Agent of the spiritual contact with Christ which imparts to us His life, and reproduces in us His life. He is the bearer of the power as well as of the holiness of Christ.'

'That God claims from His people unreserved devotion to Himself, and that what He claims He works in all who believe it, by His own power operating through the inward presence of the Holy Spirit, placing us in spiritual contact with Christ, is the great doctrine of sanctification by faith.'

The same view, that holiness is a relation, had previously been worked out very elaborately by Diestel. In what has been said on redemption and proprietorship as related to holiness (see 'Sixth Day'), we have seen what truth there is in the thought. But holiness is something more. What is holy is not only God-devoted, but God-accepted, God-appropriated, God-possessed. God not only possesses the heart, but absolutely occupies and fills it with His life. It is this makes it holy.

However much truth there be in the above exposition, it hardly meets our desire for an insight into what is one of the highest attributes of the very Being of God. When the seraphs worship Him as the Holy One, and in their Thrice Holy reflect something of the deepest mystery of Godhead, it surely means more than merely the expression of God's claim as Sovereign Proprietor of all.

The mistake appears to originate in taking first the meaning of the word holy from earthly objects, and then from that deducing that holiness in God cannot mean more than it does when applied to men. The Scriptures point to the opposite way. When Old and New Testaments say, 'Be ye holy, for I am holy, I make holy,' they point to God's Holiness as the first, both the reason and the source of ours. We ought first to discover what holiness in God is. When we read at creation of God's sanctifying the Sabbath day, we have to do, not with a thought or word of Moses as to what God had done, but with a Divine revelation of a Power in God greater and more wonderful than creation, the Power which is later on revealed as the deepest mystery of the Divine Being.

This Holiness in God, as it appears to me, cannot be a mere relation. To indicate a relation, tells me nothing positively about the personal character or worth of the related parties. To say that when God sanctifies men He claims them as His own, does not say what the nature is of the work He does for them and in them, or what the Power by which He does it. And yet that word ought to reveal to me what it is that God bestows. To say that that claim has its root in His very nature, and in His love, and that holiness is therefore an attribute, makes it an attribute, not like love or wisdom, immanent in the Divine Being, ere creatures were, but simply an effect of Love, moving God to claim His creatures as His special possession. We should then have no attribute expressive of God's moral perfection. Nor would the word holy of the Son and the Spirit any longer indicate that deep and mysterious communication of the very nature and life of God in which sanctification has its glory. In the Divine holiness we have the highest and inconceivably glorious revelation of the very essence of the Divine Being; in the holiness of the saints the deepest revelation of the change by which their inmost nature is renewed into the likeness of God.

NOTE B

On the Word for Holiness

The proper meaning of the Hebrew word for holy, kadosh, is matter of uncertainty. It may come from a root signifying to shine. (So Gesenius, Oehler, Fürst, and formerly Delitzsch, on Heb. ii. 11.) Or from another denoting new and bright (Diestel), or an Arabic form meaning to cut, to separate. (So Delitzsch now, on Ps. xxii. 4.) Whatever the root be, the chief idea appears to be not only separate or set apart, for which the Hebrew has entirely different words, but that by which a thing that is separated from others for its worth is distinguished above them. It indicates not only separation as an act or fact, but the superiority or excellence in virtue of which, either as already possessed or sought after, the separation takes place.

In his Lexicon of New Testament Greek, Cremer has an exhaustive article on the Greek hagios, pointing out how holiness is an entirely Biblical idea, and 'how the scriptural conceptions of God's Holiness, notwithstanding the original affinity, is diametrically opposite to all the Greek notions; and how, whereas these very views of holiness exclude from the gods all possibility of love, the scriptural conception of holiness unfolds itself only when in closest connection with Divine love.' It is a most suggestive thought that we owe both the word and the thought distinctly to revelation. Every other attribute of God has some notion to correspond with it in the human mind: the thought of holiness is distinctly Divine. Is not this the reason that, though God has so distinctly in the New Testament called His people holy ones, the word holy has so little entered into the daily language and life of the Christian Church?

NOTE C

The Holiness of God

There is not a word so exclusively scriptural, so distinctly Divine, as the word holy in its revelation and its meaning. As a consequence of this its Divine origin, it is a word of inexhaustible significance. There is not one of the attributes of God which theologians have found it so difficult to define, or concerning which they differ so much. A short survey of the various views that have been taken may teach us how little the idea of the Divine Holiness can be comprehended or exhausted by human definition, and how it is only in the life of fellowship and adoration that the holiness which passes all understanding can, as a truth and a reality, be apprehended.

1. The most external view, in which the ethical was very much lost sight of, is that in which holiness is identified with God's Separateness from the creation, and elevation above it. Holiness was defined as the incomparable Glory of God, His exclusive adorableness, His infinite Majesty. Sufficient attention was not paid to the fact that though all these thoughts are closely connected with God's Holiness, they are but a formal definition of the results and surroundings of the Holiness, but do not lead us to the apprehension of that wherein its real essence consists.

2. Another view, which also commences from the external, and makes that the basis of its interpretation, regards holiness simply as the expression of a relation. Because what was set apart for God's service was called holy, the idea of separation, of consecration, of ownership, is taken as the starting-point. And so, because we are said to be holy, as belonging to God, God is holy as claiming us and belonging to us too. Instead of regarding holiness as a positive reality in the Divine nature, from which our holiness is to be derived, our holiness is made the starting-point for expounding the Holiness of God. 'God is holy as being, within the covenant, not only the Proprietor, but the Property of His people, their highest good and their only rule' (Diestel). Of this view mention has already been made in the note to 'Sixth Day,' on Holiness as Proprietorship.

3. Passing over to the views of those who regard holiness as being a moral attribute, the most common one is that of purity, freedom from sin. 'Holiness is a general term for the moral excellence of God. There is none holy as the Lord: no other being absolutely pure and free from all limitations in His moral perfection. Holiness, on the one hand, implies entire freedom from moral evil; and, upon the other, absolute moral perfection.' (Hodge, Syst. Theol.) The idea of holiness as the infinite Purity which is free from all sin, which hates and punishes it, is what in the popular conception is the most prominent idea. The negative stands more in the foreground than the positive. The view has its truth and its value from the fact that in our sinful state the first impression the Holiness of God must make is that of fear and dread in the consciousness of our sinfulness and unholiness. But it does not tell us wherein this moral excellence or perfection of God really consists.

4. It is an advance on this view when the attempt is made to define what this perfection of God is. A thing is perfect when it is in everything as it ought to be. It is easy thus to define perfection, but not so easy to define what the perfection of any special object is: this needs the knowledge of what its nature is. And we have to rest content with very general terms defining God's Holiness as the essential and absolute good. 'Holiness is the free, deliberate, calm, and immutable affirmation of Himself, who is goodness, or of goodness, which is Himself' (Godet on John xvii. 11). 'Holiness is that attribute in virtue of which Jehovah makes Himself the absolute standard of Himself, of His being and revelation.' (Kubel.)

5. Closely allied to this is the view that holiness is not so much an attribute, but the 'whole complex of that which we are wont to look at and represent singly in the individual attributes of God.' So Bengel looked upon holiness as the Divine nature, in which all the attributes are contained. In the same spirit what Howe says of holiness as the Divine beauty, the result of the perfect harmony of all the attributes, 'Holiness is intellectual beauty. Divine holiness is the most perfect beauty, and the measure of all other. The Divine Holiness is the most perfect pulchritude, the ineffable and immortal pulchritude, that cannot be declared by words, or seen by eyes. This may therefore be called a transcendental attribute that, as it were, runs through the rest, and casts a glory upon every one. It is an attribute of attributes. These are fit predications, holy power, holy love. And so it is the very lustre and glory of His other perfections. He is glorious in holiness.' (Howe in Whyte's Shorter Catechism.) This was the aspect of the Divine Holiness on which Jonathan Edwards delighted to dwell. 'The mutual love of the Father and the Son makes the third, the personal Holy Spirit, or the Holiness of God, which is His infinite beauty.' 'By the communication of God's Holiness the creature partakes of God's moral excellence, which is perfection, the beauty of the Divine nature.' 'Holiness comprehends all the true moral excellence of intelligent beings. So the Holiness of God is the same with the moral excellency of the Divine nature, comprehending all His perfections, His righteousness, faithfulness, and goodness. There are two kinds of attributes in God, according to our way of conceiving Him: His moral attributes, which are summed up in His Holiness, and His natural, as strength, knowledge, etc., which constitute His greatness. Holy persons, in the exercise of holy affection, love God in the first place for the beauty of His Holiness.' 'The holiness of an intelligent creature is that which gives beauty to all his natural perfections. And so it is in God: holiness is in a peculiar manner the beauty of the Divine being. Hence we often read of the beauty of holiness (Ps. xxix. 2, xcvi. 9, cx. 3). This renders all the other attributes glorious and lovely.' 'Therefore, if the true loveliness of God's perfections arise from the loveliness of His Holiness, the true love of all His perfections will arise from the love of His Holiness. And as the beauty of the Divine nature primarily consists in God's Holiness, so does the beauty of all Divine things.'

6. In speaking of God's Holiness as denoting the essential good, the absolute excellence of His nature, some press very strongly the ethical aspect. The good in God must not be from mere natural impulse only, flowing from the necessity of His nature, without being freely willed by Himself. 'What is naturally good is not the true realization of the good. The actual and living will to be the good He is, must also have its place in God, otherwise God would only be naturally ethical. Only in the will which consciously determines itself, is there the possibility given of the ethical. The ethical has such a power in God that He is the holy Power, who cannot and will not renounce Himself, who must be, and would be thought to be, the holy necessity of the goodness which is Himself,—to be the Holy. The love of God is essentially holy; it desires and preserves the ethically necessary or holy, which God is.' (Dorner, System, vol. i.)

7. It was felt in such views that there was not a sufficient acknowledgment of the truth that it is especially as the Holy One that God is called the Redeemer, and that He does the work of love to make holy. This led to the view that holiness and love are, if not identical, at least correlated expressions. 'God is holy, exalted above all the praise of the creature in His incomparable praise-worthiness, on account of His free and loving condescension to the creature, to manifest in it the glory of His love.' 'God is holy, inasmuch as love in Him has restrained and conquered the righteous wrath (as Hosea says, xi. 9), and judgment is exercised only after every way of mercy has been tried. This holiness is disclosed in the New Testament name, as exalted as it is condescending, of Father.' (Stier on John xvii.)

8. The large measure of truth in this view is met by an expression in which the true aspects of the Holiness of God are combined. It is defined as being the harmony of self-preservation and self-communication. As the Holy One, God hates sin, and seeks to destroy it. As the Holy One, He makes the sinner holy, and then takes him up into His love. In maintaining His love, He never for a moment loses His Divine purity and perfection; in maintaining His righteousness, He still communicates Himself to the fallen creature. Holiness is the Divine glory, of which love and righteousness are the two sides, and which in their work on earth they reveal.

'Holiness is the self-preservation of God, whereby He keeps Himself free from the world without Him, and remains consistent with Himself and faithful to His Being, and whereby

He, with this view, creates a Divine world that lives for Himself alone in the organization of His Church.' (Lange.)

'The Holiness of God is God's self-preservation, or keeping to Himself, in virtue of which He remains the same in all relationships which exist within His Deity, or into which He enters, never sacrifices what is Divine, or admits what is not Divine. But this is only one aspect. God's Holiness would not be holiness, but exclusiveness, if it did not provide for God's entering into manifold relations, and so revealing and communicating Himself. Holiness is therefore the union and interpretation of God's keeping to Himself and communicating Himself; of His nearness and His distance; of His exclusiveness and His self-revelation; of separateness and fellowship.' (Schmieder.)

'The Divine Holiness is mainly seclusion from the impurity and sinfulness of the creature, or, expressed positively, the cleanness and purity of the Divine nature, which excludes all connection with the wicked. In harmony with this, the Divine Holiness, as an attribute of revelation, is not merely an abstract power, but is the Divine self-representation and self-testimony for the purpose of giving to the world the participation in the Divine life.' (Oehler, Theol. of O. T. i. 160.)

'Opposition to sin is the first impression which man receives of God's Holiness. Exclusion, election, cleansing, redemption—these are the four forms in which God's Holiness appears in the sphere of humanity; and we may say that God's Holiness signifies His opposition to sin manifesting itself in atonement and redemption, or in judgment. Or as holiness, so far as it is embodied in law, must be the highest moral perfection, we may say, "holiness is the purity of God manifesting itself in atonement and redemption, and correspondingly in judgment." By this view all the above elements are done justice to; holiness asserts itself in judging righteousness, and in electing, purifying, and redeeming love, and thus it appears as the impelling and formative principle of the revelation of redemption, without a knowledge of which an understanding of the revelation is impossible, and by the perception of which it is seen in its full, clear light. God is light: this is a full and exhaustive New Testament phrase for God's Holiness' (1 John i. 5). (Cremer.)

This view is brought out with special distinctness in the writings of J. T. Beck. 'It is God's Holiness which, taking the good which was given in creation in strict faithfulness to that good and

190

perfect will of God, as the eternal life-purpose of love, in righteousness and mercy carried out to its completion in God Himself to a life of perfection. God does this as the Alone Holy. In the world of sin Divine love can only bring deliverance by a mediation in which it is reconciled to the Divine wrath within their common centre, the Holiness of God, in such a way that while wrath manifests its destroying reality, love shall prove its restoring power in the life it gives.' (Beck, Lehrwissenschaft, 168, 547.)

'Holiness is the sum and substance of the Divine life, as, in comparison with all that is created, it exists as a perfect life, but as it, at the same time, opens itself to the creature to take it up into a Godlike perfection—that is, to be holy as God is holy. Holiness is thus so far from being in opposition to the Divine love that it is its essential feature or norm, and the actual contents of love. In holiness there is combined the Divine self-existence as a perfection of life, and the Divine self-exertion in the realizing a Godlike perfection of life in the world. Holiness as an attribute of the Divine Being is His pure and inviolably self-contained personality in its absolute perfection. Hence it is that in holiness, as the absolute unity and purity of the Divine Being and working, all the attributes of Divine revelation centre. And so holiness, as expressive of the Being of God, qualifies the love as essentially Divine.

'Love is the groundform of the Divine will, but as such it receives its Divine filling and character from the Divine Holiness, as the Divine self-existence and self-exertion. As such the Divine will manifests itself in two modes—in its pure love as Goodness, in its holy harmony as Righteousness. These two do not exist separately, but permeate each other in reciprocal immanence, just as God in His Holiness is love, and in His love is holiness. In goodness the Divine love shows itself as the pleasure in well-being. But in this goodness the righteousness of God, to secure the well-doing, also acts.' (J. T. Beck, Glaubenslehre.)

'God is holy, separate from all darkness and sin, but not in isolated majesty banishing the imperfect and the sinful from His presence: for God is light, God is love. It is the nature of light to communicate itself. Remaining pure and bright, undiminished and unsullied, it overcomes darkness and kindles light. The Holiness of God is likewise mentioned in Scripture, mostly in connection with love, communicating itself and drawing into

191

itself. "I am holy"—but God does not remain alone, separate—"be ye also holy.'" (Saphir on Hebrews xii.)

'When we think of God as light and love, we realize most fully the idea of holiness, combining separateness and purity with communion.' (Saphir, The Lord's Prayer, p. 128.)

'It is especially as the spirit of His Church, and as dwelling in the human heart, that God is the Holy One.' (Nitsch.)

That in the Holiness of God we have the union of love and righteousness, has been perhaps put by no one more clearly than Godet. In his Commentary on Romans iii. 25, 26, he writes:—

'The necessity of the expiatory sacrifice arises from His whole Divine character; in other words, from His Holiness, the principle at once of His love and righteousness, and not of His righteousness exclusively.'

'In this question we have to do not with God in His essence, but with God in His relation to free man. Now the latter is not holy to begin with; the use which he makes of his liberty is not yet regulated by love. The attribute of righteousness, and the firm resolution to maintain the Divine holiness, must therefore appear as a necessary safeguard as soon as liberty comes on the stage, and with it the possibility of disorder; and this attribute must remain in exercise as long as the educational period of the creature lasts—that is to say, until he has reached perfection in love. Then all these factors—right, law, justice—will return to their latent state....

'It is common to regard love as the fundamental feature of the Divine character; in this way it is very difficult to reach the attribute of righteousness. Most thinkers, indeed, do not reach it at all. This one fact should show the error in which they are entangled. Holy, holy, holy, say the creatures nearest to God, and not Good, good, good. Holiness, such is the essence of God; and holiness is the absolute love of the good, the absolute horror of the evil. From this it is not difficult to deduce both love and righteousness. Love is the goodwill of God toward all free beings who are destined to realize the good. Love goes out to the individuals, as holiness itself to the good which they ought to produce. Righteousness, on the other hand, is the firm purpose of God to maintain the normal relations between all these creatures by His blessings and punishments. It is obvious that righteousness is included, no less than love itself, in the fundamental feature of the Divine character, holiness. It is no offence, therefore, by God to speak of His justice and His rights.

It is, on the contrary, a glory to God, who knows that in preserving His place He is securing the good of others. For God, in maintaining His supreme dignity, preserves to His creatures their most precious treasure, a God worthy of their respect and love.'

And in his Defence of the Christian Faith Godet writes, on 'The Perfect Holiness of Jesus Christ,' as follows:—

'The supernatural in its highest form is not the miraculous, it is holiness. In the miraculous we see Omnipotence breaking forth to act upon the material world in the interests of the moral order. But holiness is morality itself in its sublimest manifestation. What is goodness? It has recently been said, with a precision which leaves nothing to be desired, Goodness is not an entity—a thing. It is a law determining the relations between things, relations which have to be realized by free wills. Perfect good is therefore the realization, at once normal and free, of the right relations to one another of all beings; each being occupying, by virtue of this relation, that place in the great whole, and playing that part in it, which befits it.

'Now, just as in a human family there is one central relation on which all the rest depend,—that of the father to all the members of this little whole,—so is there in the universe one supreme position, which is the support of all the rest, and which, in the interest of all beings, must be above all others preserved intact—that of God. And just here, in the general sphere of good, is the special domain of holiness. Holiness in God Himself is His fixed determination to maintain intact the order which ought to reign among all beings that exist, and to bring them to realize that relation to each other which ought to bind them together in a great unity, and consequently to preserve, above all, intact and in its proper dignity, His own position relatively to free beings. The Holiness of God thus understood comprehends two things— the importation of all the wealth of His own Divine life to each free being who is willing to acknowledge His sovereignty, and who sincerely acquiesces in it; and the withholding or the withdrawal of that perfect life from every being who either attacks or denies that sovereignty, and who seeks to shake off that bond of dependence by which he ought to be bound to God. Holiness in the creature is its own voluntary acquiescence in the supremacy of God. The man who, with all the powers of his nature, does homage to God as the Supreme, the absolute Being, the only One who veritably is; the man who, in His presence, voluntarily prostrates himself in the sense of his own nothingness, and seeks to draw all his fellow-creatures into the same voluntary self-annihilation, in so doing puts on the character of holiness. This holiness comprehends in him, as it does in God, love and righteousness; love by which he rejoices in recognising God, and all beings who surround God, as placed where they are by Him. He loves them and wills their existence, because he loves and wills the existence of God, and at the same time of all that God wills and loves; and righteousness, by which he respects and, as much as in him lies, causes others to respect God, and the sphere assigned by God to each being. Such is holiness as it exists in God and in man: in God it is His own inflexible self-assertion; in man it is his inflexible assertion of God.

'It is in Jesus that human nature sees how man can assert God and all that God asserts, not only humbly, but joyously and filially, with all the powers of his being, and even to the complete sacrifice of himself.'

Careful reflection will show us that in each of the above views there is a measure of truth. It will convince us how the very difficulty of formulating to human thought the conception of the Divine Holiness proves that it is the highest expression for that ineffable and inconceivable glory of the Divine Being which constitutes Him the Infinite and Glorious God. Every attribute of God—wisdom and power, righteousness and love—has its image in human nature, and was in the religion or the philosophy of the heathen connected with the idea of God. From ourselves, when we take away the idea of imperfection, we can form some conception of what God is. But holiness is that which is characteristically Divine, the special contents of a Divine revelation. Let us learn to confess that however much we may seek, now from one, then from another side, to grasp the thought, the holiness of God is something that transcends all thought, a glory not so much to be thought, as to be known, in adoration and fellowship. Scripture speaks not so much of holiness, as the Holy One. It is as we worship and fear, obey and love; it is in a life with God, that something of the mystery of His glory will be unfolded. As the Divine light shines in us and through us, will the Holy One be revealed.

NOTE D

'Our holiness does not consist in our changing and becoming better ourselves: it is rather He, He Himself, born and growing in us, in such a way as to fill our hearts, and to drive out our natural self, "our old man," which cannot itself improve, and whose destiny is only to perish.

'And how is this kind of incarnation effected, by which Christ Himself becomes our new self? By a process of a free and moral nature, described by Jesus in words which surprise, because they place His sanctification upon nearly the same footing as our own: "As the living Father hath sent me, and I live by the Father, so he that eateth me shall live by me."

'Jesus derived the nourishment of His life from the Father who had sent Him: He lived by the Father. The meaning of that, doubtless, is, that every time He had to act or speak, He first effaced Himself; then left it to the Father to think, to will, to act, to be everything in Him. Similarly, when we are called upon to do any act, or speak any word, we must first efface ourselves in presence of Jesus; and after having suppressed in ourselves, by an act of the will, every wish, every thought, every act of our own self, we are to leave it to Jesus to manifest in us His will, His wisdom, His power. Then it is that we live by Him, as He lives by the Father. The process is identical in Jesus and in us. Only in Jesus it was carried on with God directly, because He was in immediate communion with Him; whilst in our case the transaction is with Jesus, because it is with Him that the believer holds direct communication, and through Him that we can find and possess the living Father. In that lies the secret, generally so little understood, of Christian sanctification.' (Godet, Biblical Studies, N. T., p. 190.)

NOTE E

Let me once more refer all students of holiness to Marshall on Sanctification, and specially his third and fourth chapters. If they will compare him with our modern works—say, for instance, God's Way of Holiness, by so eminent an author as Dr. H. Bonar—they cannot but be struck by the prominence which Marshall gives to the one thought, that our holiness, a holy nature, is provided in Jesus, and that as faith accepts and maintains our union with Jesus in personal intercourse, sanctification is by faith. While, in other works, the union to Jesus, and faith in Him, are but incidentally mentioned, and the chief stress is laid upon duties and the motives which urge to their performance, Marshall points out how motives never can supply the strength we need: it is the power of Christ's life in us, it is Christ Himself, as we by faith are rooted in Him, who works all our works in us.

An abridgment of the work, for popular use, is published by Nisbet & Co.

NOTE F

Note from Bengel on Rom. i. 4.

'According to the Spirit of Holiness. The word hagios, holy, when God is spoken of, not only denotes the blameless rectitude in action, but the very Godhead, or to speak more properly, the divinity, or excellence of the Divine nature. Hence hagiosune (the word here used) has a kind of middle sense between hagiotes, holiness, and hagiasmos, sanctification. Comp. Heb. xii. 10 (hagiotes or holiness), v. 14 (hagiasmos or sanctification). So that there are, as it were, three degrees: sanctification, sanctity of life, holiness. Holiness is ascribed to the Father, the Son, and the Holy Ghost. And since here the Holy Spirit is not mentioned, but the spirit of holiness (prop. sanctity, hagiosune), we must further inquire what this remarkable expression denotes. The name spirit is expressly and very frequently given to the Holy Spirit; but God is also called a spirit; and the Lord Jesus Christ is called a spirit, but in contrast to the latter. (2 Cor. iii. 17.) With this we must compare the fact that, as in this passage, so often the antithesis of flesh and spirit is found where Christ is spoken of. (1 Tim. iii. 16; 1 Pet. iii. 18.) In these passages the Spirit is applied to whatever belongs to Christ (apart from the flesh, although this was pure and holy, and above the flesh), through His generation of the Father, who sanctified Him: in short, His Godhead itself. For here, flesh and spirit, and chap. ix. 5, flesh and Godhead, stand in mutual contrast. This spirit is here called not the spirit of holiness, the usual title of the Holy Spirit; but it is called in this passage the spirit of sanctity, to suggest at once the efficacy of that holiness or divinity, which led of necessity to the Saviour's resurrection, and by which it was most forcibly illustrated, and also that spiritual and holy, or Divine power of Jesus who has been glorified and yet retained a spiritual body. Before the resurrection the spirit was concealed under the flesh; after the resurrection the spirit of sanctity concealed the flesh. In reference to the former, He was wont to call Himself the Son of man; in reference to the latter, He is known as the Son of God.'

Beck, in his Lehrwissenschaft, p. 604, puts it very clearly, thus—

'Inasmuch as the innocence and purity of Christ were not present in His sufferings and death as a quiescent attribute, but were in full action in the indestructible life-power of the Spirit, as He sanctified His own self to God for us ("through the eternal spirit," Heb. ix. 14—therefore, in Rom. i. 4, hagiosune, the habit of holiness in its action or sanctity, not hagiotes, only an inner attribute, or hagiasmos, holiness in its formation)—His suffering effected an everlasting redemption.'

NOTE G

'Freed' and 'Possessed'—The Twofold Result of Redemption

(From an address by Pastor Stockmaiev)

'Who gave Himself for us, that He might redeem us from all iniquity, and purify unto Himself a people for His own possession, zealous of good works.'

'In the redemption work of our Saviour Jesus Christ, there are two definite parts. You will never find the secret of abiding in Christ, so long as you cannot see these two definite distinct parts. The first is "Jesus for me," the other "I for Jesus." Blessed be our Saviour that He came for sinners. He for us. Blessed be the Lord that there is redemption from penalty; but that is not yet all that redemption means. You must have a clear apprehension of the second part of redemption, by that same Holy Ghost who is the guide to introduce us into the full possession of all that Christ, living and dying, has wrought out for us. He gave Himself that He might redeem us from all iniquity—not that we might have the pleasure of being pleased with our own purity or holiness, or such things; but that He might have us altogether for Himself, to purify unto Himself, for Himself, not for Himself and themselves, but unto Himself, a people of His own possession.

'What is now redemption?—freedom from self, even spiritual self. We are not to be our own centre, the centre of our joy, our progress, having in our poor weak hands the threads of our spiritual life. There is no real spiritual life but Christ's life, and He must have the care of it altogether from the beginning to the end. Lift up your eyes, dear brethren, you who were creeping on the ground. We are made for the glory of God, to be possessed by Jesus. The Lord God found a way, in giving His Son, the Lamb of God, His Lamb, to get such selfish people, who even in the line of the Christian life found means to seek and to nourish self, to get such people into His own real practical possession, to be possessed by Jesus. That is redemption, and that only; that is liberty, and that is reality; that is what satisfies, not to be satisfied with any experiences of your own, but to let go your experiences, and to say, I am free, so free as the people of Israel were coming out of Egypt, free to serve God. "Let my people go, that they may serve me." You are free, free through the blood of Christ, free through the power of the Holy Ghost—no flesh, no hand, no self being able to keep you back. The Lord has stretched out His arms upon all the powers who had kept us in the bondage of Egypt, and He triumphed over them. You are free as the bird of the air to live in Jesus—that is freedom; you are free in your daily life, free in the deepest, inmost depths of your being, free for Jesus, possessed by Him, a people of His own possession. Let my people go, said God. So, I have given my blood, said Jesus; and no flesh, no sin, no self can claim against the blood of Jesus. He has redeemed unto Himself, not for us, a people of His own possession....

'You are inquiring about the secret of abiding in Jesus. Have you not seen this in the 15th of John, that abiding and bearing fruit are inseparable? You cannot abide in Jesus for His joy, and your inward satisfaction. The secret of abiding is to stand as a redeemed one, as firmly in the second part of redemption as the first. I am now living for Jesus, and I have only to ask, Lord, what wilt Thou have done now? I am for Thee. I am for Jesus. I have only to follow, to follow as a sanctified one, as a possessed one, as one who is no more living for himself, who has given his life up into the hands of Jesus. Oh, how these questions of abiding become simple! It is not mysticism; it is not some special experience. It is simply a fact. I need Jesus for every moment, and my temptations as well as my duties become opportunities of realizing this life of fellowship with Christ. Oh, yes, this is redemption! Oh, mighty power of God the Father, God the Son, God the Holy Ghost, engaged to keep such a weak, helpless, unfaithful thing as you and myself in the centre of life! Sealed by the Holy Ghost, and God will never break His own seal.'

THE END

www.ingramcontent.com/pod-product-compliance
Lightning Source LLC
LaVergne TN
LVHW030632080426
835511LV00020B/3444